ALCOHOLICS ANONYMOUS

CULT OR CURE?

Second Edition
Revised & Expanded

by

Charles Bufe

See Sharp Press ◆ Tucson, Arizona ◆ 1998

Bufe, Charles.
    Alcoholics Anonymous : cult or cure? / Charles Bufe ; with an introduction
by Stanton Peele. — 2nd. ed. — Tucson, AZ : 1998.
    192 p. ; 23 cm.
    Includes bibliographical references and index.
    ISBN 1-884365-12-4

    1. Alcoholics Anonymous. 2. Alcoholics — Rehabilitation. 3. Cults —
Psychological aspects. 4. Alcoholism — Religious aspects. 5. Alcoholism —
Psychological aspects. 6. Alcoholism — Treatment. 7. Oxford Group.
8 Psychology — Religious. 9. Twelve-step programs. 10. Moral Re-Armament.
I. Title.

                              362.29286

Cover and interior design by Chaz Bufe. Printed on acid-free paper with soy-
based ink by Thomson-Shore, Inc., Dexter, Michigan.

Contents

Introduction

Charles Bufe begins *AA: Cult or Cure* with a description of a standard AA meeting—dominated by a few people who tell their same, self-serving stories for the umpteenth time, the proceedings unfocussed and unhelpful, the environment filled with smoke and other unhealthy environmental contaminants—from which most people leave with basic psychological and social needs unmet. This opening vignette conveys a lot of information—it tells you that Chaz Bufe has been there; that AA, for all its grandiose claims, consists of meetings of typically not particularly helpful people with their own ample blind spots and personal needs; and that this is a book that takes a different slant on what has been up till now the sacrosanct topic of Alcoholics Anonymous.

Chaz Bufe writes in the great tradition of the independent scholar, someone devoted to the pursuit of knowledge and understanding without institutional support for doing so. In *AA: Cult or Cure*, Chaz combines personal experience, historical analysis, review of government, AA, and other research data, and analytic interpretation into a seamless whole. His work on the indebtedness of AA and Bill W. to the Oxford Group Movement (later known as Moral Re-Armament), AA's Carl Jung connection, and Bill W.'s fiddling with funds earmarked for publishing the Big Book breaks new ground.

But Chaz's larger task is to evaluate the overall impact of AA on the individual and on society. In conducting this evaluation, the reader feels Chaz is not an ideologue. He gives credit where credit is due, acknowledging the brilliant insights of AA-founder Bill W., represented particularly in the 12 Traditions that Bill authored for AA. Chaz sees in these a successful blueprint for ensuring the democracy of AA as an organization not beholden to commercial, political, or intellectual interests. AA is in the alcoholism business, plain and simple. Chaz likewise points out that AA has not lent itself as an institution to oppression of women, blacks, or homosexuals as have other religiously based organizations.

Unfortunately, this strength is vitiated—as Chaz's analysis shows—by the tyranny of the group and AA philosophy over the individual. There is little room for individual variation and none for individual questioning of AA. The AA attendee does not speculate that he or she may not be an alcoholic, or question any of the 12 steps—for example, the need to turn oneself over to a "higher power." Despite AA's innocuous claims that this higher power may take any form, Chaz shows through its own 12 steps that AA requires a belief in deistic authority, with a corresponding diminution of self.

Chaz also shows—often through analysis of original data sources—that AA succeeds with relatively few (5% at most) of the massive numbers of alcoholics who wander through its meetings. The data which show this are general population surveys, AA's own membership studies, and research on outcomes of AA and other 12-step treatment (which forms the over-whelming majority of treatment programs in the U.S.). But AA is not concerned with data about its effectiveness or the numbers of people it leaves out in the cold. The fundamental goal of AA is to propagate the 12-step belief system and to support the small minority that finds this approach facilitative of recovery. This single-minded purpose has led to repeated ugly instances of career-endangering attacks on those who dare to gainsay AA's methods and success.

Chaz takes as his fundamental task to evaluate whether AA (and the ubiquitous 12-step treatment programs based on AA's model) comprises a cult involvement. In reaching his conclusion, Chaz roams widely over the acknowledged cults in recent American experience—the People's Temple, the Moonies, and Scientology, among others—along with the work of cult researchers and theorists. Examining cult philosophies and indoctrination techniques, he answers with a qualified "yes": the most important therapy group/technique in the U.S., in the eyes of the public, media, and health care system, is in many ways a brainwashing factory, one whose impact has led to no reduction in alcoholism in the U.S. In fact, by discouraging alter-native approaches and free thinking about America's drinking problems, AA may have had exactly the opposite impact.

But the good news, in Chaz's analysis, is that America's honeymoon with AA is nearly over. Chaz traces this cultural shift to the recent more critical thrust of popular articles on AA and its 12-step philosophy, repeated negative court decisions on the constitutionality of forcing people to attend AA/12-step programs, and a growing awareness of AA's limited ef-fectiveness—as well as to his own and other books, many published by See Sharp Press. In the next quarter century, Chaz predicts, what has often been AA's reign of terror over American alcoholism treatment will end.

—Stanton Peele, Ph.D.
Author, *Diseasing of America*, co-author (with Archie Brodsky) *The Truth About Addiction and Recovery*

Preface
to First Edition

Alcoholics Anonymous is the most influential self-help organization for alcoholics in the United States. It is commonly believed to be the most effective treatment for alcoholism; many believe that it is the *only* effective treatment for alcoholism. It is also the basis for a great many inpatient and outpatient alcoholism treatment programs, and is an important, often mandatory adjunct to many others; and a very high proportion of the alcoholism professionals staffing those programs are former alcoholics who recovered via AA. As well, the media almost universally accord AA respectful, indeed reverential, treatment.

Still, remarkably little useful information about Alcoholics Anonymous is available to the public, and what little there is comes from AA itself and from its numerous allies. While AA and its supporters, with rare exceptions, do not deliberately disseminate false information, they do, naturally enough, disseminate only those facts and opinions which reflect favorably upon AA. This has resulted in many false impressions becoming part of "the conventional wisdom."

One such impression is the belief that AA's co-founder, Bill Wilson, invented AA's 12-step program from whole cloth. Nothing could be further from the truth. Another false impression is the idea that from its inception AA developed as an independent organization, when in fact it developed within another organization, the Oxford Group Movement/Moral Re-Armament, and operated as part of the Oxford Group Movement for the first few years of its existence.

This fact is fleetingly, if at all, mentioned in most histories of Alcoholics Anonymous, and when it is acknowledged, the information provided about the Oxford Groups is usually so incomplete as to be misleading. When the Oxford Group Movement is mentioned, more often than not it's simply referred to as an "evangelical Christian group," or something similar. While this description is accurate as far as it goes, it's in the same league with a description of Adolf Hitler as "a controversial politician who led Germany from 1933 to 1945." While these descriptions of Hitler and the Oxford Groups contain no outright lies, much more information is necessary to provide true pictures of both the "evangelical Christian group" and the "politician." So, in light of the Oxford Groups' importance in the history of Alcoholics Anonymous, one major focus of this book will be upon the Oxford Group Movement and its relationship to AA.

Another focus of this book will be upon AA's efficacy as a method of alcoholism treatment. AA is routinely presented in the media as the most effective treatment for alcoholism, and one that is applicable to all alcohol abusers. Is this in fact the case? A major purpose of this book is to sort through the studies and other evidence of AA's effectiveness in order to determine the facts; and again, the facts which emerge paint a picture far different from that routinely presented in the mass media.

AA's critics, too, have at times painted inaccurate images of the organization, portraying it as a "cult." In order to answer this accusation, two of this book's chapters are devoted to analyzing the characteristics of cults such as Synanon, Scientology, and the People's Temple, and to comparing them with the characteristics of Alcoholics Anonymous. The portrait of AA which emerges from this comparison provides a truer and more revealing image of the organization than those painted by either its friends or by some of its critics.

A final purpose of this book is to analyze AA's program and structure with a view to distinguishing its strengths and weaknesses. It's paradoxical, but AA has drawn much undeserved applause over the years for vastly overrated accomplishments, while at the same time its very real strengths have gone largely unrecognized and unappreciated. This is truly unfortunate in that many of AA's useful features, particularly its organizational principles and organizational structure, could be fruitfully adopted in a far wider social and political sphere than that of alcoholism self-help groups. The irony of the situation is that these healthy AA principles and structures are all but ignored, while the AA principles contained in the 12 steps are being loudly trumpeted as a panacea for the world's ills.

Clearly there is much to be learned from AA, and what I've attempted in this study is to note the most obvious lessons. My hope is that both AA's friends and foes will accept this book for what it is, an honest evaluation by an investigator with decidedly mixed feelings about AA. In particular, I hope that AA's friends will not reject this evaluation out of hand because, as AA's co-founders might have put it, a little deflation every now and then can be a good thing.

—Charles Bufe, June 1991

Preface
to Second Edition

In the nearly seven years since the first edition of this book appeared, my views on AA have shifted considerably. There's a very simple reason for this: I've learned more about AA.

I have several AA members to thank for prodding me into that learning. When the first edition of *AA: Cult or Cure?* hit the shelves, I did a large number of radio interviews to promote the book, and many of these interviews took place on call-in programs. At the time, my message was mild: no, AA isn't a cult, though it has cult-like aspects; there are good things about it, notably its structure and traditions; it's religious, not spiritual; the available evidence indicates that it doesn't work very well; and there are probably better alternatives to it. Many of the AA members who called during my interviews were polite and respectful, and wanted to discuss issues. But a fair number of others were just the opposite. They had no interest in discussing issues—all that they wanted to do was to attack me personally. I particularly remember one fake-friendly caller who, after bragging about his time sober, accused me of lying purely for personal profit, and ended his *ad hominem* attack with, "You sound might *thirsty* to me!" I remember another vociferous defender of AA, on another program, who insisted that AA was the only route to recovery and that it had worked beautifully for him, but who was obviously drunk when he called.

At about the same time, newspaper and journal book reviews began to appear, and I fairly quickly noticed a pattern: those written by addictions "professionals" were extremely negative, and in two cases, it seemed to me, deliberately misrepresented what I'd said. As well, from their assertions and phraseology, I felt quite sure that the authors of these reviews were members of AA, but hadn't revealed it to their readers. I felt outraged by this. It seemed to me that their behavior was simply dishonest. I considered it—and still consider it—cowardly and deliberately deceptive.

Taken together, these two things—the sheer hatefulness of many of the pro-AA talk show callers and the hatchet-job reviews by AA members who hid their affiliation with AA—caused me to begin to question my own conclusions about AA's relative harmlessness. I started to wonder whether there was more to AA than had met my eye; and I planned to investigate AA further. But I had other writing and publishing projects in the works, so I let the matter rest.

Over the next several years, I began to publish alcohol-related books by other authors, and I learned a considerable amount by working with them. In particular, Vince Fox (*Addiction, Change & Choice*) showed me that the way AA's supporters had treated me was hardly out of the ordinary. From Audrey Kishline (*Moderate Drinking: The New Option for Problem Drinkers*—now published by Crown Books), I learned how damaging 12-step "treatment" is for many people. And from Ken Ragge (*The Real AA*), I gained a much better understanding of AA's indoctrination program. The writings of many other writers were also useful to me in deepening my knowledge of AA; in particular, I should acknowledge the writings of Stanton Peele and Jack Trimpey here.

Finally, about a year ago, I began to work on this second edition of *AA: Cult or Cure?* with the determination that I would do a much more thorough examination of AA this time. As a result, I went back over my old research, and I spent hundreds of hours reading additional books and journal articles, prowling around addictions-related web sites, talking with non-12-step professionals, and interviewing former 12-step-treatment patients and "therapists." In June, I began to write this second edition, and gradually a much more comprehensive portrait of AA emerged than I had painted in the first edition; but it's also a much darker portrait.

One indication of how much more comprehensive this edition is than the first edition is its sheer size: the new text is roughly 50% longer than the first edition. Significant new material appears in a good majority of the chapters, and good portions of the book are entirely new. I've added a new chapter ("AA's Influence on Society"—the longest chapter in the book), a new appendix ("AA and the Law"—which deals with coerced attendance), and a much-expanded appendix on the secular self-help groups, in which they present themselves in their own words.

Some defenders of AA will undoubtedly complain that virtually all of the new information and new analysis presented here reflects badly on AA, and is, in fact, "AA bashing." All that I can say in reply is that, as in the first edition of this book, I've done my best to honestly present and evaluate the available evidence. As well, it's not terribly surprising that the bulk of the new evidence is unfavorable to AA. AA has a well-oiled propaganda machine that loudly trumpets *every* finding and assertion favorable to AA, 12-step treatment, and the disease concept of alcoholism. This material is readily available, to say the least. In contrast, evidence that reflects badly on

AA is often hidden away in obscure professional journals and government reports. Thus, by digging deeper this time, I found much new negative evidence and little new positive evidence regarding AA.

It's also well to remember that in addition to AA itself, there are literally hundreds of presses churning out pro-AA/pro-12-step titles. These presses have published thousands of pro-AA titles in recent years, and almost all chain bookstores carry dozens if not hundreds of such works. In contrast, only a handful of books critical of AA and the 12-step approach to addictions have appeared over the past decade. Amazingly, See Sharp Press is the only publisher in the country specializing in books critical of AA and 12-step treatment, and advocating alternative approaches. So, if the material in this book didn't appear here, it almost certainly wouldn't appear elsewhere.

To put the matter a bit differently, because of the preponderance of pro-AA/pro-12-step materials, there's value in pointing out that the emperor (AA) wears no clothes. It helps to produce a more balanced, more realistic public view.

As for the new findings in this edition, probably the most significant is that AA is *not* what it presents itself to be. (I took AA largely at face value when I wrote the first edition of this book). AA portrays itself as an all-volunteer organization (except for a few paid service workers) whose only goal is to help alcoholics—an organization that innocently offers its program on a take-it-or-leave-it basis.

The facts paint a very different picture. At present, fully a third, probably over 40%, of AA's members are—or at least were originally—coerced into attendance (by the courts, prisons, employers, and professional diversion programs). As well, more than half a million Americans per year are forced into 12-step "treatment" by these same agencies. These coerced individuals constitute a *majority* of those undergoing "treatment"; and a great many of them are required to attend "aftercare" (that is, AA) after "treatment." Thus, lily-white AA, the program built on "attraction rather than promotion," is actually a program built on massive coercion.

AA's approach to researchers, critics, and alternative programs is equally hypocritical. While carefully cultivating its take-it-or-leave-it image, AA has taken pains to ensure that it's the only game in town. AA members have set up "educational" and "medical" front groups to promote AA and its ideology (especially the 12 steps and the disease concept of alcoholism). In addition to promoting AA and its concepts, the hidden AA members (in "professional" guise) in these front groups have repeatedly and viciously attacked critics of AA and researchers who've published findings contrary to AA dogma. They have also attempted to suppress alternative alcoholism treatment approaches—and to a great extent they've succeeded.(See Chapter 8 for a detailed discussion of all these points.)

I feel that it's healthy to point out these things—I believe that the public has a right to know and a need to know the facts about Alcoholics Anonymous and the 12-step treatment industry.

Others will undoubtedly disagree.

—Charles Bufe, November 28, 1997

ACKNOWLEDGEMENTS: I would like to thank all those who helped me in my research efforts for this second edition: Paul Amyx, Chris Cornutt, Vince Fox, Earl Lee, Stanton Peele, Ken Ragge, Jeffrey Schaler, Jack Trimpey, and Emmett Velten. This book is far better than it would otherwise have been because of the valuable contributions of all of these individuals. I would particularly like to thank Stanton Peele and Lynaea Search for their many useful comments, suggestions, and criticisms during the writing of this book. My thanks also to all those who contributed personal stories and anecdotes about the treatment industry, but whom I didn't quote in the book; their input was very valuable in giving me a fuller, more personal understanding of 12-step treatment.

A NOTE ON LANGUAGE: Throughout this book I've attempted to use gender-neutral language where possible. Unfortunately, in a few places, such as passages leading out of quoted material, it would have been awkward to do so; in such places, I chose what I consider the lesser of two evils and opted for masculine pronouns rather than clumsy constructions.

1

A Typical AA Meeting

What is a "typical" AA meeting like? Is there such a thing? A look in the AA "meeting book" for any large metropolitan area reveals a bewildering variety of meetings. A San Francisco meeting book from the early '90s, for example, lists meetings seven days a week with the first starting at 6 a.m. and the last starting at midnight; it lists beginners' meetings, step meetings, open meetings, closed meetings, speaker meetings, discussion meetings, candle-light meetings, women's meetings, lesbian and gay meetings, nonsmokers' meetings, writers' and artists' meetings, meetings for retired seamen, meetings conducted in Spanish—there are even meetings for atheists and agnostics.[1]

Meeting places range from church basements to library conference rooms to hotel lobbies to rented halls. Meeting sizes range from as few as three or four people up to several hundred at the larger weekend meetings. About all that can be said with reasonable certainty is that meetings last an hour to an hour and a half, and even that's not always the case. Still, certain features are common to virtually all AA meetings, and there are many other features which, while not universal, are typical.

If you were to go to a meeting you selected at random, it would probably go something like this:

It's ten minutes before meeting time as you walk through the front door of the AA hall, a large, dingy room reeking of stale tobacco smoke. You walk across the grimy linoleum floor to the coffee urn, pour yourself a cup of what appears to be used motor oil (rumor has it that the stuff will dissolve pencils), grab a couple of cookies, and wander over to one of the 40 or so folding metal chairs facing the table at the front of the room.

The meeting's secretary and the evening's speaker are already seated at the table, smoking cigarettes and slurping coffee. Other people, mostly casually dressed men in the 30s and 40s, are filing in, gradually filling the seats, and gradually filling the air with tobacco smoke. Perhaps half the chairs are taken when the meeting starts.

Precisely on the hour the secretary raps his gavel, introduces himself, and asks two pre-selected members to read the AA Preamble and the Serenity Prayer. Then, since it's a small meeting, everyone in the room introduces himself or herself and is then greeted by the crowd: "My name is Mike. I'm an alcoholic." "Hi Mike!" "My name is Bob. Alcoholic." "Hi Bob!" "Ed. Alcoholic." "Hi Ed!" . . . until everyone present has stated his or her name and muttered the magic word, "alcoholic." The secretary then asks any newcomers with less than 30 days sobriety to introduce themselves; he adds that this is only so that the rest of the members can get to know them. One hand timidly goes up in the back row and, after being prompted by the secretary, its owner introduces himself as "Tom"; everyone else loudly says, "Hi Tom," and applauds. The secretary next asks if there are any out-of-towners at the meeting. Since there are none, he goes on to ask if anyone has an anniversary (of months or years of sobriety) that day. No one does, so the secretary concludes by making his only announcement, that of an upcoming "clean and sober" dance at a local AA hangout.

The speaker rises, steps to the podium, introduces himself, and launches into a history of his alcoholism, describing at length and with apparent relish some of his more lurid drinking episodes. He pauses, lights a cigarette, and speaks of how he "bottomed out"—the degradation, humiliation, and hopelessness he felt when he finally realized what alcohol had done to him. He lights another cigarette and recounts how finally, in desperation, he hesitantly walked into an AA meeting despite fears about "the God stuff." After deeply inhaling a puff of tobacco smoke, he describes how his life has never been the same since that day. He kept coming to meetings, even though he still had doubts, because he was attracted to "something" the AA members had which he felt lacking in himself. He lights another cigarette and continues, saying that once he overcame his doubts, began to work the steps, and found his "Higher Power," his life has been transformed and that he literally owes his life to AA. He sits down to polite applause as his cigarette smoke curls upward toward the humming fluorescent lights.

By this time there are only 25 minutes left, and the secretary throws the meeting open to questions and discussion. A hand goes up in the front row and a nearly incoherent but boastful drunkalogue (a recitation of drunken escapades) ensues for ten minutes. Toward the end of it, the secretary passes the collection basket; most of those present chip in a buck or some pocket change. The next member to speak, who has been chafing at the bit during the drunkalogue, takes off on a tangent and describes how by working one of the steps he overcame his frustration after a car accident. One or two others take off on different tangents, and then it's time to end the meeting.

The secretary announces the fact and everyone rises, joins hands, and most say the Lord's Prayer. About a quarter, looking pained or disgusted, remain mute. After a moment of silence, everyone chants, "Keep coming back. It works!" And the meeting is over.

About half of those present leave immediately, while a few busy themselves cleaning up the room, and the rest stand around drinking coffee, smoking cigarettes, and chatting, two of them paying special attention to the newcomer. Finally, a half-hour after the meeting formally closed, the secretary ushers everyone out into the night.

Not all meetings are like this, however—just a majority. Other writers have described supportive meetings with friendly socializing in a cozy, club-like atmosphere.[2] Such meetings probably exist in abundance, but in my estimation they're outnumbered by meetings of the type I've described here.

I should also point out that only those who blindly, and vocally, embrace the 12 steps are fully welcome at most meetings. Those who have doubts and those who have disagreements with AA dogma are normally ostracized if they express their opinions; and those who remain silent and sit on their doubts will normally be the objects of proselytization and dire warnings, and, if they continue to refuse to mouth accepted AA wisdom, will win, at best, grudging acceptance—if they're strong enough to stand up to the ridicule and condescension they're sure to encounter.

If doubters are fortunate, there will be an "agnostics" or "atheists" meeting in their city where they can commune with their fellow second-class citizens; but such meetings are normally found only in large cities such as San Francisco. In many, probably most, rural areas, small towns, and small cities, a majority of meetings are even more overtly religious than the one I've described here.

---

1. "Step meetings" feature discussion of the 12 steps; at "open meetings" both alcoholics and nonalcoholics are welcome; and at "closed meetings" only self-proclaimed alcoholics are welcome. The names of the other types of meetings are self-explanatory.

2. See, for example, *Getting Better*, by Nan Robertson. New York: William Morrow and Company, 1988. Chapter 5, pp. 109–126.

2

The Oxford Group
Movement:
The Forerunner of AA

" . . . Many a channel had been used by Providence to create Alcoholics Anonymous. And none had been more vitally needed than the one opened through Sam Shoemaker and his Oxford Group associates . . . the early A.A. got its ideas of self-examination, acknowledgment of character defects, restitution for harm done, and working with others straight from the Oxford Groups and directly from Sam Shoemaker, their former leader in America, and from nowhere else. . . . A.A. owes a debt of timeless gratitude for all that God sent us through Sam and his friends in the days of A.A.'s infancy."
—Bill Wilson in *Alcoholics Anonymous Comes* of Age, pp. 39–40

In order to understand Alcoholics Anonymous, it's first necessary to understand the movement which gave birth to AA: The Oxford Group Movement, also known as the Oxford Groups, Buchmanism, and, in its later days, Moral Re-Armament (MRA). The importance of the Oxford Group Movement to the structure, practices, and, especially, the ideology of Alcoholics Anonymous cannot be overstated. The two founders of AA, Bill Wilson and Dr. Robert Smith, were enthusiastic members of the Oxford Groups; the early AA-to-be groups in both Akron and New York operated as part of the Oxford Groups; and both Bill Wilson and "Dr. Bob" believed that the principles of the Oxford Groups were the key to overcoming alcoholism. Thus, AA's bible, *Alcoholics Anonymous*, the so-called Big Book, in large part reads like a piece of Oxford Group Movement literature, and the 12 steps, the cornerstone of AA ideology, are for all intents and purposes a codification of Oxford Group principles.

The Oxford Group Movement was very much the creature of its founder, Dr. Frank Nathan Daniel Buchman. He was born on June 4, 1878 in Pennsburg, Pennsylvania, of conservative, apparently prosperous,

Lutheran parents. He attended Muhlenberg College in Allentown, Pennsylvania and graduated in 1899. Following his studies at Muhlenberg, he entered Mount Airy Seminary (Pennsylvania) and graduated in 1902 as an ordained Lutheran minister.

Buchman's first parish was in Overbrook, now a section of Philadelphia, where shortly after his appointment he opened a small hospice for young men. The hospice apparently prospered, because in June 1905 the Evangelical Lutheran Ministerium of Pennsylvania and Adjacent States called upon him to open a larger hospice for young men in Philadelphia. He proceeded to do so, but the enterprise was plagued by financial problems. In 1908 Buchman became embroiled in a dispute with the Ministerium's Finance Committee and resigned his position in a huff.

Shortly after resigning, he went to an evangelical conference in Keswick, England. While there he had a "conversion experience" complete with "a poignant vision of the Crucified" while listening to a Salvation Army speaker at a local chapel. Following this experience, he wrote letters of apology to the six members of the Ministerium with whom he had quarreled. (In Oxford Group/Moral Re-Armament literature, much is made of the fact that he received not a single reply. But according to the superintendent of the Ministerium, Dr. J.F. Ohl, world-traveler Buchman didn't bother to put a return address on his letters.[1]) He also "shared" his experience with the family with which he was staying, thus making his first convert, their son.

After returning from England, he applied for and was given a position as YMCA secretary at State College, Pennsylvania effective as of July 1, 1909. At that time the "Y" was more than a series of health clubs; it was an active evangelical association with considerable influence on American college campuses. Buchman built a reputation at State College for conducting well-attended Bible classes and evangelical crusades, and for building up the membership of the YMCA. According to one report, he inflated "Y" membership figures by handing out "free" Bibles to incoming freshmen and then later billing them for "Y" dues.[2] He also instituted the practice of the "Morning Watch" (later called "Quiet Time") in which devotees spent time reading the Bible, praying, and "listening to God."

In 1915 he resigned to go traveling once again, this time to the Far East with evangelist Sherwood Eddy. Upon his return in 1916, he was appointed Extension Lecturer in Personal Evangelism at the Hartford (Connecticut) Seminary. At first, he lived in the students' dormitory—a rather odd thing for a man of 38 to do—but he was asked to move out after students complained of his intrusive methods. He also began to rely on "guidance" (from God) to run his daily life, and encouraged students to do the same. In this way he developed a reputation for being unreliable—"God" would "guide" him to miss appointments, etc.—and students were supposedly "guided" to do things such as booking steamship passage to Europe without having the funds to pay for it.[3] One former Buchmanite (at a different college) later recalled, "I put my trust in guidance and failed my examinations."[4] Buchman also gained a reputation for dwelling on the importance of sexual sin in his dealings with students.

To make matters worse, he was having trouble with members of the faculty at Hartford. Buchman was an evangelical fundamentalist who emphasized emotional experience, and he regarded the classes of his colleagues as not "vital." They returned the contempt by regarding Buchman as a simpleton.

So, it seems probable that this was not an especially happy period in Buchman's life; and he must have been at least somewhat relieved when he received the "guidance" to resign his position. In 1922 he quit his job at Hartford in order to devote himself to "personal evangelism" and to living off the largesse of wealthy backers, activities which he would pursue for the rest of his life. Buchman remained unrepentant about his lavish lifestyle, and that of his close associates, to the end of his days. On many occasions he made remarks similar to one quoted in *Time* in 1936: "Why shouldn't we stay in 'posh' hotels? Isn't God a millionaire?"[5]

While in Hartford, Buchman had much free time, and thus the opportunity to travel. In Kuling, China in 1918 he organized his first "houseparty," a type of gathering which was to become a Buchmanite trademark. Houseparties were in some ways a form of religious retreat and were, at least for their first decade or so, gatherings of no more than a few dozen people in spacious private homes or, more often, expensive inns or hotels. Participants were normally invited to attend through friends or acquaintances already involved with Buchman's movement.

That atmosphere at houseparties was always informal, and activities ranged from Bible study and "quiet times" to bridge playing and golf. There were also voluntary general meetings in which attendees "shared," confessing their "sins" and offering witness to the "change" in their lives caused by adherence to Buchman's principles. A noteworthy feature of houseparties was the upscale economic status of their attendees, and the frequent well-advertised presence of prominent individuals. It was the norm for Buchman and his cohorts to go to great lengths to attract the rich and famous, and, when they were hooked, to shamelessly exploit their names, a tendency which would become more pronounced in the coming years.

While still at Hartford Seminary, Buchman began to hold houseparties at Ivy League colleges in the U.S. and at Oxford and Cambridge in England. This was entirely in keeping with Buchman's background as a YMCA secretary at State College and as a lecturer at Hartford Seminary.

Through the mid-1920s, the focus of his ministry would be evangelical work at colleges such as Harvard, Yale, Princeton and Bryn Mawr. Throughout this period—and indeed throughout his entire life—Buchman retained his obsession with sex. One Harvard graduate is reported to have said, "He started asking me intimate questions about sex before I'd been alone with him for five minutes. I left in a hurry."[6]

Strangely, some Oxford Group/MRA literature almost *brags* about Buchman's obsession with sex. Perhaps the best examples of this are found in *Frank Buchman's Secret*, a hagiography by Peter Howard (Buchman's successor as head of MRA) published a few months after Buchman's death in 1961. In describing one of Buchman's "soul surgery" victories, Howard records the following revealing scene:

> Buchman said, "You have a very unhappy home."
> The atheist answered, "Yes, I have. I hate my father. I always have since I was a boy."
> Buchman then said, "You are in the grip of an impure habit which you cannot bring yourself to talk about with anyone."
> The atheist answered, "That is a lie." There was silence.
> Buchman said, "I must go." . . .
> "No, don't go."
> Buchman then said, "Well, I'll stay on one condition—that you and I listen to God together."
> The atheist made a surprising reply. He said, ". . . I told you a lie a few minutes ago. I am in the grip of that habit."
> Buchman said, "I know."[7]

In a later chapter, Howard records another instance of Buchman's "soul surgery":

> [Buchman] literally shook with the strength of his feelings. "I may have the wrong details," he said, "but I have the right girl, the right diagnosis and the right cure. You are the girl, the diagnosis is that you are sex mad, the cure is Jesus Christ."[8]

In 1924, Buchman's sexual obsession and the obtrusive zeal of some of his converts caused Princeton University's president to ban him. As was usual in his campus crusades, Buchman's followers engaged in high-pressure attempts to get fellow students to "change," followed dubious "guidance" religiously—with predictable social and academic results—thought nothing of invading other students' privacy, and engaged in inappropriate "sharing," much of it of a sexual nature. One chronicler reports that a Buchmanite took "the young and rather innocent daughter" of a Princeton professor out on a date, and proceeded to "share" with her a confession of his sexual sins in fulsome detail.[9]

Such incidents did little to increase Frank Buchman's popularity with either students or faculty. Buchman himself, though, seems to have precipitated his own banishment by telling John Hibden, Princeton's president, that 85 percent of Princeton undergraduates were either "sexually perverted or [self-]abusive."[10] Hibden evidently didn't appreciate this assessment of his students, and soon declared Buchman *persona non grata* at Princeton.[11] While this undoubtedly annoyed Buchman, it certainly didn't deter him from pursuing his "good work" at other colleges. But by the mid-'20s, the influence of the Buchman movement had peaked on American campuses, and Buchmanism quickly faded into obscurity at virtually every institution where it had taken root.

Throughout what could be termed the "collegiate" period of the Oxford Group Movement, Buchman's program was remarkably consistent. It consisted of "personal evangelism" with emphases upon: 1) both public and private confession of sin, especially sexual sin; 2) reception of divine "guidance" during "quiet times"; 3) complete surrender to this "guidance"; 4) the living of a "guided" life in which every aspect of one's actions, down to the choice of dinner entree, was controlled by God; 5) the practice of the Buchmanite "four absolutes"—purity, honesty, love, and unselfishness; 6) making restitution to those one has harmed; and 7) carrying "the message" to those still "defeated."

The "message" was delivered one-to-one by individual Buchmanite "life changers," also known as "soul surgeons," or en masse by "traveling teams" which ranged in size from about half-a-dozen to several dozen persons. These teams would spread the word on campuses through individual contacts and through the ever-popular houseparties. A notable feature of the Buchmanite movement at this stage was that it was directed at the "up-and-out" on prestigious campuses, and that its primary aim was to convert "key men"—football stars and other athletes, student body officers, and the sons of the prominent, the powerful, and the very rich.

During this period, four other key features of Buchmanism became prominent: its emphasis on nonprofessionalism; its antipathy toward formal organization; its complete disregard of social, political, and economic causes of individual social problems; and its virulent anti-intellectualism. The emphasis on nonprofessionalism was implicit in the concept of divine "guidance" available to all who would listen, and the accompanying command that all "guided" individuals should "change" others. The antipathy to formal organization was also implicit in the concept of "guidance." (If individuals are being directly controlled by God, what need do they have for formal organization?) In practice this led to dictatorial control of the movement by Buchman and a small clique surrounding him. The neglect of political, social, and economic factors as causes of individual and social problems was due to Buchman's belief that "guidance" in itself was sufficient to solve all problems, and to the implicit Buchmanite belief in social inequality—that there is nothing inherently wrong with coercion, domination and submission, with some giving orders and others taking them, and with an unequal distribution of wealth and income. And the anti-intellectualism of Buchman's message likewise stemmed from his fixation on "guidance" as a cure-all. Anything that could call "guidance" into doubt was inherently undesirable; thus logic, careful consideration of facts, and a questioning attitude were deadly enemies to the Oxford Group Movement. A Group axiom expresses this attitude succinctly: "Doubt stifles and makes abortive our attempt to act upon God's Guidance."[12] A former Buchmanite recalled that when he was a member of the Groups, "thinking seemed to me atheism."[13]

Following the collapse of his campus movement in the U.S., Buchman moved his base of operations to England and conducted evangelical crusades at Oxford and Cambridge. It was through recruits garnered in these crusades that the group acquired its name. While the Buchman movement never attracted more than a small minority of students at Oxford, a traveling team consisting largely of Oxford students went to South Africa in 1929 where it was dubbed "the Oxford Group" by the press, and shortly after that Buchman and his minions began to refer to themselves as the "Oxford Group Movement." Whether this was "absolutely honest" is open to question: Buchman had never studied at Oxford University; he held no position there; and his movement had no official connection with the university and very limited influence among its students.

Nonetheless, the use of the Oxford name was very advantageous to the Buchmanites, suggesting as it did connection with a venerable and respected institution. Another advantage was that the centenary of the Oxford Movement—John Henry Newman's attempt to Catholicize the Anglican Church—was to be celebrated in 1933, and the names Oxford Movement and Oxford Group Movement would inevitably become confused in the public mind, much to the benefit of the Oxford Group Movement. The Buchmanites used the name "Oxford Group Movement" for a decade, and dropped it only in the opening days of World War II for all but certain legal purposes.[14]

Concurrent with the transfer of his base of operations to England, Buchman began to shift the focus of his movement on both sides of the Atlantic from well-to-do students to their parents. In the early 1930s, the Buchman movement began to hold mass meetings which, like the much smaller meetings of the 1920s, were called "houseparties." For several years the Buchmanites held an annual houseparty in Oxford. Attendance in 1930 was 700; by 1935 it had risen to 10,000. In 1936, a houseparty in Birmingham, England attracted 15,000 persons. The smaller '20s-style houseparties were, however, also a prominent feature of the Oxford Group Movement throughout the 1930s.

A feature common to both types of houseparty was the ostentatious use of the names of the rich and famous. One friendly observer noted, "No feature of the Oxford Group Movement so strikes the casual observer . . . as its studious attention to position, title, and social prestige. No meeting is properly launched without its quota of patrons of rank and social standing."[15] In the U.S., prominent—and trumpeted—supporters included Russell Firestone, Mrs. Thomas Edison, Admiral Byrd, Mr. And Ms. Cleveland Dodge, Mrs. Harry Guggenheim, and Mr. and Mrs. Henry Ford. As this list suggests, money, power, and prestige were what mattered to Buchman and his followers, not politics (as long as the powerful and prestigious didn't hold "communist" views). If politics had mattered to the Buchmanites, it's highly unlikely that they would have publicized their association with the prominent, vocal anti-semite and Nazi sympathizer, Henry Ford.[16]

Another notable feature of the Oxford Group Movement in this period (and indeed throughout its history) was its routine and extreme exaggeration of its own importance and influence. The Groupers' estimation of their influence in South Africa is illustrative. During the years following 1929, when Buchman accompanied the "team" (and the Buchman movement acquired the name "Oxford Group"), "traveling teams" visited South Africa many times. In his estimate of the Buchmanites' influence, Deputy Prime Minister J.H. Hofmeyr, who had fallen under Buchman's sway, stated that Buchman's 1929 visit had "started a major and continuing influence for racial reconciliation throughout the whole country, white and black, Dutch and British."[17] Similar estimations appeared after every "traveling team" visit.

The South Africans, curiously, didn't seem to notice the effect of the Buchmanites. Writing in the South African religious newspaper, *The Church Times*, on September 14, 1934, the Cape Town correspondent stated: "The English Newspapers continually bring us news of the wonders which the Group Movement is effecting in South Africa. To it they ascribe the formation of the coalition Government, and the melting away of the barriers between Dutch and English, European and native, Indian and Bantu; . . . It is curious that in South Africa we should know so little of these wonders. It seems clear to us that the coalition Government came into being through sheer weariness of strife; certainly it was never attributed here to the influence of the Groups. And the Groups have long since ceased to attract any attention to speak of."[18]

Undeterred by facts, Oxford Group Movement/Moral Re-Armament (MRA) spokesmen continued to give glowing accounts of their effectiveness in healing racial divisions in South Africa over the coming years. In 1955, South African delegates attended a Moral Re-Armament World Assembly in Washington, D.C. The Allentown *Morning Call*, Buchman's hometown newspaper, reported: "Speakers from South Africa said MRA was replacing racial supremacy and bloody revolution with 'a new dimension of racial unity.'"[19] As late as 1960, Frank Buchman wrote in his birthday message, "A Hurricane of Common Sense," that "White and black leadership in South Africa want their Cabinet and the whole country to see this movie [the MRA film, *The Crowning Experience*]. They say it holds the secret that alone can cure the racial divisions that are tearing South Africa apart, dividing her from other countries, and undermining her economic life."[20] This was written when the apartheid system had already been in place for over a decade, and less than a year before the Sharpeville massacre. Yet Buchman makes no demand that the apartheid system be dismantled; in fact, he makes no criticism of it at all. In his view it was enough that the South Africans see his MRA film.

Such political naïvete was nothing new to Buchman. In 1936, at the height of his movement's prestige and influence, he stated in an interview published in the August 26, 1936 *New York World Telegram:*

> I thank heaven for a man like Adolf Hitler, who built a front line of defence against the anti-Christ of Communism . . .
> Of course I don't condone everything the Nazis do. Anti-semitism? Bad, naturally. I suppose Hitler sees a Karl Marx in every Jew.
> But think what it would mean to the world if Hitler surrendered to the control of God. Or Mussolini. Or any dictator. Through such a man God could control a nation overnight and solve every last, bewildering problem . . . Human problems aren't economic. They're moral and they can't be solved by immoral measures. They could be solved within a God-controlled democracy, or perhaps I should say a theocracy, and they could be solved through a God-controlled Fascist dictatorship.[21]

It's worth noting that Bill Wilson and his fellow AAs-to-be *must* have known about this interview, which caused a public furor, yet they continued to work as part of the Oxford Groups for more than another year in New York and another three years in Akron.

It's also worth noting that AA, in its official "Conference-approved" biography of Bill Wilson, *Pass It On*, treats this matter in what can only be described as a dishonest manner. This is all the more surprising and disappointing in that the book's dust jacket proclaims, "Every word is documented, every source checked."

In the section of *Pass It On* dealing with Buchman's remarks, the anonymous author states:

> In August [1936], the New York *World Telegram* published an article about Buchman, charging that he was pro-Nazi. The newspaper quoted Buchman as saying: "Thank Heaven for a man like Adolf Hitler who built a front-line defense against the Anti-Christ of Communism. Think what it would mean to the world if Hitler surrendered to God. Through such a man, God could control a nation and solve every problem. Human problems aren't economic, they're moral, and they can't be solved by immoral measures."
> While most discussion of the incident, even by Buchman's critics, have since vindicated him, the article brought the group into public controversy.[22]

There are several remarkable features in this passage. The first is that the *World Telegram* piece is referred to as an "article" when in fact it was an *interview* in which Buchman's comments comprised well over half the text, with almost all of the remaining text consisting of descriptive passages, transitions between Buchman's statements, and uncontroversial background information on Buchman and the Oxford Group Movement. There is a tremendous difference between an "article" in which Buchman was "charged" with being pro-Nazi and an *interview* in which he himself clearly expressed pro-Nazi opinions, a fact which undoubtedly was not lost on the author of AA's official Wilson biography.

Another remarkable feature of the passage just quoted from *Pass It On* is that Buchman's statements are carefully edited to put his best possible face forward. The anonymous AA author took fragments separated by hundreds of words and patched them together as if they were a single statement, while dropping a number of words within the fragments. For example, by dropping the word "But" before the words "think what it would mean . . . ," the author made the fragments appear to fit together snugly—thus hiding the fact that the "statement" is a patchwork.

In normal literary practice, it's considered proper to separate patched-together fragments with ellipses if the intervening material doesn't alter the meaning of the quoted material. If the intervening material does alter the meaning, as it does in the "statement" cited in *Pass It On*, it's considered unethical to quote it even with ellipses, and blatantly dishonest to quote it as if it were a single unitary statement. It should also be noted that the author of *Pass It On* quoted Buchman's "statement" in such a way as to leave the impression that it was the *only* such "statement" in the "article."

Perhaps most remarkably, the anonymous AA author concludes that, "most discussions of the incident, even by Buchman's critics, have since vindicated him." One remarkable aspect of this statement is its deliberate fuzziness. What was Buchman "vindicated" of? Of making pro-Nazi statements? Of being pro-Nazi? Our AA author leaves that crucial matter unresolved.

Further, I've done my best to read *all* of the widely circulated criticisms of Buchman's remarks, and *none* "vindicate" him of making pro-Nazi statements. I should also point out that Buchman never denied that he made the statements quoted in the *World Telegram*, and that he never repudiated them.[23] (Since he believed that he was "guided" to make the remarks, if he had repudiated them it would have been a tacit admission that the "guidance" he received was in error; and that would have brought down his whole ideological house of cards, built as it was on the infallibility of "guidance.")

As for "vindicating" Buchman of being pro-Nazi, several of his critics pointed out that Buchman was a political simpleton who believed—as Buchman himself stated in the *World Telegram* interview—that the world's problems could be solved through "a God-controlled democracy," a "theocracy," or a "God-controlled Fascist dictatorship." It must be admitted, though, that in the *World Telegram* interview, Buchman showed decided enthusiasm for the latter option.

As *The Christian Century* pointed out two weeks after Buchman's remarks were published:

> Indeed the worst thing about a religion which undertakes to be purely individualistic and to concern itself not at all as to the way in which the corporate life of society is organized is that it cannot succeed in that undertaking—it is forced to take a political position, and its utter lack of understanding of political realities predetermines what that position shall be.
>
> Such a religion enters the social arena inevitably on the side of reaction. God works through individuals it [Buchmanism] argues. The way to make institutions good is to make the individuals who run them good. The fewer these individuals are, the simpler the operation. The only way to make a good government is to convert the governors, and if there could be but one governor dictating the policies of the nation under God's guidance, the ideal type of state would have been achieved. Individualism in religion thus leads by the straightest of roads to fascism in politics.[24]

If this is "vindication" of Frank Buchman, it's vindication of a very strange sort.

Another "incident" is also revealing of Buchman's attitude toward the Nazis. At the 1936 Berlin Olympics, Buchman offered to introduce British MP Kenneth Lindsay to Heinrich Himmler, who Buchman referred to as "a great lad."[25] At the time, that "great lad" was the head of the Gestapo. It should be remembered, however, that Buchman always took great pains to ingratiate himself with "key men" of all political persuasions (except

Communists). It seems probable that in this incident Buchman was revealing no special love for Himmler, but was simply being his normal, oily self.

Not quite two years after the *World Telegram* interview, Buchman launched his "Moral Rearmament" campaign in Britain on May 28, 1938 in a speech in London. The implication of the slogan "Moral Rearmament" seemed to be that if the people of Britain relied on "guidance" they had no need to physically rearm to fend off Hitler. Three weeks before the Munich conference, Buchman coined the slogan "Guns or Guidance" and— remembering that the influence of Buchman's movement was strongest among rich Tories, that is, members of the ruling class—one can only speculate on the possible contribution of Buchman's Moral Rearmament/ Guns or Guidance campaign to Chamberlain's policy of appeasement.

(Remarkably, in the years since World War II, Moral Re-Armament has attempted to paint Buchman as an advocate of preparedness. The lead sentence in an article posted on MRA's official web site baldly states: "Throughout the 1930's [sic], Frank Buchman continued to arouse the European democracies to the danger of totalitarianism of Left and Right, and to fight strenuously for the concept of true democracy."[26] And in *Moral Re-Armament: What Is It?*, the authors assert that "Buchman's efforts in the 1930s led in many European countries to . . . [an] awakening to the realities of the aims of both Hitler and Stalin . . ."[27] How this jibes with Buchman's "Guns or Guidance" campaign and his enthusiasm for "a theocracy . . . [or] a God-controlled Fascist dictatorship," they don't explain.)

Within three years of Buchman's launching the Moral Re-Armament campaign, the Buchmanites had abandoned the name Oxford Group Movement for all but certain legal purposes, and they began calling themselves Moral Re-Armament, or MRA. Coincidentally with the adoption of the MRA name, the Buchmanites shifted their emphasis from "personal evangelism" to mass propaganda through full-page newspaper advertisements, worldwide radio broadcasts, mass distribution of Buchmanite books and pamphlets, and the holding of huge public rallies. This shift in emphasis did little to reverse the declining fortunes of the movement, which had been on a downhill slide since the time of Buchman's "thank heaven for Hitler" remarks in 1936.

A contributing factor to the decline of Buchmanism was the fact that in both the U.S. and Britain during World War II, several dozen Oxford Group members attempted to obtain exemptions from the draft on the grounds that they were "lay evangelists" and that their work was essential to national morale. *None* of these "lay evangelists" were pacifists or conscientious objectors; they actually favored the war, but had been "guided" not to take part in it because of the importance of their "work." Their "work" consisted of the production of heavy-handed MRA morality plays with titles such as "You Can Defend America." The authorities were impressed by neither their arguments nor their "chicken hawk" attitude, and the Buchmanite "lay evangelists" were soon sporting khaki and crewcuts and marching in lock-step with other conscripts.[28]

The "Moral Rearmament" campaign, the attempts at draft evasion by MRA members, and Buchman's 1936 interview in which he thanked heaven for Hitler contributed to marked public disenchantment with Buchman and his Groups. A good indication of the decline in interest can be found in the number of articles on the Groups listed in the *Reader's Guide to Periodical Literature.* From first mention with only three articles in the January 1929 to June 1932 volume, the total quickly rises to 38 in the July 1932 to June 1935 volume, nosedives to 12 in the following volume, and ultimately bottoms out at zero in the July 1943 to June 1945 volume.[29]

Following the war, Buchman's fortunes revived somewhat, and wealthy backers bought luxurious hotels for his movement at Mackinac Island, Michigan and Caux, Switzerland. This isn't surprising. Buchman's doctrine of individual responsibility for all personal and social ills posed absolutely no threat to the wealth of his backers, allowed them to feel virtuous while retaining their privileges, and even showed some prospects of further domesticating the labor movement.

That was a difficult task given the corrupt, hierarchical, and visionless nature of most American and British unions, but the Buchmanites felt themselves up to the job. From the mid-1930s on, one finds numerous Oxford Groups/MRA claims of successful interventions in labor struggles. The scenarios outlined by MRA were often drearily the same: one of the parties in a dispute, often a labor "leader," was "changed" by the Buchmanites, realized his wrongs, confessed them to someone on the management side who was so touched by the confession that he confessed his wrongs to the original wrongdoer, and the conflict was peacefully resolved; and wages, working conditions, and productivity all improved sharply.

Needless to say, these scenarios were usually pure fantasy. In *The Mystery of Moral Re-Armament,* Tom Driberg cites numerous examples of MRA's false claims. One example is a claim made at the January 16, 1952 MRA "Assembly of the Americas" in Miami, Florida, where a British delegate, "Bill Birmingham, Union Secretary of the Mosley Common Pit, Lancashire," stated that because of MRA activity at the mine "production had increased from 11½ to 15 tons per man per shift," while wages had increased from 37 to 52 shillings per day. According to figures from Lord Robens, chairman of the National Coal Board (which oversees all mine operations in Britain), production had actually increased from 2110 *pounds* per man in 1947 to 2190 pounds per man in 1952, while wages increased from 27 shillings 6 pence to 38 shillings per day.[30]

But fallacious claims of successful interventions in labor disputes were nothing new to the Buchmanites. More than a decade before the Miami Assembly, even *Time* magazine had seen fit on two occasions to make snide comments about Oxford Group Movement/MRA false claims in the labor-dispute field.[31] And MRA's outrageous claims in this area have persisted to the present day. In the previously cited article posted on MRA's web site, one finds the claim that "One group of men, for instance, tackled unemployment [in Denmark in the late '30s] which was running at over 20 per cent. It was reduced eventually to 4.7 per cent."[32] How and when MRA accomplished this amazing feat is not revealed. Perhaps MRA's success occurred during World War II, when Adolf Hitler "tackled [Danish] unemployment" and drastically reduced it through forced labor.

Despite the exaggerated and often wholly unrealistic claims made by MRA, Buchman's movement did have some influence in the upper echelons of the labor bureaucracy. MRA publicly bragged of this influence: "Illustrations of the effectiveness of this ideology in industry could be taken from all around the world. One of the 'five giants of American labor' lay dying. [MRA never identifies the "giant."] He said to a Senator, 'Tell America that when Frank Buchman changed John Riffe [Executive Vice-President of the CIO], he saved American industry 500 million dollars."[33] In April 1953, 13 years after he fell under Buchman's influence, Riffe listed his aims for American labor. One of them sounded as if it could just as easily have been issued by a leader of a Nazi or Soviet official trade union: "With the united strength of labor and industry to back the government in a foreign policy that will win all nations.[34]

MRA's focus on labor was but one part of its post-war strategy to present Moral Re-Armament as the *only* alternative to Communism. In *Ideology and Co-Existence*—a Moral Re-Armament pamphlet distributed by the millions in 1959 in the U.S. and Britain—its anonymous MRA author states: "There are two ideologies bidding for the world today. One is Moral Re-Armament . . . ; the other is Communism . . ."[35] This is a rather grandiose self-assessment, but hardly a surprising one from an organization whose members and leadership believed that it was guided by God.

One ideological prong of MRA's post-war strategy was its emphasis on influencing organized labor; the other two prongs were a McCarthyite brand of anti-Communism and crude homophobia. The Buchmanites could not conceive of anyone disagreeing with them, much less attacking them, unless he or she were under Communist influence or otherwise morally tainted—a fact abundantly obvious from reading their literature of the period. One 1950s MRA book states: "Moral Re-Armament cannot be honestly opposed on intellectual grounds because it is basic truth . . . Opposition to Moral Re-Armament has special significance. It always comes from the morally defeated."[36] Like many other MRA pronouncements, this statement is very arrogant, but hardly surprising. MRA believed (like many deranged murderers—"God told me to do it") that it had a direct line to the Almighty, and hence The Truth; and who but someone morally tainted would opposed God's chosen spokesmen? This is the cardinal article of faith in every religious fanatic's creed: s/he has The Truth, and anyone who criticizes that Truth, or its bearer, *must* be immoral.

MRA really did believe that there was a Communist under every bed (and a "pervert" in it). In *Ideology and Co-Existence,* we read that "Chiang Kai-Shek was sold out and the mainland and Manchuria lost to Red China . . . Men, later found to be giving the Communist Party line, were successful with their deceptions and achieved the change of direction in American policy [which led to the "loss" of China]."[37]

An even clearer echo of McCarthy—but in reference to homosexuals, "security risks," in MRA terms—can be found in a book written by Peter Howard, Buchman's successor as head of MRA, which was published a few years after *Ideology and Co-Existence*: "At one point, 264 homosexuals were reported to have been purged from the American State Department. Many of them moved from Washington to New York and took jobs in the United Nations . . ."[38] This startling information appears in a chapter titled "Queens and Queers." It's very reminiscent of Joe McCarthy's famous speech in Wheeling, West Virginia on February 9, 1950, in which he said: "I have here in my hand a list of 205—a list of names that were made known to the Secretary of State as being members of the Communist Party and who are, nevertheless, still working and shaping policy in the State Department." (Despite repeated challenges, McCarthy, of course, never produced the "list.") Another example of Buchmanite homophobia can be found in a 1963 advertisement in the *New York Times* in which Moral Re-Armament attacked "sexual deviants in high places who protect potential spies."[39 40]

MRA's attacks on homosexuals were not always purely venomous; at times they were also ludicrous. A 1954 Moral Re-Armament tract instructs readers on how to spot homosexuals:

> There are many who wear suede shoes who are not homosexual, but in Europe and America the majority of homosexuals do. They favor green as a color in clothes and decorations. Men are given to an excessive display and use of the handkerchief. They tend to let the hair grow long, use scent and are frequently affected in speech, mincing in gait and feminine in mannerisms. They are often very gifted in the arts. They tend to exhibitionism. They can be cruel and vindictive, for sadism usually has a homosexual root. They are often given to moods.
>   . . . There is an unnecessary touching of hands, arms and shoulders. In the homosexual the elbow grip is a well-known sign.[41]

Moral Re-Armament's virulent homophobia and obsession with homo-sexuality seem odd at first glance, but they make sense when one realizes that Frank Buchman was quite probably a "closeted" homosexual, per-petually at war with his own desires. Thus, in all likelihood, his own inner battle (against homosexual inclinations, or "perversion," as he often called it) ultimately became MRA's battle.

Buchman certainly exhibited many signs of being a "closet case": 1) he never married; 2) it was never even hinted in any of the numerous books and magazine articles written about him and his movement that he had sexual relations with women; 3) he was obsessed with sexual "sin," specifically self-"abuse" and "perversion"; 4) from the time he was ordained in his early 20s until he was nearly 50, his primary concern was working with young men; 5) he apparently relished discussing intimate sexual matters with young men; and 6) he was markedly homophobic, which is often a defense mechanism used by "closet cases" to conceal their true desires from both themselves and others.

As well, I've uncovered some slight direct evidence that Buchman was indeed homosexual: shortly after publication of the first edition of this book, the son of a member of Buchman's inner circle told me that among that circle "Buchman's homosexuality was taken for granted."[42] This all makes Buchman's and MRA's obsession with "purity" and "perversion" much easier to understand.

Frank Buchman died in Freudenstadt, Germany on August 6, 1961, and his long-time disciple, Peter Howard, took the reins of Moral Re-Armament. MRA continued much as it had under Buchman for the next few years, but the loss of its guru was a blow from which it never recovered. Howard died suddenly in 1965 without designating a successor, and the organization quickly shriveled.

The leadership vacuum and the unsavory reputation Moral Re-Armament had acquired through its red-baiting and gay-baiting evidently combined to nearly put an end to MRA. By 1970 the organization had effectively ceased to exist in the U.S.[43]; and by 1972 it was in serious decline in Britain. At that point, its reputation was so tarnished that the liberal Protestant weekly, The Christian Century, reported that MRA, through its actions, had acquired "a sinister mafia image, and to be identified with it in any way remains a serious liability for anyone seeking public support."[44] At present, Moral Re-Armament continues to exist in both Britain and the U.S., but only as a shadow of its former self. (A few MRA books have been published over the last quarter century, and MRA currently publishes a slick, expensively produced monthly magazine, For a Change; as well, MRA maintains offices in Washington and London, retains its conference/hotel complex in Caux, Switzerland, and has added conference centers in India and Zimbabwe. But MRA has been out of the public spotlight for decades, and its membership is undoubtedly but a small fraction of what it was during its heyday in the 1930s.)

In the U.S., Moral Re-Armament lived on in the form of Sing Out!/Up with People!, the cloyingly wholesome kiddie vocal group cum traveling pep rally, whose "message" was, and is, taken straight from MRA. For well over a quarter century, Up with People! performances have been inflicted upon many millions of high school students (including the author on one dreary afternoon in the late 1960s).

Sing Out! was founded in 1965 by MRA member J. Blanton Belk, at Peter Howard's behest, and for its first two years was sponsored by MRA and the Reader's Digest Foundation. It retained its original name for roughly two years before becoming Up with People! in 1967. Sing Out!/Up with People! was almost certainly intended to be MRA's "antidote to hippies and peaceniks," as the *Dallas Times Herald* put it in 1967. The group's formal ties with Moral Re-Armament were, however, short-lived, probably because its association with MRA created fundraising difficulties.

Following its incorporation in 1968, Up with People! became organizationally independent of Moral Re-Armament, though MRA's influence was, and still remains, obvious. One former cast member from Sing Out!'s early days told me that boys and girls were forbidden to sit together on buses because of "purity" concerns, and that he distinctly remembers one assembly for male cast members, the specific purpose of which was to warn them against taking warm showers lest they become aroused and engage in self-"abuse." Another area where MRA's influence is evident is in Up with People!'s inflated self-concept. In 1967, Calvin Trillin archly commented, "Any place that 'Up with People!' has visited tends to sound like a battleground in the struggle . . . the show always seems to have arrived in a foreign country 'just weeks after violent demonstrations'; the names of Negro urban areas are normally preceded by 'the streets of,' so that cast members talk of having sung in 'the streets of Watts.'"[45]

In 1990, Up with People!'s annual budget was $19 million, much of it contributed by corporations such as General Electric, Coca-Cola, and Volvo. Members of the cast and their sponsors (often Rotary Clubs or the like) kicked in the rest. In 1990, cast members were expected to pay $9,200 for the privilege of being in the group for one year, though more than 30 percent of them received financial help from the organization.[46] In all likelihood, Up with People! will be around for some time, as the messages in its songs are music to corporate ears.

Today, Frank Buchman, the Oxford Group Movement, and Moral Re-Armament are nearly forgotten. Probably not one person in a hundred under the age of 50 would recognize Buchman's name or the names Oxford

Group Movement or Moral Re-Armament; and probably not one in a thousand could provide even the meagerest information about Buchman or his groups. But the influence of Frank Buchman and his minions lingers on. His doctrines are almost certainly more widely adhered to and more influential now than they ever were during his lifetime—even if not one person in a thousand knows their origin.

---

1. *The Mystery of Moral Re-Armament,* by Tom Driberg. New York: Alfred A. Knopf, 1965. Quoted on p. 37.

2. *The Oxford Group: Its History and Significance,* by Walter Houston Clark. New York: Bookman Associates, 1951, p. 41. The source given for this information is an unnamed alumnus.

3. Ibid., p. 49.

4. "Report on Buchmanism," *Time,* Jan. 4, 1943, p. 68.

5. *Time,* April 20, 1936, p. 37.

6. Driberg, op. cit., p. 256.

7. *Frank Buchman's Secret,* by Peter Howard. New York: Doubleday, 1961, p. 12.

8. Ibid., p. 83.

9. *The Confusion of Tongues,* by Charles W. Ferguson. Grand Rapids, Michigan: Zondervan Publishing House, 1940, p. 16.

10. Ibid.

11. Writers sympathetic to Buchman, the Oxford Group Movement, and Alcoholics Anonymous have put a different interpretation on these events. A good example is provided by Bill Pittman in *A.A. The Way It Began* (Seattle: Glen Abbey Books, 1988). In his carefully sanitized chapter on the Oxford Groups, Pittman omits mention of Buchman's comments to Hibden but notes that Buchman "claimed that the problem at Princeton was that most of the criticism of the Group's frankness on sexual matters came from a group of sexual perverts." (pp. 118–119) And he lets the matter rest with that.

12. *Saints Run Mad,* by Marjorie Harrison. London: John Lane the Bodley Head, 1934. Quoted on page 39.

13. "Report on Buchmanism," *Time,* January 4, 1943, p. 68.

14. *On the Tail of a Comet: The Life of Frank Buchman,* by Garth Lean. Colorado Springs, Colorado: Helmers & Howard, 1988, pp. 261-263.

15. "Apostle to the Twentieth Century," by Henry P. Van Dusen, *The Atlantic Monthly,* July, 1934, p. 13.

16. During World War I, Ford published a series of viciously anti-semitic articles in *The Dearborn Independent,* a Michigan newspaper that he owned. He later published these articles in book form as *The International Jew: The World's Foremost Problem.* In the early 1920s, this book was published in Germany under the title, *The Eternal Jew.* It reportedly had a major influence on Adolf Hitler, and he almost certainly plagiarized parts of it in *Mein Kampf.* The admiration was mutual. Following Hitler' assumption of power, Ford sent Hitler 50,000 Deutsch Marks every year on Hitler's birthday. Ford's anti-semitic views were well known during the period that the Buchmanites bragged of Ford's support of their movement. For more information on Ford's Nazi connections, see *Who Financed Hitler?,* by James and Suzanne Pool. New York: Dial Press, 1978.

17. Driberg, op. cit., p. 174.

18. Quoted in *The Groups Movement*, by the Most Rev. John A. Richardson. Milwaukee: Morehouse Publishing Co., 1935, pp. 23-24.

19. Quoted in Driberg, op. cit., p. 175.

20. Ibid.

21. Quoted in Driberg, op. cit., pp. 68-69.

22. *Pass It On.* New York: Alcoholics Anonymous World Services, 1988, pp. 170-171.

23. Half a century later, MRA writer Garth Lean, in *On the Tail of a Comet* (op. cit., p. 240), denied that Buchman had said "Thank God for Hitler." (It should be noted that this is not the wording in the *World Telegram* interview, nor, to the best of my knowledge, is Buchman's statement quoted in this form in any source except Lean's book.) Lean quotes a fellow MRA member, Garrett Stearly, who was supposedly present at the interview, as stating that Buchman "said that Germany needed a new Christian spirit, yet one had to face the fact that Hitler had been a bulwark against Communism there—and you could at least thank heaven for that," a remark which Stearly regarded as "no eulogy of Hitler at all." Given the nature of journalism, it is certainly possible that the phrasing of Buchman's statement was that quoted by Stearly rather than that quoted in the *World Telegram* interview. In either case, however, it's quite clear that Buchman was happy that Hitler's rise to power had created a "front-line of defense" or a "bulwark" against Communism.

In his defense of Buchman, Lean makes no denial that Buchman waxed enthusiastic over the possibilities of a "God-controlled Fascist dictator." Indeed, it would be very surprising if Buchman didn't harbor such sentiments. The main thrust of Buchmanism was to persuade "key men" to place themselves under "God-control," so that they could carry out "God's will"; and there is virtually no one in a more "key" position than a fascist dictator.

24. "A God-Guided Dictator," *The Christian Century*, September 9, 1936, p. 1183.

25. Driberg, op. cit., pp. 64-65.

26. In the site's "Discovering MRA" section: "Arousing Europe to the gathering storm," http://www.mra.org.uk/discovering/06arouse.html

27. Op. cit., p. 55.

28. For a fuller description of these events see Driberg, op. cit., pp. 105-111. See also Clark, op. cit., p. 81; *Drawing Room Conversion: A Sociological Account of the Oxford Group Movement*, by Allan W. Eister. Durham, North Carolina: Duke University Press, 1950, pp. 62-63; "Less Buchmanism," *Time*, November 24, 1941, pp. 59-60; and "Buchman's Kampf," *Time*, January 18, 1943, pp. 65-66.

29. The actual numbers are Jan. 1929–June 1932, 3 articles; July 1932–June 1935, 38 articles; July 1935–June 1937, 12 articles; July 1937–June 1939, 12 articles; July 1939–June 1941, 5 articles; July 1941–June 1943, 5 articles; July 1943–June 1945, zero articles.

30. Driberg, op. cit., pp. 127-128.

31. See *Time*, November 24, 1941, p. 59, and July 31, 1939, p. 34.

32. "Arousing Europe to the gathering storm," op. cit., p. 2.

33. *Ideology and Co-Existence.* Moral Re-Armament, 1959, p. 14.

34. Ibid.

35. Ibid., p. 1.

36. *Remaking Men*, by Paul Campbell and Peter Howard. New York: Arrowhead Books, 1954, p. 66.

37. Op. cit., p. 23.

38. *Britain and the Beast*, by Peter Howard. London: Heinemann, 1963, p. 47.

39. Quoted by Calvin Trillin in *The New Yorker*, December 16, 1967, p. 134.

40. In a choice bit of irony, at roughly the same time that MRA was conducting its red-baiting/gay-baiting campaign against homosexual "security risks," the Communist Party had a policy of expelling gay members because it too considered them "security risks." Harry Hay, a longtime Communist and founder of the first American gay rights group, the Mattachine Society, states: "About the fall of 1951 I decided that organizing the Mattachine was a call to me deeper than the innermost reaches of spirit, a vision-quest more important than life. I went to the Communist Party and discussed this "total call" upon me, recommending to them my expulsion. They rejected 'expulsion,' and, in honor of my eighteen years as a member and ten years as a teacher and cultural innovator dropped me as a 'security risk but as a life-long friend of the people.'" Quoted in *Gay American History: Lesbians and Gay Men in the U.S.A.*, by Jonathan Ned Katz. New York: Meridian, 1992, p. 413.

41. Campbell and Howard, op. cit., pp. 60-62.

42. Unfortunately, I cannot disclose my source for this information. Shortly after publication of the first edition of this book, I lost touch with him. I've made several attempts to find him during preparation of this expanded edition, without success; but I'm convinced that he was telling me the truth about this matter.

43. See "Moral Re-Armament RIP" in *National Review*, October 20, 1970, p. 1099.

44. "When the White Begins to Fade," *The Christian Century*, June 28, 1972, p. 704.

45. Trillin, op. cit., p. 132.

46. "1960s Troupe Celebrates 25 Years of Enthusiasm," by Dirk Johnson. *New York Times*, July 29, 1990, p. 18, section 1.

3

A Brief History of AA

The purpose of this chapter is *not* to give a detailed history of Alcoholics Anonymous. AA's story has been told at length by other writers in other books.[1] The purpose of *Alcoholics Anonymous: Cult or Cure?* is to analyze AA as it exists today; and while readers will require a certain amount of historical information in order to understand AA, they will not require an intimate knowledge of AA's history. So, this chapter will provide an overview of AA's history, while emphasizing facts pertinent to its organizational development and to the development of its "program."

William Griffith (Bill) Wilson, the co-founder and the driving force behind Alcoholics Anonymous, was born on November 24, 1895 in East Dorset, Vermont. His father, Gilman, a heavy drinker, was the foreman at a marble quarry. In 1905, his parents divorced, and Bill and his sister were entrusted to the care of their maternal grandparents while their mother studied osteopathy in Boston. Bill's grandfather was a landlord with extensive holdings, and the richest man in East Dorset, so despite the trauma of his parents' divorce and his separation from both his father and mother, Bill was at least materially well off during his late childhood and adolescence.

In 1917, following an unsuccessful attempt to get into MIT, Wilson joined the army and became a second lieutenant. He took his first drink that same year. On January 24, 1918 he married Lois Burnham, his sweetheart from Vermont, who remained his wife until his death in 1971. Later in 1918 he was shipped with his unit to Europe, though he never saw combat; and in 1919 he was shipped home, discharged, and began living in New York City.

Like many other returning veterans he had a tough time finding regular employment, and at one point he quit a job on the docks because he refused to join a union.[2] That's not surprising given Wilson's background, conservative politics, and admiration for businessmen—"power drivers" as he called them. (In the "Big Book, he comments that "Business and financial leaders were my heroes."[3]) In *Pass It On*, AA's official Wilson biography, he's quoted as saying, "I objected very much to joining the union, and I was threatened by force, and I left the job rather than join the union."[4] Given the nature of the AFL unions, it wouldn't have been surprising if he was threatened. Eventually, Wilson landed a job as an investigator for a brokerage firm and began his rise on Wall Street, a rise which would make him a rich man and which would last until the stock market crash in 1929.

All through the 1920s, Wilson's drinking had gradually worsened, and when the crash came he went on a bender. He was ruined. He had been a margin trader and lost everything in the crash. Eventually, he and Lois moved in with her father, she took a job in a department store, and his drinking continued to worsen. He couldn't hold a job and his drinking resulted in blackouts, bar room brawls, temporary separation from his wife, panhandling, DTs, and pawning household items to pay for booze. He was on the ropes physically and emotionally. In 1933 and 1934 he was hospitalized several times at the Charles B. Towns Hospital in Manhattan under the care of Dr. William Silkworth, with his brother-in-law, Leonard Strong, paying his hospital bills.

Bill Wilson finally escaped from his alcoholic nightmare at the end of 1934. In the fall of that year, Ebby Thatcher, an old boarding school friend, stopped by to visit him. Like Bill, Ebby had been an extremely heavy drinker, so Bill was quite surprised when Ebby refused to drink with him. When Bill asked him why, Ebby replied that he had gotten religion, and that he was a member of the Oxford Group Movement.

Ebby had been introduced to the Movement by Roland Hazard, another alcoholic. Like Ebby, Roland was a "hopeless" alcoholic from a privileged background. Several years earlier he had been in desperate straits and had traveled to Switzerland and placed himself under the care of Dr. Carl Jung, the mystically inclined former pupil of Freud, in an attempt to find a cure for his abusive drinking. Roland had been sober for a year while under Jung's direct care, but when he left Jung he had gotten drunk almost immediately. In frustration, Jung told him that his only chance lay in religious conversion, an option Roland had seized upon by joining the Oxford Groups. When Roland told him about this way of overcoming alcoholism, Ebby had seized upon this "chance" as readily as had Roland.

Sitting in the Wilson kitchen, Ebby outlined the Groups' teachings to Wilson: 1) Admission of personal defeat; 2) Taking of personal inventory; 3) Confession of one's defects to another person; 4) Making restitution to those one has harmed; 5) Helping others selflessly; 6) Praying to God for the power to put these precepts into practice. Bill was unimpressed, however, and continued to drink for the next several weeks.

On December 11, 1934, Wilson's drinking came to a screeching halt. On that day he was readmitted to Towns Hospital, sedated, and subjected to Dr. Silkworth's "belladonna cure," a treatment regimen which included morphine and other psychoactive drugs in addition to belladonna (which in large doses is a powerful hallucinogen).[5] While under the influence of the "cure," Bill Wilson experienced his "spiritual awakening." He described the experience in *Alcoholics Anonymous Comes of Age:*

> I found myself crying out, "If there is a God, let Him show Himself!" I am ready to do anything!"
> Suddenly the room lit up with a great white light . . . All about me there was a wonderful feeling of Presence, and I thought to myself, "So this is the God of the Preachers."[6]

The day after Bill Wilson's "spiritual awakening," Ebby Thatcher brought him a copy of *The Varieties of Religious Experience*, by William James. Wilson read it cover to cover. He later wrote in the "Big Book" that he found the idea in it that spiritual experiences—which could come in many forms—had the power to transform lives. Nearly 20 years after he wrote the "Big Book," in *Alcoholics Anonymous Comes of Age*, Wilson also credited James with the idea that "deflation at depth" was necessary before a spiritual experience could occur.[7] Curiously, neither the words "deflation at depth" nor the single word "deflation" occur anywhere in James' book; James does, however, state that some type of extremely jarring event often occurs before a "spiritual experience." Another important idea found in *Varieties*, and one which is the cornerstone of AA, is the suggestion that the "only radical remedy . . . for dipsomania is religiomania."[8]

For several months following his stay at Towns Hospital and his "spiritual awakening," Bill Wilson attempted to singlehandedly put Oxford Group principles into practice in the field of alcoholism. He worked tirelessly, seeking out drunks to "work on." He devoted all of his energies to attempts to help other alcoholics sober up, by carrying the Oxford Group Movement message to them, and even by allowing many to live in his home.

While Bill devoted his energies to fruitless attempts to sober up drunks, Lois continued to work in a department store. She wasn't making much money, and they were in a precarious financial position. Eventually, Bill decided to seek employment, and in May 1935 he traveled to Akron, Ohio to take part in a proxy fight for control of a machine tool firm, the National Rubber Machinery Company. The fight went badly and Wilson quickly found himself alone in a hotel lobby with ten dollars in his pocket—and within a few feet of an inviting bar.

He didn't succumb to the temptation to seek companionship in such familiar surroundings; instead, he went to the nearest phone and called

Walter Tunks, an Episcopalian minister and the leading supporter of the Oxford Groups among the Akron clergy. He told Tunks that he was a drunk and a member of the Oxford Groups who needed to find another drunk in order to stay sober. Tunks gave him ten numbers to call. After nine fruitless calls, he dialed the last number on the list, that of Henrietta Seiberling.

She was delighted to hear from Bill Wilson because she was very concerned about the destructive drinking of an Oxford Group friend, Dr. Robert Smith. Smith, a judge's son, was a Dartmouth graduate and an M.D. who had become a proctologist and skilled surgeon; but he was also a hardcore abusive drinker with severe financial problems. The day that Bill Wilson called Henrietta Seiberling, Smith was unavailable because he had passed out at home, dead drunk. So, Seiberling arranged for Wilson and Smith to meet late the following afternoon at her home.

Dr. Smith, who was very shaky that day, agreed to meet with Wilson only to please his wife Anne and his friend Henrietta. He expected to talk with the stranger from New York for no more than 15 minutes. They ended up talking for more than six hours, and Dr. Smith was deeply affected. The man who would later become known within AA as "Dr. Bob" immediately quit drinking.

Seeing the surprising change in her friend, Henrietta Seiberling was determined to keep Bill Wilson in Akron. At the time, however, Bill was dead broke; so, Henrietta arranged with a neighbor to allow Bill to stay at a local country club for two weeks. At about the same time, Bill received additional money from New York to continue the proxy fight over the machine tool company. After his two-week stay at the country club, he moved into the Smiths' home at the invitation of Anne Smith.

Wilson's stay at the Smiths' went smoothly. While he lived with them, Bill Wilson and the Smiths made the practice of Oxford Group principles a focus of their lives. In particular, they held a daily "quiet time" in the morning which they devoted to meditation, Bible reading, and receiving "guidance" from God. As importantly, Bill and Dr. Bob almost immediately began to "work on" other drunks.

Shortly after they began this regimen, Dr. Bob decided to attend the annual AMA convention in Atlantic City. Within a week of his leaving, he arrived back in Ohio blind drunk. Bill and Anne sobered him up, and on June 10, 1935, Dr. Bob took his last drink (to steady his nerves before an operation). This is often cited as the founding date of Alcoholics Anonymous.

Wilson and Smith wasted no time in continuing the search for other drunks. Despite several failures, they did succeed in sobering up two more alcoholics during the summer of 1935. By late that summer, however, the proxy fight for control of the machine tool company had failed, and Wilson was obliged to return to New York. He left behind him Dr. Smith and two other ex-drunks, all three of whom were attending Oxford Group meetings and faithfully practicing Oxford Group principles. Some time during or shortly after this period, Dr. Bob's small group of alcoholics started to call themselves "the alcoholic squadron [or "squad"—there are references to both] of the Akron Oxford Group."

Once back in New York, Bill Wilson continued to devote most of his energies to working with other alcoholics, turning his home into a halfway house for drunks, again with no success. A particularly jarring failure was that of Bill C., a lawyer who lived with the Wilsons for almost a year. After repeatedly (and without detection) stealing from them, he committed suicide. When Bill and Lois returned home after a visit to a member of their fledgling society in Maryland, they found Bill C.'s decomposing body and a house reeking of gas.[9]

In late 1935, at a time when the Wilson home still functioned as a halfway house, small groups of alcoholics and their wives began to meet there for an open house on Tuesday evenings; thus the second de facto AA group was born. It didn't take long for the Wilsons to notice that some of the drunks who turned up on Tuesday nights were staying sober, while none of those who were living in their home managed to do so. The members of the Tuesday night group also attended Oxford Group meetings, a practice which would continue until late 1937. At that time, the still-unnamed New York group of ex-alcoholics severed its connections with the Oxford Group Movement.

There were several reasons for the split. An important one was that Wilson and his band of ex-drunks were only interested in working with other alcoholics. As time went on, this caused friction with an ever-growing number of non-alcoholic Oxford Group members; increasing numbers of them received "guidance" that Wilson should quit working with alcoholics and instead concentrate his energies directly on Oxford Groups work. For their part, the alcoholics found the Oxford Groups too "authoritarian," and took no part in the Groups Movement other than attending meetings. From his writings, it seems clear that while Bill Wilson agreed wholeheartedly with Oxford Group Movement principles, he felt that for alcoholics, "These ideas had to be fed with teaspoons rather than by buckets."[10] (This statement largely explains why Oxford Group Movement principles are clearly presented, but are expressed so unforcefully, and at times euphemistically, in the "Big Book.")

These differences alone would probably have been enough to ensure the eventual disaffiliation of the reformed New York alcoholics from the Oxford Groups. It's also possible that Oxford Group founder Frank Buchman's interview in the August 26, 1936 *New York World Telegram*, in which he was quoted as saying, "I thank heaven for a man like Adolf Hitler," provided additional incentive for Wilson to put distance between his group of ex-drunks and the Oxford Group Movement. That's impossible to know, however, as Bill Wilson apparently left no written record of the matter, and AA's official literature treats it in a very circumspect manner. (It is possible that Wilson commented on the matter, but that his comments lie hidden somewhere in that large portion of his correspondence that AA refuses to open to researchers.)

There were two further reasons why Wilson's group left the Oxford Group Movement. One was that the Catholic Church was very critical of the Buchmanites, and Wilson didn't want to run the risk of Catholics being forbidden to join his group. The other was that the easiest way to avoid controversy and divisiveness was to concentrate solely on alcoholism. So, formal ties were severed between Wilson's ex-alcoholics and the Oxford Groups; nevertheless, the New Yorkers continued to be guided by many of the Oxford Group Movement's principles.

In the fall of 1937, Bill Wilson made a second business trip to Akron. While there, he met with Dr. Smith. By this time, Wilson had decided that their organization needed to expand through paid missionaries, hospitals for alcoholics, and publication of its principles in book form, and that they needed to raise funds for those purposes. While he supported the idea of a book, Dr. Bob had doubts about paid missionaries and hospitals. Neverthe-less, he supported all of Wilson's proposals at a meeting of the Akron "alcoholic squadron" and all of Bill's ideas were approved by a narrow margin after heated debate. Upon returning home, his proposals were enthusiastically approved by the New York group.

In the spring of 1938, Bill Wilson began to write what was to become the "Big Book" of Alcoholics Anonymous. After several months of work, Wilson completed the book. It's worth noting that because he was a firm adherent to Oxford Group Movement principles, and so believed that he lived a "guided" life, Wilson very probably believed that he wrote the entire "Big Book" under divine "guidance." It's certain that he believed that he had written the 12 steps under such "guidance"; in *Lois Remembers*, Lois Wilson recalls that, "He relaxed and asked for guidance. When he finished writing and reread what he had put down, he was quite pleased. Twelve principles had developed—the Twelve Steps."[11]

He apparently wrote the entire portion which outlined the AA program, with the exception of "The Doctor's Opinion," which was written by Dr. William Silkworth of Towns Hospital. The remainder of the book consisted of members' stories. The New Yorkers wrote their own, while the Akronites composed theirs with the help of a member who had been a professional journalist. In addition to contributing their stories, members in New York and Akron read the sections Bill wrote and contributed criticisms and suggestions, many of which were incorporated into the book.

During the book's writing, serious disputes had arisen over both its title and contents. Before *Alcoholics Anonymous* was settled on as the title, several others had been proposed. One title in particular, *The Way Out*, was quite popular and would probably have been adopted but for the fact that there were 25 books listed by that name in the Library of Congress, while there were none listed under the name *Alcoholics Anonymous*.

More serious disagreement arose over the 12 steps. They were a distillation of Oxford Group Movement principles, principles which some members of Wilson's New York group found unpalatable. In the original version of the steps, Wilson had included the words "on our knees" in step 7, but many members felt that this was too overtly religious and would drive away alcoholics. A few even objected to the use of the word "God," but they were outvoted. Some concessions, however, were made to nonbelievers—the elimination of the offensive words in step 7, the additions of the words "as we understood Him" after the word "God" in steps 3 and 11, and the substitution of the phrase "a Power greater than ourselves" for the word "God" in step 2. Additionally, the steps were prefaced with the statement: "Here are the Steps we took which are suggested as a Program of Recovery." The changes made to the steps were relatively insignificant, but the prefacing statement was important. Because it stated that AA's "Program" was only "suggested," it (in theory) allowed nonbelievers to participate in AA without embracing the religiosity of the steps.[12] (For a fuller discussion of the steps, see Chapter 5.)

It's interesting to note that in the "Big Book" Bill Wilson gives no credit whatsoever to the Oxford Groups as the source of the AA program, even though every single one of the 12 steps is directly traceable to Buchman's teachings. This deliberate omission was, almost certainly, the result of Wilson's desire not to incur the wrath of the Catholic clergy. The only influences he mentions in the "Big Book" are Carl Jung's advice to seek a cure for alcoholism through "vital spiritual experiences" and the idea expressed in William James' *Varieties of Religious Experience* that such experiences can take many forms.

A revealing sidelight to these attributions is that it's quite possible that Jung had borrowed the idea of "religiomania" as a cure for "dipsomania" directly from *Varieties*, which had been translated into German in 1907. What's even more revealing is the fact that the suggestion in James' book that religion could be a cure for drunkenness had come directly from William S. Hadley, an American alcoholic who underwent his own "conversion experience" in New York City in 1871 and then immersed himself in evangelical missionary work—thus placing himself as a spiritual ancestor of the later evangelist and missionary, Frank Buchman.[13] So, it certainly seems possible that the idea of "religiomania" as a cure for "dipsomania" came full circle: from New York ex-drunk and evangelist William Hadley to William James, from James to Carl Jung, and from Jung via Roland Hazard and Ebby Thatcher to ex-drunk Bill Wilson back in New York, who failed to credit the immediate evangelical source of AA's "program" (the Oxford Groups), while pointedly mentioning both Jung and James. Whatever the case, it seems probable that Wilson cited Jung and James in the "Big Book" in an attempt to lend it intellectual respectability, and that he failed to cite the Oxford Groups in order to avoid trouble with the Catholic Church.

While the "Big Book" was being written, Bill and his fellow AAs moved to set up a formal non-profit organization to unify the fellowship and to enable the wealthy to give tax-deductible donations to it. The name they settled upon was the Alcoholic Foundation, and in May 1938 it held its first meeting. Its trustees (now the General Service Board of Alcoholics Anonymous) were divided between alcoholics and nonalcoholics, with the nonalcoholics having a majority of one vote on the board.

The first steps toward obtaining financial backing from the rich were made in late 1937. Through his brother-in-law, Leonard Strong, Bill was able to see Willard Richardson, an ordained minister and an aide to John D. Rockefeller, Jr. Richardson arranged a meeting between Bill, Dr. Bob, and other Oxford Group/AA members, and several friends and advisers of Mr. Rockefeller. The meeting went smoothly, and one Rockefeller adviser, Frank Amos, was appointed to further investigate the group. After traveling to Akron and observing Dr. Bob and company in action, Amos recommended that Rockefeller give $50,000 to AA, with more to follow. Rockefeller, however, refused, citing the fear that "money will spoil this thing."[14] He did, however, donate $5000 (equivalent to about $57,000 today) to relieve Bill's and Dr. Bob's immediate financial problems. A portion of the money was used to pay off Dr. Smith's home mortgage, and the remainder was put in a trust fund from which AA's two co-founders began to draw $30 per week apiece (equivalent to about $340 per week apiece today).

While Bill Wilson was writing the "Big Book," it was still unclear who would publish the book once it was finished. Wilson had received a contract offer with provision for a $1500 advance from a commercial publisher, Harper & Brothers, but after much contemplation—he was in serious financial straits despite Rockefeller's gift, and $1500 was a lot of money in 1938—he decided that AA should publish its own literature.

The Alcoholic Foundation, however, did not raise any money for the project. So, Wilson and Hank P., a member of the New York AA group and Wilson's business partner in Honor Dealers, a gasoline-buying cooperative, set up an ad hoc publishing venture, Works Publishing Co. They expected to sell shares to the by-now 50 or so AA members, but, to their surprise and disappointment, they were unable to sell a single share. Finally, after they talked to a member of the *Reader's Digest* staff and believed that they had obtained a promise of a story upon publication of the book, they managed to sell 200 shares at $25 each, Charles Towns lent them an additional $2500, and an AA member's sibling, "Fitz's sister, Agnes," lent them an additional $1000.[15][16] As for the loans, *Pass It On* doesn't mention the $1000 loan, but presents the Towns loan as if it were to Works Publishing,[17] while Lois Wilson clearly states that the purpose of both loans was for living expenses.[18] As for ownership of the company, the shareholders owned one-third of the company, while Bill and Hank, who had awarded themselves 200 shares apiece, each owned an additional third.[19] But even after raising $8500, they didn't have the money to print the book the following year, and they would have had great difficulty in publishing it but for a sympathetic printer, Edward Blackwell at Cornwall Press, who agreed to print the book with $500 down and no further guarantee other than Bill's and Hank's promise of eventual payment.[20]

This is most surprising given that $8500 in 1938 (the amount that Bill and Hank raised) translates to over $97,000 in 1997 dollars, according to the Federal Reserve Bank.[21] As well, according to Lois Wilson, the per-unit cost of printing the "Big Book" was only 35 cents apiece,[22] which—given the initial print run of 5000—yields a total printing cost of only $1750 (in 1938 dollars).[23] Amazingly, out of the $8500 they raised, Bill Wilson and Hank P. didn't even have enough money to pay the under-$2000 printing bill; they only had $500 left. Somehow, during the course of the year before the "Big Book's" printing, the equivalent of over $91,000 in today's currency evaporated. (Subtracting the $3500 apparently borrowed for living expenses [equivalent to just over $40,000 today] still leaves a very large unexplained deficit.) In *Pass It On*, Bill Wilson's biographer comments: "That [$8500] was enough to support the work during the writing process, although it would not cover the printing costs."[24] And he leaves it at that.

In contrast, the pre-printing costs for this book, *Alcoholics Anonymous: Cult or Cure?*, came to under $1000 in 1997 currency; that translates to a cost of about $88 in 1938 dollars—under 2% of what Bill and Hank raised through sale of stock, and about 1% of the total that they raised. (Most of the several hundred dollars spent for the pre-printing costs of this book went for research expenses: xeroxing, buying books and journals, mailing expenses, long distance calls to addictions professionals, etc.; Bill Wilson and Hank P. would have had virtually no such expenses, as Bill Wilson did virtually no research for his book.) Of course, Works Publishing would have had to pay for the 400 multilithed copies of the "Big Book" they had run off prior to publication, and those copies might have cost them as much as two dollars apiece (just under $23 apiece today), though that seems highly unlikely, especially as the multilithed version was much shorter than the printed book.[25] As well, they undoubtedly mailed some of the multilithed copies, so they would have had some mailing costs. Other than that, they should have had no pre-printing expenses beyond those of self-publishers today (which are usually very low). Thus, their pre-publication costs of printing the 400 multilithed copies, any mailing of those copies, and any normal self-publishing expenses, such as buying typing paper, typewriter ribbons, postage stamps, and envelopes, should have come to under $1000, and probably to under $500. This leaves $3500 to $4000 (in 1938 dollars— roughly $40,000 to $45,000 today) unaccounted for.

Perhaps the disappearance of the $3500 to $4000 from Works Publishing had something to do with the fact that Bill and Hank's other small business, Honor Dealers, their gasoline-buying co-op, was failing,[26] and that, almost certainly, the only persons overseeing the finances of the two companies were Bill and Hank.[27] Both Honor Dealers and Works Publishing shared office space; Works Publishing had only two "employees"—Bill and Hank; and Honor Dealers' only other employee was Ruth Hock, a secretary being paid $25 a week.[28] (It seems that Honor Dealers' and Works Publishing's' operations were intermixed to at least some extent, as Ruth Hock typed up the "Big Book" manuscript at the Honor Dealers office.[29])

It seems entirely possible that Bill and Hank could well have regarded two-thirds of the money raised for Works Publishing, if not all of it, as their personal property (as they owned two-thirds of the stock), and simply took the money and used it for personal expenses and/or to support Honor Dealers. They could have done this by paying themselves salaries from Works Publishing for the small amount of work they did, and by having Works Publishing pay rent to Honor Dealers. (The normal term for this sort of thing is "milking"; it's a form of fraud.)

One indication of their financial irresponsibility can be found in how fast and loose they played with Works Publishing's stock. Lois Wilson flatly states that Honor Dealers' secretary, Ruth Hock, "was paid, when paid at all, with book stock."[30] And Bill and Hank simply issued certificates to pay her (thus devaluing those owned by the Works Publishing investors).[31]

Even if all of this was done in a technically legal manner (which seems highly unlikely), it would have been fair neither to the investors who had put $5000 into Works Publishing to finance publication of the "Big Book," nor to Charles Towns or Agnes who had loaned them money for living expenses. As well, since Bill and Hank apparently never bothered to incorporate Works Publishing, they could well have been guilty of unauthorized sale of securities (the stock), a criminal offense.[32] And by selling stock in a company with no assets, they quite possibly violated the Blue Sky laws, designed to protect investors from fraud.

One indication that Bill and Hank might have known that they were engaging in illegal activity can be found in the afterword of sorts, titled "The Alcoholic Foundation," in the back of the 400 multilithed copies of the "Big Book" produced in January 1939. In it, they mention neither the loans nor the $5000 raised from sale of stock when they touch on the finances of the "Big Book's" publication. Instead of acknowledging the loans and stock sale, they state: "This volume is published by the Works Publishing Company, organized and financed mostly by small donations of our members."[33] Unless they knew (or at least suspected) that their financial dealings were illegal, it's difficult to see why Bill Wilson and Hank P. would have written and published this lie about the finances of Works Publishing.[34] [35] [36]

For that matter, assuming that they did so, why would Bill Wilson and Hank P. have engaged in such unseemly, small-time financial scamming? Why would they have sold unregistered securities, violated the Blue Sky laws, and milked Works Publishing for the equivalent of at least $40,000 (in today's currency)? The answer almost certainly is that they were dogmatic religious believers who believed that they were "guided" to do so by God. One of Bill and Hank's most basic beliefs was that they were receiving direct guidance from the Almighty; and if the Almighty "guided" them to engage in financial malfeasance in pursuit of His ends, who were they to object? This would hardly have been the first time that religious believers have adopted an ends-justify-the-means rationale while carrying out "God's will."

The exact details of how the Works Publishing money evaporated have never come to light, and probably never will. It is, though, quite possible that the details of this financial mess lie hidden somewhere in that large portion of Bill Wilson's correspondence that AA refuses to open to researchers' examination. Whatever the case—whether the money was used in a legal or an illegal manner—the disappearance of the Works Publishing money in 1938 and 1939 remains one of the sleazier episodes in AA's history.

In any event, the "Big Book" was finally printed—on promises of eventual payment—in April 1939, a time when AA still had fewer than 100 members.

While Bill Wilson was busy in New York hauling drunks to Oxford Group meetings, raising money, founding the Alcoholic Foundation and Works Publishing Co., and writing what was to become the "Big Book," Dr. Bob Smith was busy in Akron attending to the day-to-day business of searching out and attempting to sober up drunks. The usual procedure was for Dr. Smith and the other reformed drunks to visit a hospitalized alcoholic, give him the "facts" on alcoholism, tell their stories, and ask him he wanted to quit drinking and was willing to do what was necessary to stop.

If he was, Dr. Bob would make him get out of bed, get on his knees, and "surrender" to God. Those who for some reason were not hospitalized were forced at their first Oxford Group meeting to go to an upstairs room with Dr. Bob and the other reformed alcoholics and to "surrender" before they were allowed to participate.

In those days, hospitalization for upwards of a week was the normal practice in Akron. Dr. Bob customarily prescribed it even for alcoholics who had no physical need of it, in order that they be isolated and thus have time to contemplate their situation and to be properly "worked on." The only reading material that they were allowed was the Bible. By making hospitalization routine, Dr. Bob's group quickly ran up huge hospital bills, even though (unbelievable though it may seem to present-day readers) the daily cost of hospitalizing a patient then was less than the cost of renting an expensive hotel room for a night.

A notable practice of the reformed alcoholics in Akron at this time (and, shortly after, in Cleveland as well), was that Dr. Smith and his band aggressively pursued prospects. Besides dropping in uninvited on hospitalized alcoholics, they would call on alcoholics at their homes in order to explain their program and to try to recruit them. Clarence S., the founder of AA in Cleveland, is even reported to have hauled prospects off barstools. This is in marked contrast to AA's present approach: AA has now abandoned its early practice of aggressively and overtly pursuing prospects in order to *persuade* them to join, and instead presents a "take it or leave it" posture to the public while it simultaneously cooperates with treatment and diversion programs (run by AA members and sympathizers) and traffic courts that *force* patients and drunk drivers to attend AA meetings.

In early 1937, alcoholics from Cleveland began to make the trip to Akron in order to attend Oxford Group meetings with Dr. Bob and the other Akron alcoholics. Their numbers gradually grew, and by early 1939 they had decided to start meeting in Cleveland. Many of them were Catholics, which was probably the key consideration in their decision to not only begin meeting in Cleveland, but to meet separately from the Oxford Groups. This provoked a minor furor, as many of the alcoholic members of the Akron Oxford Group felt betrayed; but they followed the Clevelanders out of the Oxford Groups by the end of the year. For their name, the Cleveland alcoholics chose the name of the just-published "Big Book": Alcoholics Anonymous. They thus became the first group to officially use the AA name.

The "Big Book" was well received in the popular and religious press, but not in the scientific or medical press. It received a favorable review in the *New York Times*, and several religious publications printed a glowing review written by the influential clergyman, Dr. Harry Emerson Fosdick. The book received scant notice in medical and scientific publications, however, other than a scathing review in the October 14, 1939 *Journal of the American Medical Association* which stated:

> [The book] is a curious combination of organizing propaganda and religious exhortation. It is in no sense a scientific book . . . The book contains instructions as to how to intrigue the alcoholic addict into the acceptance of divine guidance in place of alcohol in terms strongly reminiscent of Dale Carnegie and the adherents of the Buchman ("Oxford") movement. The one valid thing in the book is the recognition of the seriousness of addiction to alcohol. Other than this, the book has no scientific merit or interest.

Despite Dr. Fosdick's enthusiastic and widely published review, very few copies of the "Big Book" sold initially. The *Reader's Digest* article, which Bill Wilson and the other AA members had been counting on so heavily, never appeared, and spirits were at a low ebb until one of the New York members, Morgan R., managed to arrange a three-minute interview on a national radio show. After ten days of being locked up and guarded night and day by other AA members (so he wouldn't drink),[37] Morgan R. appeared on Gabriel Heatter's "We the People" program on April 25, 1939. The interview went well, and Bill and the other early AAs sat back and waited for orders for the book to pour in. To stimulate demand, they had raised $500 and had used the money to mail promotional postcards announcing the broadcast and the book to every physician east of the Mississippi River. Three days after the broadcast they arrived at the post office, empty suitcases in hand, to reap what they expected would be a harvest of hundreds if not thousands of orders for the "Big Book." They were rudely surprised. They received a total of 12 replies, with only two of them being book orders.

Further publicity quickly rescued AA from the depression induced by the postcard fiasco. In June, the *New York Times* ran its favorable review of *Alcoholics Anonymous*, and shortly thereafter *Liberty* magazine, a popular national weekly, published an article lauding AA. The article, titled "Alcoholics and God" and written by Morris Markey, appeared in *Liberty's* September 30, 1939 issue. The New York AAs weren't especially happy with the piece because of its title, its emphasis on the religious nature of AA, and Markey's explanation of 12th-step work: "These men were experiencing a psychic change. Their so-called 'compulsion neurosis' was being altered—transferred from liquor to something else. Their psychological necessity to drink was being changed to a psychological necessity to rescue their fellow victims from the plight that made them so miserable."[38] Still, the Markey article did lead to 800 inquiries—most of them from the South and overtly religious, according to one chronicler[39]—and resulted in a burst of book sales, growth, and, eventually, the formation of AA's first "mail order" group in Little Rock, Arkansas. AA's final stroke of luck in 1939 was the publication of a series of highly laudatory articles in the *Cleveland Plain Dealer*. The articles led to a spurt of growth in Cleveland and surrounding areas, and Cleveland-area AAs quickly outnumbered those in Akron and New York combined.

That was a temporary situation, as within two years AA would receive its most important publicity boost, and its effects would dwarf those of everything previously published or broadcast about AA; it would be responsible in large part for AA's transformation into a nationwide movement. On March 1, 1941, the *Saturday Evening Post*, then one of the most important magazines in the country, published Jack Alexander's article, "Alcoholics Anonymous: Freed Slaves of Drink, Now They Free Others." It generated an avalanche of responses and, according to AA's own estimate, 6000 new members.[40] The article was so laudatory and so important to AA history that AA subsequently reprinted it and still distributes it as a pamphlet.

In June of the same year, while perusing the obituary column in the *Herald Tribune*, a New York AA discovered a short incantation which would be repeated millions of times in the following years at AA meetings, The Serenity Prayer: "God grant me the serenity to accept the things I cannot change, the courage to change the things I can, and the wisdom to know the difference." The prayer is often credited to Protestant theologian, Reinhold Niebuhr. If he did write it, there's more than a trace of irony in the fact that the author of this prayer, which is so much a part of AA, had acidly attacked AA's spiritual father, Frank Buchman, because of Buchman's pro-Hitler remarks in 1936.[41]

While AA was rapidly growing as a result of all the free publicity it was receiving, its co-founders' financial problems were finally being resolved. Despite the $30-a-week stipend from the Rockefeller money, and the money from Works Publishing, the early years of AA were apparently a financially difficult period for Bill Wilson. In 1939 the mortgage company which held the title to Lois' father's house evicted them and sold the building. They were homeless for the next two years. How this jibes with Wilson's receiving the equivalent of $340 per week from Rockefeller, and his and Hank P.'s receiving the equivalent of at least $40,000 from Works Publishing in 1938, remains a mystery.

In any event, in early 1940 the Alcoholic Foundation trustees, at Bill's urging, had decided that AA itself should own the rights to the "Big Book." The foundation soon managed to acquire all of the stock in Works Publishing, and the foundations trustees voted to pay both Bill and Dr. Bob royalties on book sales. As sales increased, those royalties became substantial enough that Bill was able to drop his sporadic attempts to obtain outside employment, and to devote all of his energies to AA.

(Before his death in 1971, Bill Wilson received several hundred thousand dollars in royalties from sales of the "Big Book" and his three other AA books. Nan Robertson reports that as of the late 1960s, "Big Book" sales were generating royalties "from $30,000 to $40,000 annually," [equivalent to approximately $140,000 to $190,000 annually today] and that after Bill's death royalties paid by AA on Bill's four books "made Lois rich."[42])

In November 1940, after well over a year of being the guests of various AAs, Bill and Lois moved into a room in the first AA clubhouse, a small building on 24th Street in New York City. Six months later they moved into their own home. It was in Bedford Hills, in expensive Westchester County, but they were able to buy it because its owner was willing to sell it to them for $6500 with no money down and payments of $40 a month.

Dr. Bob's financial condition had been desperate before the 1938 Rockefeller donation, and even after his mortgage was paid off and he began to receive his stipend, he was still in bad financial shape. He was devoting most of his time to AA work, and his practice, though gradually recovering, was still poor. As the 1940s progressed, though, his practice improved, and the income from it and the ever-increasing royalties from "Big Book" sales allowed him to spend the last years of his life in relative comfort.

The early years of World War II would have been quite difficult for him and for Bill Wilson, though, if Rockefeller hadn't once again lent a helping hand. In early 1940 Willard Richardson, now a member of the Alcoholic Foundation's board of trustees, revealed that John D. Rockefeller, Jr. wanted to hold a dinner for AA to which he would invite a large number of his wealthy friends. It was held on February 8, 1940 at New York City's Union Club. Of the 400 guests Rockefeller invited, 75 showed up. They were treated to speeches by Bill, Dr. Bob, Harry Emerson Fosdick, and Dr. Foster Kennedy. Rockefeller was sick that evening and was unable to attend, so his son, Nelson, delivered the after-dinner summation. He reiterated his father's sympathetic interest in AA, and then added, "Gentlemen, you can all see that this is a work of good will. Its power lies in the fact that one member carries the good message to the next, without any thought of financial income or reward. Therefore it is our belief that Alcoholics Anonymous should be self-supporting so far as money is concerned. It needs only our good will.[43] And with that, the guests applauded, shook hands with the assembled AAs, and filed out into the night.

Bill, Dr. Bob, and the other AAs were extremely disappointed, but John D. Jr. did end up giving them some assistance. Shortly after the dinner, he donated $1000 to AA, bought 400 copies of the "Big Book" at full cover price, and sent them, along with a letter hinting that AA needed additional financial help, to all 400 persons to whom he had sent invitations. They responded by donating $2000, and would contribute a similar amount annually for the next four years. John D. also had his publicist, in conjunction with AA, draft a press release which generated a considerable amount of favorable publicity for AA.

Thanks largely to the free publicity it was receiving, AA grew rapidly during the opening days of World War II. When the "Big Book" was published in 1939, AA had two groups (one in Akron, one in New York), a membership of no more than 100, and no national office. Two-and-a-half years later, in the final days of 1941, AA had 200 groups, a membership of 8,000, and a national office in New York City.[44] By 1944, AA had 360 groups with a total membership of 10,000, and in June of that year it had begun publication of what was to become its official organ, *The Grapevine*, which had originally been a newsletter for AAs in the armed forces.

In October of that year there was a second development. The National Committee for Education on Alcoholism (NCEA, later the National Council on Alcoholism, and currently the National Council on Alcoholism and Drug Dependence—NCADD) opened its first office. Marty Mann, the first woman to achieve lasting sobriety in AA, was its founder, and both Bill Wilson's and Dr. Bob's *full* names appeared on its letterhead as sponsors. This caused a storm of controversy within AA in 1946, when the NCEA mailed a fundraising appeal on its letterhead stationery, with some copies of the appeal going directly to AA groups. The names of Bill and Dr. Bob quickly vanished from the letterhead.[45] (The 10th tradition forbids AA from involving itself in "public controversy." And, conveniently, because of AA's anonymity strictures, 12-step "professionals" almost never reveal their AA membership publicly; instead, they appear in the guise of "professionals" when promoting 12-step dogma and when attacking those who publicly disagree with it.) Since then, great care has been to taken to avoid any *formal* ties between AA and the NCADD, though the NCADD has consistently functioned as AA's lobbying arm and spokesman—in the guise of a *professional* organization—on matters of "public controversy."

During this early period of growth, Bill Wilson was on the road a great deal of the time visiting members and groups scattered across the country. He also spent a lot of time at headquarters dealing with correspondence from AA groups and members, where he quickly noticed that many problems and questions recurred over and over again. In an attempt to formulate a set of guidelines to help groups deal with these recurring problems and questions, Bill wrote the 12 traditions. Just as the 12 steps were his, and subsequently AA's, principles for the conduct of individuals' personal lives, the 12 traditions were Wilson's principles for the conduct of AA's organizational life. They were first published in the April 1946 *Grape-*

vine; and, strange as it now seems, they were not universally well received within AA. Bill Wilson spent a good part of the next few years on the road stumping for them before they were unanimously adopted by AA's first international convention in 1950.

During the 1940s, both Bill and Dr. Bob were avidly pursuing a common interest outside of, but related to, AA: spiritualism. They believed that it demonstrated the existence of the "Higher Power" so central to their AA program. Thus, shortly after the Wilsons moved into their Bedford Hills home, they began to hold regular "spook sessions," complete with mysterious messages on a Ouija board, and on at least one occasion they held a "spirit rapping" session (a seance in which spirits supposedly rap out messages with an "a" being one rap, a "b" two, a "c" three, and so on, spirits evidently being too dense to learn the far more efficient Morse code.)[46]

The 1940s were not, however, a uniformly happy time for AA's cofounders. In 1944, despite his new home, new-found financial security, and AA's continuing growth and increasing respectability, Bill Wilson fell into deep depression; it was a problem which would plague him for more than a decade. For Dr. Bob Smith, the 1940s brought tragedy. In 1948, he learned that he had incurable prostate cancer; in 1949 his wife Anne died; and in 1950 he too died following a prolonged, painful illness. He was buried next to his wife in an Akron cemetery. At his request, as a final expression of his dedication to the principle of anonymity, he had a simple gravestone which made no mention of Alcoholics Anonymous.

Despite his ongoing problems with depression, Bill Wilson was extremely active during this period. In addition to stumping for the 12 traditions, he was also promoting a plan for AA to become self-governing. It says much about his dedication to Alcoholics Anonymous, rather than to personal aggrandizement, that he devised the plan which would eventually make it impossible for him, or any other individual, to control AA. Briefly, the plan called for AA's affairs to be directed by a constituent assembly, called the General Service Conference, that would meet once a year and would be elected at area conferences. In turn, the delegates to the area conferences would be the elected representatives of the individual AA groups, the Group Service Representatives (GSRs), and the District Committee Members elected by the GSRs. To ensure continuity, delegates to the General Service Conference were to be elected to staggered terms, with approximately half being elected in even years and half elected in odd years, with terms of office running two years. The plan called for every state and Canadian province to have one delegate, with states and provinces with large numbers of AA members to have additional representation.

The plan was approved for a probationary five-year period at the 1950 international convention, and the first General Service Conference was held in New York in 1951. Only 37 delegates attended that first conference, but even so, it was considered a success. Following the conference's conclusion, Bill Wilson commented, "As I watched all this grow, I became entirely sure that Alcoholics Anonymous was at last safe—even from me."[47] An additional 38 delegates were elected to the conference the following year. In 1955, the second international AA convention declared that the General Service Conference plan had successfully completed its probationary period and was an accepted part of AA. At present, delegates are still elected for staggered two-year terms, and as of 1997 there were 92 delegates.

The year 1955 saw another significant development—publication of the second edition of the "Big Book." Except for a few minor changes, such as the elimination of the term "ex-alcoholic" and the substitution of the euphemism "illness" for "disease," very little was changed in the section written by Bill Wilson. The major changes were in the section consisting of members' stories; several were added and several deleted to make the book more up to date.

Bill Wilson wrote two additional books in the 1950s. In 1953 AA published *12 Steps and 12 Traditions*, commonly called "the 12 & 12," Wilson's at-length explication of the principles in both the steps and traditions, and his explanation of how to properly work the steps as "a way of life" that will "enable the sufferer to become happily and usefully whole."[48] As Ken Ragge has pointed out, Bill Wilson wrote this guide to wholeness and happiness while he was severely depressed, and had been so for nearly a decade.[49]

Wilson's other new book appeared four years later. In 1957 AA published *Alcoholics Anonymous Comes of Age*, which was Wilson's history and evaluation of AA up to the point where formal control was turned over to its members at the 1955 international convention.

There was one other development in the early and mid-'50s which, though not a part of AA's organizational history, should be mentioned: the formation of the first non-AA groups that adopted the AA "program," especially the 12 steps, with only minimal modifications. The first of these was Al-Anon, an organization for family members of alcoholics, which appeared in 1951. The second was Alateen, a group for the teenage children of alcoholics, which appeared in 1957. In the years to come there would be literally hundreds of other AA spin offs.

AA grew rapidly during the ten years following World War II. During the first few years especially, AA's membership mushroomed. In 1951 AA had 112,000 members and 4,000 groups; and in 1955 AA had 132,000 members and nearly 6,000 groups.[50] In the years to come, AA would continue to grow very rapidly. By the end of 1957, AA had over 7,000 groups and 200,000 members scattered across 70 countries, but with the vast majority in the United States.[51] AA abroad, however, had sufficient numerical strength that the first overseas General Service Board of Alcoholics Anonymous was created in the U.K. and Ireland in that same year, 1957.

As a sign that AA had "come of age," Bill Wilson largely disengaged himself from the day-to-day administration of the General Service Office, AA's national service center in New York. One indication of how much work he had been doing is that, following his disengagement, AA set up a Public Information Committee to take charge of the public relations work which Bill had formerly handled.

Shortly before the second international AA convention, Bill Wilson discovered a new interest—LSD. At the time it was considered a promising therapeutic agent for the treatment of alcoholism, which is what aroused Bill's interest in it. He first took the drug in 1956 and was quite enthusiastic, believing that the drug had the ability to sweep away mental barriers which keep people from directly experiencing the presence of God.[52] Secrecy was never one of Bill Wilson's strong points, and he soon had a coterie of friends and acquaintances, including clergymen and psychiatrists, joining him in his LSD experiments. Word of this traveled fast, and controversy soon followed, the nation being then, as now, in the grip of anti-drug hysteria. Even though initial studies involving LSD treatment of alcoholics had shown promising results, and even though LSD produced no physically damaging side effects and definitely was not addictive, the press began circulating sensational, wildly inaccurate reports of LSD's effects. So, because his name would inevitably be linked with AA even though he had formally withdrawn from its day-to-day administration, Bill Wilson ended his LSD experiments in 1959.[53]

In early 1961, Bill Wilson wrote to Carl Jung, expressing his appreciation of Jung's influence (via Roland Hazard) in the formation of AA. By chance, he wrote just a few months before Jung's death. Jung replied with a gracious letter which became one of Wilson's treasured possessions.[54]

Just two months after Jung died, Frank Buchman, who had contributed far more to AA than Jung, also died. Bill Wilson had never bothered to write to Buchman to express his thanks, and regretted that he had not done so. He commented in a letter to a friend: "Now that Frank Buchman is gone and I realize more than ever what we owe to him, I wish I had sought him out in recent years to tell him of our appreciation."[55]

At about the same time as his correspondence with Jung, Bill Wilson was developing another new interest: niacin (vitamin B-3) as a treatment for alcoholism. He believed that it was the long-sought-after cure for the "allergy" mentioned by Dr. Silkworth in the "Big Book." By the mid-1960s, Wilson was zealously promoting niacin to both the medical community and to the members of AA. This, naturally enough, caused still another controversy, and in 1967 the AA General Service Board requested that he not use the General Service Office address on his stationery.

In that same year, AA published Bill Wilson's final book. Its original title was *The A.A. Way of Life*; it has since been retitled *As Bill Sees It*. The book is a collection of Wilson's writings, and resembles nothing so much as a prayer book, complete with a long ribbon at the top of its spine. *The A.A. Way of Life* marked Bill Wilson's last significant contribution to Alcoholics Anonymous. The year before it was published, the General Service Conference had finally approved, after years of dragging its heels, Wilson's plan to reverse the ratio of alcoholic to non-alcoholic trustees on AA's board of directors, the General Service Board. Following the Conference's decision, the board's composition was reversed, and for the first time alcoholic members held a majority of the votes. When this was done, Bill felt that AA had finally become truly mature.

It was fortunate that Bill Wilson lived to see this change which he so fervently desired, as his health was rapidly failing during the late 1960s. Bill Wilson was an addicted smoker, and by the late '60s he had developed emphysema, which caused him increasing pain and debilitation as the decade advanced. Still, even while his health deteriorated, he continued to smoke. He finally quite in 1969, but by then the damage had been done, and his last two years of life were plagued by tobacco-caused disease, debilitation, and misery. He did attend the AA international convention in Miami in 1970, but he barely managed to speak for four minutes. Finally, after a lingering bout of pneumonia, he died on January 24, 1971.

While Bill Wilson had been attempting to have the trustee ratio altered, promoting niacin, and overseeing production of his final book, AA was in a period of change and expansion. The 1960s saw significant AA growth overseas, and by 1967 20 percent of AA members lived outside of the United States.[56] A second trend in the '60s was that relatively large numbers of newcomers had drug problems in addition to alcohol problems. This eventually led to the formation of other 12-step groups, such as Narcotics Anonymous, for those whose problems are not primarily alcohol related. Another trend which became noticeable in the 1960s (though it had certainly been present in the 1950s) was the incorporation of AA as an integral part of hospital and institutional alcoholism programs. In the 1970s and 1980s the trend toward AA integration into hospital and institutional programs mushroomed. There was also a major increase in the numbers of new members with multiple "dependencies" (with the concomitant trend of new 12-step groups with names taken from those "dependencies").

In the 1970s, another trend emerged which deserves comment: the formation of "special meetings" for members who share special interests, identities or desires. Examples include lesbian and gay meetings, non-smokers meetings, and (in a very few places) atheists and agnostics meetings. No AA member is turned away from these special meetings, but when those not sharing a group's common interest or identity show up, they are oftentimes advised that though they are welcome they might feel more comfortable at other meetings. This trend from the 1970s, as well as those begun in the 1960s, continues into the 1990s.

During the 1980s, the percentage of overseas AA members increased significantly, and by 1996 nearly 33 percent of AA's members lived outside of the U.S. or Canada.[57] As well, between 1977 and 1989 the percentage of AA members also "addicted" to drugs rose from approximately 19 percent to approximately 46 percent.[58] And, of late, AA's membership (at least in the U.S. and Canada) has aged considerably. AA's 1989 triennial survey showed that fully 22 percent of AA members were under 31 years of age,[59] while the percentage of those under 31 had fallen to 13 percent by 1996[60]; at the same time, those older than 50 increased from 23 percent in 1989[61] to 28 percent in 1996.[62]

In the last decade of the 20th century, AA is a mass organization, and one with great influence in both the United States and abroad. In January 1996, there were 50,671 AA groups in the U.S., with 1,153,795 members; and worldwide there were 95,166 groups with 1,866,281 members.[63] The irony is that during its 60-plus years of expansion and external changes, the core of AA's program has remained virtually unchanged, and at present probably not one member in 100 of AA or other 12-step groups has more than the foggiest concept of where the ideas at the core of 12-step programs originated.

---

1. Those interested in more detailed, though more sympathetic, histories should consult *Alcoholics Anonymous Comes of Age*, by Bill Wilson; *Getting Better*, by Nan Robertson; *A.A. The Way It Began*, by Bill Pittman; *Turning Point: A History of AA's Spiritual Roots*, by Dick B.; *Design for Living: The Oxford Groups Contribution to Early AA*, by Dick B.; *The Sober Alcoholic*, by Irving Peter Gellman; *Not God: A History of Alcoholics Anonymous* (later retitled, in an updated edition, *The A.A. Story*), by Ernest Kurtz; *Pass It On* (AA's official Wilson biography); *Dr. Bob and the Good Old Timers* (AA's official Smith biography); *Bill W.*, by Robert Thomsen; *Lois Remembers*, by Lois Wilson; and *The A.A. Service Manual*.

2. *Getting Better*, by Nan Robertson. New York: Wm.. Morrow & Co., 1988, p. 41.

3. *Alcoholics Anonymous*, Third Edition, by Bill Wilson. New York: Alcoholics Anonymous World Services, Inc., 1985, p. 2.

4. *Pass It On*. New York: Alcoholics Anonymous World Services, Inc., 1984, p. 63.

5. For details of the "cure," see *A.A. The Way It Began*, by Bill Pittman. Seattle: Glen Abbey Books, 1988, pp. 163-169.

6. *Alcoholics Anonymous Comes of Age*, by Bill Wilson. New York: Alcoholics Anonymous World Services, 15th printing, 1989, p. 63.

7. Ibid., p. 64.

8. *The Varieties of Religious Experience*, by William James. New York: New American Library, Inc., 1958, p. 213 (footnote).

9. *Lois Remembers*, by Lois Wilson. New York: Al-Anon Family Group Headquarters, 1987, p. 105.

10. *Alcoholics Anonymous Comes of Age*, op. cit., p. 75.

11. Lois Wilson, op. cit., p. 113.

12. *Alcoholics Anonymous Comes of Age*, op. cit., pp. 166-167.

13. See "The Ideology of a Therapeutic Social Movement: Alcoholics Anonymous," by Leonard Blumberg in *Journal of Studies on Alcohol*, Vol. 38, Nov. 1977, pp. 2122-2143.

14. *Alcoholics Anonymous Comes of Age*, op. cit., p. 150.

15. *Pass It On*, op. cit., pp. 195-196.

16. Lois Wilson, op. cit., pp. 112-113.

17. *Pass It On*, op. cit., pp. 195-196: "Bill and Hank soon sold 200 shares for $5000, and Charlie Towns lent them $2500."

18. Lois Wilson, op. cit., pp. 112-113: "Charlie Towns lent Bill and Hank $2500 to live on while working on the book, and it was then that Agnes, Fitz's sister, offered them the $1000."

19. Ibid., p. 194.

20. Ibid., p. 204.

21. http://woodrow.mpls.frb.fed.us/economy/calc/cpihome.html

22. Lois Wilson, op. cit., p. 112.

23. The per-unit cost of the "Big Book" in 1938 is more or less in line with printing costs today. I asked Thomson-Shore, Inc., the printer of this book, to do an estimate using the specifications for the first edition of the "Big Book," and their quote came in at just under $15,000 for 5000 copies. That translates to almost exactly $1300 in 1938 dollars—26 cents per book. The lower per-unit cost today might, at least in part, reflect the fact that the cost of typesetting was probably included in the printing costs in 1938.

24. *Pass It On*, op. cit., p. 196.

25. The term "multilithed" refers to copies printed on a Multilith press, a small offset press referred to in the trade as an "offset duplicator" to distinguish it from larger presses. The press actually used to print the 400 copies of the "Big Book" was probably the Multilith 1250, a sheet-fed press with an image area of 10" x 15" that was commonly used at the time in small print shops. In the hands of a skilled operator, it could produce work close in quality to that produced by larger, commercial presses.

26. Lois Wilson, op. cit., p. 113: "The Honor Dealers plan was by then [1938] nearly defunct."

27. For information on Honor Dealers, see *Pass It On*, op. cit., pp. 191, 192, 200, and *Getting Better*, op. cit., pp. 69, 76.

28. *Pass It On*, op. cit., p. 191.

29. Lois Wilson, op. cit., p. 113.

30. Ibid.

31. *Pass It On*, op. cit., p. 235: "There were 49 subscribers. Bill and Hank each held a third of the stock, and Ruth had also received shares, in lieu of pay."

32. Ibid., p. 195: "Hank bought a pad of stock certificates at a stationery store, typed the name of the new company at the top of each certificate, and signed his name, with the title 'President,' at the bottom. 'When I protested these irregularities,' Bill recalled, 'Hank said there was no time to waste; why be concerned with small details?'"

33. "The Alcoholic Foundation" page from the back of the multilithed "Big Book" is reproduced on at least two sites maintained by AA enthusiasts on the World Wide Web. I downloaded my copy from
http://www.recovery.org/aa/bigbook/ww/manuscript/alcfound.html

34. Although it's within the realm of possibility that Hank P. wrote "The Alcoholic Foundation" page, it's much more likely that Bill Wilson was the author. Except for "The Doctor's Opinion," by Dr. Silkworth, and the two personal stories it contained (one of them Dr. Bob's), Wilson wrote everything else in the multilithed edition of the "Big Book," with the possible exception of Chapter 10, "To Employers," which Hank might have written. In any event, Bill Wilson certainly knew of the lie about Works Publishing's finances, and, even if he didn't write it, he at least must have agreed to its inclusion.

35. It's relevant to note that former Wall Street insider Bill Wilson almost certainly had at least a passing familiarity with the securities and exchange laws.

36. It's also relevant that those who bought stock in Works Publishing were investors, not donors. If they had intended to "donat[e]" their money to Works Publishing through buying its stock, they would have done so before Bill and Hank promised them national publicity in The Reader's Digest. That they only bought the stock after this promise indicates that they intended to make a profit on their investment.

37. Pass It On, op. cit., pp. 115-116.

38. "Alcoholics and God," by Morris Markey. Liberty, September 30, 1939, p. 7.

39. Not God, by Ernest Kurtz. Center City, Minnesota: Hazelden Educational Services, 1979, p. 284.

40. Pass It On, op. cit., p. 249.

41. "Hitler and Buchmanism," by Reinhold Niebuhr in The Christian Century, October 7, 1936, p. 1315.

42. Getting Better: Inside Alcoholics Anonymous, by Nan Robertson. New York: Wm.. Morrow, 1988, pp. 83-84. Robertson reports that in 1986 alone Lois Wilson received $912,500 in royalties, and that according to "an agreement between Wilson and A.A. World Services, the publisher: 13.5 percent of the books' retail price [went to] Lois and 1.5 percent [to] Helen W., Bill's last and most enduring mistress."

43. Alcoholics Anonymous Comes of Age, op. cit., pp. 184-185.

44. Figures cited in AA's conference-approved literature are seemingly at odds. In Pass It On, the figure cited is 6,000 members in November 1941 (p. 266); and in Alcoholics Anonymous Comes of Age, the figure cited is 8,000 members "at the end of 1941" (p. 192). Considering the inherent difficulties in accurately estimating AA membership, especially at this early stage, this minor discrepancy isn't surprising.

45. Pass It On, op. cit., p. 230.

46. Ibid., pp. 275-280.

47. A.A. Service Manual, p. S19.

48. 12 Steps & 12 Traditions, New York: Alcoholics Anonymous World Services, Inc., 1953, p. 15.

49. More Revealed, by Ken Ragge. Henderson, Nevada: Alert Publishing, 1992, pp. 151-152. (This book has been retitled; its new title is The Real AA: Behind the Myth of 12-Step Recovery.)

50. *Pass It On*, op. cit., pp. 344 & 358.

51. *Alcoholics Anonymous Comes of Age*, op. cit., p. ix.

52. In this belief, he wasn't alone; those who have taken large amounts of LSD report that one of its most common effects is the sweeping away of ego barriers and a feeling of oneness with the universe.

53. See *Pass It On*, pp. 368-377 for fuller details of Wilson's LSD experimentation.

54. As mystically minded as ever, Jung, in his letter, contemptuously dismissed "mere rationalism," and stated, "An ordinary man, not protected by an action from above and isolated in society, cannot resist the power of evil, which is called very aptly the Devil." This seems less like an attempt at insight than an attempt to evade it. Jung's remarks bring to mind Wilhelm Reich's caustic comment in *The Mass Psychology of Fascism* that "every form of mysticism is reactionary, and the reactionary man is mystical."

In regard to Hitler and Nazism, Jung's reactions were almost as naive as those of Frank Buchman, AA's spiritual father. Jung was ambivalent about the rise to power of the Nazis, and he foolishly allowed himself to be used for propaganda purposes by the Nazi media. At a time when the mystical, anti-semitic, anti-union, militaristic, and police-state tendencies of the Nazis were already blindingly obvious, and after they had first set up concentration camps, Jung still didn't realize what Nazism meant. He willingly appeared on Berlin radio in June 1933 where a Nazi Jungian psychiatrist interviewed him and elicited comments about "times of leadership," "the aimless conversation of parliamentary deliberation," and the older generation's acquiescence "to this natural course of events." Jung's biographer, Gerhard Wehr, called this interview "a thoroughly shameful business." (*Jung: A Biography*, by Gerhard Wehr. Boston: Shambala, 1987, pp. 320-321.)

Later, in an article, Jung noted, "The ultimate outcome of this unmistakable mass movement [Nazism] still seemed to me uncertain, just as the figure of the Fuhrer at first struck me as being merely ambivalent." He also stated that because of the "archetypal" nature of the forces driving such "psychological mass movement[s]," "it is impossible to make out at the start whether [they] will prove to be positive or negative." (Quoted in *Jung's Last Years*, by Aniela Jaffe. Dallas, Texas: Spring Publications, 1984, pp. 79-80.) Other observers—even though many labored under the handicap of utilizing "mere rationality" —had no such difficulty in determining whether the Third Reich would be a "positive or negative" development.

Those interested in meaningful analyses of Nazism and the reasons for its rise would do well to consult *The Mass Psychology of Fascism*, by Wilhelm Reich; *Fascism and Big Business*, by Daniel Guerin; *Who Financed Hitler?*, by James and Suzanne Pool; and *The Irrational in Politics*, by Maurice Brinton.

55. Quoted in *Pass It On*, p. 387.

56. *Alcoholics Anonymous Comes of Age*, op. cit., p. X.

57. From AA's web site: http://www.alcoholics-anonymous.org/factfile/doc07.html

58. "Comments On A.A.'s Triennial Surveys," 1990, p. 10, figure B-2.

59. Ibid., p. 2.

60. "Alcoholics Anonymous 1996 Membership Survey" brochure.

61. "Comments On A.A.'s Triennial Surveys," op. cit., p. 2.

62. "Alcoholics Anonymous 1996 Membership Survey" brochure.

63. AA web site document, op. cit. The total worldwide AA membership reported at the site does not match the total arrived at by adding the broken-down (by country) membership totals listed there. The total listed by AA is 1,922,269 members, while the figure one arrives at by adding all of the discreet totals is 1,866,281.

4

The Oxford Groups & AA: Similarities & Differences

"Our debt to them [the Oxford Group Movement] . . . was and is immense."
—Bill Wilson in *Alcoholics Anonymous Come of Age*, p. 73

It would be surprising if anyone who read the two preceding chapters didn't notice certain similarities between Alcoholics Anonymous and the Oxford Group Movement, for similarities abound in ideology, operation, and style.

AA took its central doctrines virtually unchanged from Frank Buchman's Oxford Groups. This can be seen clearly in the 12 steps, the cornerstone of AA's program. The following chapter is devoted entirely to the 12 steps, so for now suffice it to say that the Buchmanite principles of *personal powerlessness* and the necessity of *divine guidance* are embodied in steps 1, 2, 3, 6, 7, and 11; the principle of *confession* is embodied in steps 4, 5, and 10; the principle of *restitution* to those one has harmed is embodied in steps 8 and 9; and the principle of *continuance*, of continuing to practice the other Buchmanite principles and to carry the word to other "defeated" persons ("alcoholics," in the steps) is embodied in steps 10 and 12.

To spell out some of these correspondences in more detail: AA inherited the Oxford Group Movement belief that human beings in themselves are powerless, and that only submission to God's will is sufficient to solve human problems. It also inherited the belief that God will guide anyone who "listens." An additional Buchman legacy is the belief that it's necessary for human beings to confess their "wrongs" (in AA) or "sins" (in the Oxford Groups); as well, both groups employ(ed) both private and public confessions. The Oxford Groups emphasized private confessions from "sinners" to individual "soul surgeons," and public confessions at houseparties, while AA emphasizes private confessions from "pigeons" (newcomers being indoctrinated with the AA program) to "sponsors" (experienced members responsible for indoctrinating individual newcomers) and public confessions at AA meetings.

A closely related concept, common to both AA and the Oxford Groups, is belief in the necessity of "sharing." This term embraces both private and public confessions, but also encompasses giving "witness," both private and public. In AA, this concept is embedded in the twelfth step as the injunction "to carry this message to alcoholics." While AA has for the most part dropped the term "sharing" (which is now usually associated with new agers and the Brie and Chablis set), it still adheres to it religiously.

Another point of ideological correspondence between the two organizations is that AA, in exactly the same manner as the Oxford Groups, ignores social, political, and economic factors as causes of personal and social problems. AA concerns itself solely with alcohol abuse (more properly, with its own program for "alcoholics"), but even though its focus is narrower than that of the Oxford Groups, its approach is identical. Nowhere in the dozens of books and pamphlets published by AA will you find even a hint that there is any cause of alcoholism (or even contributory factors) other than the alcoholic him (or her) self.

This extreme emphasis on individual responsibility rather than social factors, and the accompanying belief in the necessity of divine guidance, implies acceptance of the political-economic status quo and a marked disinterest in, and at times outright hostility to, political activism. Critics recognized this tendency in the Oxford Groups well *before* Bill Wilson and Dr. Bob joined the Oxford Group Movement and organized within it what was to become AA.[1] In 1932, Frank Buchman expressed his anti-political activist attitude in as callous a manner as is imaginable. In that year, when tens of millions were unemployed, with a very large number of them homeless and hungry, well-fed Frank Buchman stated: "The President's social trends report indicates there will surely be a revolution in this country. We are going to make it a spiritual revolution. What hunger marchers need is to be changed."[2] Buchman didn't say a word about food, housing, or employment; he knew what the poverty stricken *really* needed—"guidance."

In present-day AA, this anti-activist tendency is not as extreme as it was in the Oxford Groups, but it's still so obvious that observers who know next to nothing of AA's history or that of its predecessor, the Oxford Group Movement, find it striking. One such observer, Ellen Herman, notes: "The [12-step] programs' core concept . . . is decidedly apolitical . . . In particular, the programs' philosophy . . . emphasizes the person and problem in isolation from any outside social forces."[3]

Another ideological correspondence between AA and the Oxford Groups can be found in their attitude toward recruitment of those who have (had) doubts about their programs. The Oxford Groups encouraged doubters, including agnostics, to pray and to practice "quiet times" acting "as if" they believed in God. The assumption was that God would make himself known to the supplicator, God having a "plan" for every human life and being ready to reveal it to anyone who would "listen." In AA, the approach to doubters and the assumptions underlying that approach are identical to those of the Oxford Groups. AA even has a prescriptive slogan for newcomers harboring doubts: "Fake it until you make it." In the "Big Book," Bill Wilson devotes an entire chapter, "We Agnostics," to this idea. In it, he comments: "We [atheists and agnostics] found that as soon as we were able to lay aside prejudice [that is, rational thought] and express even a willingness to believe in a Power greater than ourselves, we commenced to get results . . ."[4]

The concept of God implied in this belief is less than subtle. The AA/Oxford Group Movement concept of a deity has little to do with Einstein's impersonal God who doesn't play dice with the universe, while it has much to do with—and is in fact indistinguishable from—the Old Testament concept of a God who is jealously concerned with the most picayune aspects of his followers' lives.

A related similarity is that even though the roots of both AA and the Oxford Groups are in evangelical Protestantism, AA is, and the Oxford Group Movement was, nonsectarian. Frank Buchman and his followers always insisted that they were not a religious organization and were in fact a "movement" which intended to revitalize existing religious organizations. AA, like the Oxford Groups, has no ties to any particular religious bodies; but it goes one step further than the Oxford Groups and argues, not very convincingly, that its program is "spiritual" rather than religious.

An additional ideological similarity between the Oxford Groups and AA is a distinct hostility to formal organization. In the Oxford Groups this stemmed from a belief in ever-present divine guidance which would render formal organization unnecessary. (The primary purposes of organization are coordination and communication, and who or what could better fulfill those functions than an all-powerful God making his will known to all those willing to "listen"?) AA inherited this hostility to formal organization and, ironically, spelled it out in one of the 12 traditions, AA's organizational principles. The ninth tradition states, in part, that "A.A., as such, ought never be organized." The results of this hostility to organization were, however, vastly different in AA and the Oxford Groups. AA, thanks largely to Bill Wilson, developed an organizational structure which is completely noncoercive and very democratic, and is in fact quite similar to organizational models developed by anarchist theorists. The Oxford Group Movement, on the other hand, was always a prime example of what has been called "the tyranny of structurelessness"; it was always under the informal but dictatorial control of its founder, Frank Buchman, and remained so until his death—thanks in part, in all probability, to the fact that there was no organizational structure through which disaffected members could challenge him.

A further point of similarity between the Oxford Group Movement and AA, and one which reflects favorably on both, is their emphasis on human equality. Unfortunately, this emphasis is based in the shared belief that human beings are equally powerless without God's guidance; but the fact remains that there was no institutionalized racism or sexism (with the marked exception of virulent homophobia) in the Oxford Group Movement, and there is none in AA. While it's certainly true that the Oxford Groups had no real understanding of racism and did nothing effective to combat it (and were blissfully unaware of sexism), and that Frank Buchman hobnobbed with rich and powerful anti-semites, it's also true that the Oxford Groups did in theory oppose racism; and while AA was hardly a leader in the fight for desegregation, it's also true that AA has always made real efforts to make its program available to all alcoholics regardless of their race, sex, or sexual orientation. This is not to say that many AA members are not racist, sexist, and homophobic—many are—but AA has always officially frowned on such prejudice. And, indeed, as AA's membership, though somewhat whiter than average, is fairly representative of the U.S. population as a whole, it would be surprising if AA's members didn't hold many of the prejudices common in American society.[5]

A final, and very important, point of ideological correspondence between AA and the Oxford Groups is their anti-intellectualism. Given the religious basis of both organizations, this isn't surprising. Both AA and the Oxford Groups were based upon belief in a God who would make "His" plans known to anyone who would "listen." This belief leads directly to anti-intellectualism in that, first of all, there is no evidence that God exists, and thus a questioning intellectual approach is a direct threat to belief in God. In the second place, even if you grant that God does exist, how can you be sure that any "guidance" you receive is from God rather than from your own imagination? A related question is how do you reconcile conflicting "guidance" received by different persons unless some "guidance" doesn't come from God? And if that's the case, how do you tell which "guidance" is genuine? Obviously, there is no satisfactory answer to these questions, so an intellectual approach to these problems becomes a real threat to belief. Thus, Oxford Group members were told, "Doubt stifles and makes abortive our attempt to act upon God's guidance," and AA newcomers are often told, "Your best thinking got you here."

A related stylistic similarity between AA and the Oxford Groups is an emphasis upon emotional experience. This stems from their common evangelical roots. Oxford Group Movement meetings were openly evangelical and often very emotional, and a great many observers have commented upon the revival-like quality of Alcoholics Anonymous meetings with their prayers, confessions, collections, rituals, and witnessing.

A rather odd correspondence between AA and the Oxford Groups is the extensive use of slogans, aphorisms, and folk sayings. Some MRA slogans sound downright bizarre to the modern ear: "P-R-A-Y: Powerful Radiograms Always Yours"; "A spiritual radiophone in every home"; "F-A-I-T-H: Forsaking All I Take Him"; "Crows are black the world over"; "When man listens, God speaks"; "Minute Men of God"; "World-changing through life changing"; and "J-E-S-U-S: Just Exactly Suits Us Sinners." In AA, one frequently hears "One Day at a Time"; "Easy Does It"; "Let Go and Let God"; "Keep It Simple" (sometimes "Keep It Simple, Stupid"—KISS); "Utilize, Don't Analyze"; "Fake It Until You Make It"; "One Drink, One Drunk"; and a number of similar homely homilies.

A harmless, and indeed attractive, stylistic feature of both AA and the Oxford Groups is informality. Until late in his life, his followers usually referred to Frank Buchman simply as "Frank," and by all accounts Oxford Group Movement houseparties were extremely informal affairs with attendees coming and going as they pleased, addressing each other by first names, and spending much time on leisure activities. AA is similarly informal. First names are habitually used at AA meetings, service workers at AA offices are almost invariably friendly and helpful, and members often engage in informal socializing, such as going out for coffee, after meetings. Given the terrible problem of loneliness in American society, it would be surprising indeed if many alcoholics didn't find the friendliness and informality of AA to be its most attractive features.

A not-so-attractive stylistic similarity between the two organizations is self-preoccupation. Again, this stems directly from their shared belief in divine guidance. Frank Buchman and his followers believed that their movement was directly controlled by God and was *the* answer to all human problems. Therefore, all attempts at social improvement outside of the Oxford Groups' sphere were dead ends, as well as distractions from the *only* essential work, that of the Oxford Groups. AA isn't as grandiose in its claims as the Oxford Groups, but probably a large majority of AA members would vocally affirm that AA is the *only* route to lasting sobriety, and one often hears comments at meetings to the effect that "AA always works" for those who "honestly" try it. Since AA "always works" (except for those who lack "honesty" or have other "defects of character"), there is no need to develop alternative treatments, and attempts to develop and implement such alternatives are useless at best and could be harmful, in that they might lead alcoholics away from the *only* effective treatment for alcoholism—AA. The blindness and arrogance such irrational beliefs engender are so obvious as to need no further comment.

One initial similarity between AA and the Oxford Groups disappeared decades ago. The Oxford Group Movement was always aimed primarily at the influential and well to do, just as AA originally was. That AA initially attracted upper class and upper middle class alcohol abusers isn't terribly surprising given the fact that AA's founders were a Wall Street insider and a surgeon, both of whom came from privileged backgrounds, and were, to boot, both members of the Oxford Group Movement before they met.

Within a relatively few years of AA's inception, however, AA's composition had changed dramatically, probably due to its emphasis upon a desire to give up drinking being the sole requirement for membership, and the 12th-step injunction to "carry this message to alcoholics." This is in stark contrast to the Buchmanites' emphasis upon recruiting "up-and-outers" and "key men." At present, AA membership cuts across all class lines, though it does seem to be drawn primarily from the lower middle class.

One important dissimilarity between the two groups regards the matter of anonymity. The Oxford Group Movement went to great lengths to attract the wealthy and prominent and, once they were hooked, assiduously used their names in its self-promotions. In addition, the Oxford Groups routinely went to great lengths to obtain endorsements, or statements that could be misrepresented as endorsements, from presidents, prime ministers, tycoons, and sports and show business figures. The Oxford Group Movement also built a veritable cult of personality around its founder, Frank Buchman, and Buchman left no stone unturned in his efforts to inflate his own reputation.

In contrast, AA has always insisted that members maintain strict anonymity in relations with the media. AA's insistence in this matter was motivated by fear that famous and prominent members would announce their AA membership and then get drunk in public, bringing disgrace upon AA. This policy has served AA well. In addition to protecting AA from public ridicule, it has also allowed AA members involved in the addictions field to issue pronouncements beneficial to AA while hiding their AA membership and posing as disinterested professionals.[6]

These are only the most outstanding similarities and differences between Alcoholics Anonymous and the Oxford Group Movement. Anyone thoroughly familiar with AA and the Oxford Groups should be able to discover other points of correspondence and divergence.

1. See, for example, "The Oxford Group Movement," by Henry P. Van Dusen in *The Atlantic Monthly*, August 1934, p. 249; and *Saints Run Mad*, by Marjorie Harrison. London: John Lane the Bodley Head, 1934, pp. 27-29.

2. Quoted in "The Oxford Group—Genuine or a Mockery?," *Literary Digest*, January 28, 1933, p. 17.

3. "The Twelve-Step Program: Cure or Cover?," in *The Utne Reader*, November/December 1988, p. 61 .

4. *Alcoholics Anonymous*, by Bill Wilson. New York: Alcoholics Anonymous World Services, 1985, p. 46.

5. According to the "Alcoholics Anonymous 1996 Membership Survey," AA is 86% white, with both blacks and hispanics being under-represented in its membership.

6. For instance, the first edition of this book received an absolutely horrendous review (which contained a glaring and important factual error) in an important library review journal by an addictions "professional" who was almost certainly an AA member, but who did not disclose her membership in the review, and, almost certainly, did not reveal it to the editors of the review journal either.

5

The 12 Steps

This chapter draws heavily upon two sources: The paper "Divine Intervention and the Treatment of Chemical Dependency," by Drs. Albert Ellis and Eugene Schoenfeld,[1] and *The Real AA: Behind the Myth of 12-Step Recovery* (formerly *More Revealed*), by Ken Ragge.[2] The material regarding the relationship of the Oxford Group Movement's teachings to the content of the 12 steps is mine. But many of the other insights contained in this chapter are the responsibility of the above-mentioned authors; and any inaccuracies are my responsibility alone.

The 12 steps are the backbone of the AA "program." A majority of Alcoholics Anonymous members regard them in the same reverent manner that fundamentalist Christians regard the 10 Commandments. This is no accident, considering the overtly religious nature of the steps. They were drawn directly from the teachings of the Oxford Groups, the evangelical Christian movement to which Bill Wilson and Dr. Bob Smith belonged, and which AA was a part of until the late 1930s. As well, Bill Wilson believed that he was acting under divine "guidance" when he wrote the 12 steps,[3] and any-one who accepts that he was doing so must necessarily place the 12 steps in the category of "revealed wisdom." One indication that Wilson and his fellow AAs believed that he was divinely inspired is found in *Pass It On*, where Wilson, or a fellow AA in his company, is quoted as follows in replying to a suggestion that Wilson make changes in the "Big Book": "Why [change it]? What is the matter with it? It is perfect."[4] One doubts that Bill Wilson was so egotistical as to think that he, as a "powerless" individual, could write a "perfect" book; he undoubtedly believed that he had God's help in doing so. Many current AA members almost certainly believe that Wilson did indeed have divine help. One service worker in AA's General Service Office recently stated: "I consider the Big Book as an inspired text, written by Bill under the guidance of the spirit."[5]

Bill Wilson makes the connection between the Oxford Groups and the AA "program" crystal clear in *Alcoholics Anonymous Comes of Age*, in which he directly credits the Oxford Groups as the source of the religious teachings codified in the 12 steps.[6] In the Oxford Groups, the concepts embodied in the steps were prescribed as the cure for *sin.* In AA, these same principles are prescribed as the cure for *alcoholism.* Thus, *religion* is presented as the cure for what is commonly considered a *disease.*

Unfortunately, the hold of AA upon the field of alcoholism treatment is so tight that this obvious fact is almost never mentioned in either the popular press or professional journals. When this fact is (rarely) pointed out in the mass media, more often than not it's "balanced" by the disingenuous claim that AA's program is "spiritual" rather than "religious."

A great many members of AA, probably a large majority, regard the steps as fundamental to their own recovery, and often vocally maintain that recovery is *impossible* without following the steps. Is this true? Are the 12 steps essential to recovery, and are alcohol abusers who reject them doomed to an early death from alcoholism? Fortunately, the answer is "no" to both parts of the question. If it were "yes," the many thousands of members of Moderation Management, S.M.A.R.T. Recovery, Rational Recovery, Women for Sobriety, and Secular Organizations for Sobriety wouldn't be sober today,[7] nor would the multitude—undoubtedly millions—of persons who have recovered from alcohol abuse without participating in *any* recovery program.

Why then do so many members of Alcoholics Anonymous zealously promote the 12 steps, and why—in the face of convincing contradictory evidence—do they maintain that the steps are essential to recovery? The answer can only be that their position is the result of religious belief, not the result of honesty and logical thinking.

Fully half of the 12 steps explicitly mention "God," "a Power greater than ourselves," or "Him." Most religious AA members have little or no problem with this terminology. It fits their belief system. And just as they have no problem believing, in the absence of evidence, that God exists, they have no problem insisting, in the presence of crushing contradictory evidence, that the 12 steps are essential to recovery.

But what of formerly nonreligious alcoholics who embrace the 12 steps? Virtually without exception they "got religion" when they were in desperate straits. They underwent religious conversion.

Normally, happy, well-adjusted persons do not radically change their views; and, especially, they do not normally adopt views that they regard as silly and irrational. On the other hand, when a person is in an emotional crisis, radical alteration in beliefs, including religious conversion, is not unusual. As Drs. Ellis and Schoenfeld point out, "A person may be so desperate and beaten that his or her normal beliefs can be temporarily suspended, as in 'there are no atheists in foxholes.' Yes, the drowning may grasp at any straw."[8] In probably 999 cases out of 1000, then, the acceptance of the 12 steps by formerly nonreligious alcohol abusers is no more based in rationality and respect for facts than is the acceptance of the 12 steps by religious alcohol abusers.

Another likely reason that many members of AA tightly embrace the 12 steps is that the steps provide structure, a well groomed path to follow, in shattered lives. That can look awfully attractive when your world has turned upside down and you no longer have your best friend—alcohol—to lean on. It seems probable that to a great extent the substance of the steps is irrelevant; what is seemingly more important is simply that the steps are there and that those dependent on them believe that they're the means of overcoming alcoholism. Another way of spelling recovery-via-the-steps could well be p-l-a-c-e-b-o e-f-f-e-c-t. That would largely explain why those who believe in the steps cling to them so stubbornly.

Nevertheless, their religious content is probably a more important reason for blind adherence to the steps. Life is filled with annoyances, dangers, and uncertainties, and like most people, AA true believers don't want to face such unpleasant things. They want a "Higher Power" to take care of their problems; and since there is no evidence that their heavenly Big Brother exists, they desperately cling to the belief that it does. As Albert Ellis notes, "This is like a young boy's believing that he must have a kindly father in order to survive; and then, when his father is unkind, or perhaps has died, the boy dreams up a father . . . and insists that this dream-father actually exists."[9]

Still another reason for religious adherence to the steps is fear. As Ken Ragge has pointed out, while the Oxford Group Movement exploited *guilt* in its indoctrination process, AA exploits *fear* in its indoctrination process.[10] Newcomers to AA are routinely and repeatedly told that the only alternatives to AA and "working" the steps are "jails, institutions, and death."

In itself, this is a sad state of affairs. What makes it truly worrisome is that many, probably most, members of Alcoholics Anonymous not only embrace the irrational belief in a "Higher Power," but they actively promote the idea that their irrational belief system is the *only* road to sobriety. I believe that they do this primarily for self-validation; they *want* to assure themselves that they're doing the right thing *and* that it "works." And because "believers" invariably have doubts (about themselves, if not about received wisdom), "belief" becomes much easier to maintain if there are no dissenting voices to be heard. This largely explains the routine and extreme hostility to those who question accepted wisdom at AA meetings.

This attempt at self-validation with its accompanying fixation on the AA program often leads to a lack of concern for those who have alcohol problems but reject AA. In fact, from what I've observed, at least a few members of AA enjoy seeing nonreligious alcoholics drink themselves to death. It provides confirmation of their "spiritual" beliefs.

Unfortunately, many non-religious alcoholics *do* drink themselves to death after investigating AA and rejecting it because of its religiosity. In all too many cases, that appears to be the result of their acceptance of the AA myth that alcoholics who reject AA are doomed to an alcoholic hell. This belief frequently becomes a self-fulfilling prophecy. If those too honest to "fake it until [they] make it" believe that their only choice is between abandoning their integrity (by embracing AA and participating in an endless series of dreary religious meetings) or continuing to drink, it's little wonder that a great many eventually do drink themselves to death.

But what of the 12 steps themselves? Are they the magic key to sobriety? The key to becoming "happily and usefully whole," as AA claims? Are they a formula for mental enslavement? Or are they a combination of good, useful principles and unhealthy, pernicious dogma? The best way to answer the question is to consider the steps individually:

1. We admitted we were powerless over alcohol . . . that our lives had become unmanageable.

This, like all of the other steps, stems directly from Oxford Group Movement/Moral Re-Armament beliefs. A central tenet of Oxford Group Movement dogma is that the vast majority of "men" (the terminology is theirs) are "defeated" and are powerless in themselves to overcome their "defeat." The original version of the first step shows its lineage very clearly: "We admitted that we were licked, that we were powerless over alcohol."[11]

To put it plainly, this first step can only be seen as harmful in that it stresses personal powerlessness. It's difficult to see how it can do anything for those who accept it other than contribute to low self-esteem. This is pernicious in that if there's one common denominator among those who do harmful things to themselves, such as drinking excessively, it's that they have a low opinion of themselves.

Some—including myself in the first edition of this book—have attempted to interpret this step as a healthy admission of having a problem. But this is simply at odds with the first step's wording and intent. This step is an admission alright, but it isn't a healthy one. There's a huge difference between stating that you have a problem and are going to do something about it, and stating that you have a problem and are "powerless" to do anything about it.

As Ken Ragge points out, the first step is a step toward *learned helplessness*, toward personal *irresponsibility*. In fact, there is evidence that AA's emphasis upon individual powerlessness over alcohol consumption—where taking a single drink is considered a catastrophe *inevitably* leading to a bender—significantly contributes to worsening relapses. In the March-April 1987 issue of the professional journal *Social Work*, Dennis Daley states:

> Teaching clients to expect one episode of use to lead to total loss of control may set the expectation that initial use cannot be curtailed before a full-blown relapse occurs . . . In the course of treating hundreds of relapsed substance abusers, my colleagues and I found that our clients reported that they thought total loss of control was inevitable or that the initial substance use behavior meant that they could not recover.[12]

In addition to the anecdotal evidence offered by Daley, there is also experimental evidence that the learned helplessness induced by AA (as expressed in the first step) leads to binge drinking. In the most sophisticated controlled study yet done of AA's effectiveness, after several months' exposure to AA, the court-mandated offenders assigned to AA were engaging in *four times* as much binge drinking as the no-treatment control group.[13]

In short, the first step leads to low self-esteem, learned helplessness, personal irresponsibility, and binge drinking. The first step is a step toward disaster; it has no redeeming features.

2. Came to believe that a Power greater than ourselves could restore us to sanity.

Again, this stems directly from Oxford Group Movement teachings. Oxford Groupers fervently believed that the individual was powerless and that there was an all-powerful God who could, and would, solve *all* human problems if "men" would only turn their lives over to "Him." Of course, this belief implies the existence of a God which can only be described as crudely anthropomorphic—a God vitally concerned with human problems, including the most trivial. It's difficult to see the results of such a belief as anything other than atrocious. In the Oxford Groups, it led, as *The Christian Century* pointed out (see p. 13), to Frank Buchman's desire for "a God-controlled Fascist dictator"; and in AA it leads to personal powerlessness, learned helplessness, and other-directedness.

As well, the very religiosity of step 2 is a major problem for many persons. Like steps 3, 5, 6, 7 and 11, step 2 refers to "God," "Him," or "a Power greater than ourselves." (Note the capitalization.) This poses obvious problems for those who believe that the existence of God is no more likely than the existence of Mother Goose. It's little wonder that a great many atheists and agnostics reject AA and its steps rather than renounce their honest beliefs—though often only after being pushed in self-destructive directions by AA's "one drink, one drunk," "progressive" illness, and "AA is the last house on the street" dogmas.

When AA newcomers express doubts about the religiosity of the second step, they're normally told that their "Higher Power" can be anything they choose. Doorknobs, bedpans, and AA itself are often suggested as "Higher Powers" for atheist and agnostic newcomers. It doesn't seem to bother those making such suggestions that the very next step explicitly mentions "God."

The second step is also harmful to religious persons in that it reinforces individual powerlessness and learned helplessness. It encourages AA members to be dependent. This is directly contrary to the normal therapeutic goal of helping individuals to become independent and self-directed.

3. Made a decision to turn our will and our lives over the care of God *as we understood Him.*

As Jack Trimpey, founder of Rational Recovery, has pointed out, steps 2 and 3 are a con—a classic "bait and switch." Specifically, step 3 poses obvious problems for atheist and agnostic newcomers who have chosen, for example, a doorknob as their "Power greater than [themselves]." How does one turn one's life over to a doorknob? Obviously, one can't. One is left with the choice of God, or, more likely, God's interpreters—in this case, AA. This is clearly dangerous. The submission of the individual to the collectivity is a hallmark—indeed a defining criterion—of religious cults and authoritarian political groups. Submission of the individual to the collectivity, to the "collective wisdom" if you will, is a recipe for producing masses of other-directed true believers.

Unsurprisingly, this step was lifted directly from the Oxford Group Movement dogma mentioned in the discussion of step 2. Indeed, the central tenet of the Oxford Groups was that God would reveal "Himself" to anyone who would "listen," and that "He" had a minutely detailed plan for every human life. The sheer *chutzpah* of this belief is positively breathtaking. It's the most grandiose excuse imaginable for the evasion of individual thought, responsibility, and decision making.

A particularly harmful aspect of this step is that it demands dependence on a God whose existence has never been demonstrated. If someone truly believed that God was keeping him or her from drinking and—perhaps because of the death of a loved one or some other traumatic event—was shocked into the realization that God very probably doesn't exist, s/he could well begin to drink abusively again (especially if he or she bought AA's "one drink, one drunk" dogma). Of course, those who have chosen AA as their "Higher Power" don't face this particular hazard, as they've turned their "will" and "lives" over to AA, not God.

As Drs. Ellis and Schoenfeld point out, *anything* encouraging individual effort and responsibility—even the religious saying, "God helps those who help themselves"—would be preferable to this step.

4. Made a searching and fearless moral inventory of ourselves.

This could be a very useful principle—and not just for alcoholics. A searching and fearless self-examination is obviously useful to those attempting to rebuild shattered lives (or to those simply attempting to live happier, more productive lives). Few things are more useful to former alcoholics than discovering the reasons *why* they drank excessively. For once they've discovered those reasons, and especially the irrational beliefs which made drinking seem attractive, they can deal with them.

Unfortunately, the fourth step doesn't call for an inventory of irrational beliefs, physical causes, or other contributory factors; it calls for a *moral* inventory. What this has to do with recovery from alcoholism is anybody's guess. Unless one believes that alcoholism is caused by *sin*, this step makes no sense whatsoever.

Unfortunately, Bill Wilson was an enthusiastic Oxford Grouper and *did*, at bottom, believe that alcoholism was caused by sin. If Wilson actually believed that alcoholism was caused by an "allergy," as Dr. Silkworth speculates in the "Big Book,"[14] it's extremely difficult to see why he would have included the guilt-inducing, religious term "moral" in this step. But at the time he wrote the steps, Wilson regarded the Oxford Group Movement as his rescuer, and so it was natural that he would share the assumption of the Groups that all human problems are a direct result of sin.

In sum, this step is designed to produce guilt, and hence low self-esteem, which tends to contribute to self-damaging rather than self-caring behavior. Step four performs one other function: it prepares those being indoctrinated into AA for the next step, *confession.*

5. Admitted to God, to ourselves, and to another human being the exact nature of our wrongs.

This is still another legacy of the Oxford Groups. "Confession" was an integral part of the Oxford Group program, and Group Movement founder Frank Buchman was an expert at extracting confessions (often of a sexual nature) from potential converts. Confession of sin was considered so important by Buchman that he included it as one of the "5 Cs," which were a schematic outline of the Group program, and were reportedly utilized by conservative AA groups well into the 1940s: "Confidence, Conviction, Confession, Conversion, Continuance." Thus it was natural that Grouper Bill Wilson would include confession as a key element of the AA program.

It should be noted, though, that in order to make this step more palatable to nonreligious alcoholics, Wilson used the euphemism "our wrongs" when what he undoubtedly really meant was "our sins." It should also be noted that confession in AA consists of more than confessing one's "wrongs" to "another human being"; it also consists of public "sharing" and "witnessing" at meetings. Finally, it should be noted that such use of confession is a classic means of deepening individual immersion in groups, and of fostering individual identification with groups. Robert Jay Lifton goes into great detail about the techniques and purposes of such public confession in his classic study of Chinese Communist indoctrination methods, *Thought Reform and the Psychology of Totalism.*[15]

Unsurprisingly, many commentators on the steps have attempted to torture the meaning of the fifth step into a recommendation of openness and honesty—which it isn't. The wording of this step is unambiguous; it's concerned with admission (confession) of "wrongs," period. While it's quite understandable that humane individuals would attempt to interpret the steps in a humane manner—much as liberal Christians attempt to interpret scripture in a humane manner—such interpretations jibe with neither the actual wording of the steps nor with the concepts and intent of the religious movement (Buchmanism) that produced them. Like it or not, the steps do not have the humane meanings ascribed to them by wishful thinkers.

Finally, the reference to "another human being" introduces us to the concept of "sponsors." Newcomers ("pigeons") in AA are routinely urged to find a sponsor (a more experienced member of AA with whom they develop a special relationship, to whom they make a confession of their "wrongs," and from whom they receive guidance and indoctrination) shortly after they enter "the program." Sponsors, of course, vary greatly. Some genuinely try to be helpful, while others are meddlesome busybodies who enjoy controlling other human beings. The therapeutic value of the sponsor relationship—like that of public confession—seems suspect in that it, like virtually everything else in the AA program, encourages dependence.

6. Were entirely ready to have God remove all these defects of character.

This is yet another step which invokes "God" and encourages dependence rather than independence. It echoes the first three steps' declarations of personal "powerlessness" (first step), personal "[in]sanity" (second step), and the "decision to turn our will and our lives over to the care of God" (third step). (As an aside, it's most interesting to speculate how those who chose doorknobs or bedpans as their "Higher Power" work this step.")

The sixth step is yet another expression of the Oxford Group belief in an all-powerful, anthropomorphic God with a detailed plan for every human life, which "He" will reveal if human beings will only "listen." Needless to say, "defects of character" is almost certainly another euphemism for "sins," and is employed to disguise the religious nature of the steps.

7. Humbly asked Him to remove our shortcomings.

Humility is the virtue of those with poor self-images. In our cultural context, it's a purely religious, Christian concept: human beings are sinful wretches and should be properly humble before a perfect God who will resolve all of their problems if they properly abase themselves. Nonbelievers often find this concept revolting, and it would be surprising if this step in and of itself didn't drive countless alcoholics away from AA. It's interesting to note that the original version of step 7 included the words "on our knees" after the word "humbly." In light of this step, it seems absurd that AA continues to maintain that its program is "spiritual" rather than "religious."

Step 7 is yet another assertion of individual helplessness and defectiveness, and the desirability of dependency and guilt—things which were at the heart of the Oxford Group program. In the Oxford Groups (after "Confidence" in the "soul surgeon" was established), guilt was considered a desirable and necessary precursor to "Conviction, Confession, Conversion, Continuance." It plays a similarly vital role (though one subservient to the role played by fear) in AA.

8. Made a list of persons we had harmed, and became willing to make amends to such people wherever possible.

This and the next step stem directly from the personal experience of Oxford Group Movement founder Frank Buchman, specifically from his much ballyhooed writing of apologetic letters after his "conversion" at Keswick in 1908. After writing the letters, Buchman reportedly felt a great sense of release, and henceforth regarded making amends as an essential aspect of his spiritual program.

Making a list of those one has harmed is a useful practice in so far as it goes, and can be a helpful tool in coming to a full realization of the effects one's alcoholism (or other destructive behavior) has had on other people. But this step begs the question of whether those one has harmed *want* to be contacted by the person responsible for their irritation, inconvenience, loss, or suffering. In a great many cases, they've probably forgotten about minor harmful incidents, and in others are happy to have the perpetrator out of their lives; and recontacting them could easily reopen old wounds.

As well, the eighth step (and, indeed, the entire AA program), with its emphasis on individual culpability and total disregard of social factors, bears more than a passing resemblance to the more reactionary strands of "new ageism," with their insistence that we are all "totally responsible" for everything that happens to us. New ageism and AA's eighth step both ignore the fact that most people (including alcoholics) are the victims of more wrongs than they commit. We're all the victims of government and corporate intrusions into our private lives and finances; the vast majority of us are economically exploited and have little choice but to work at jobs that we barely tolerate, if not outright hate; we're all victims of environmental despoliation for private profit; and huge numbers of us are the victims of racism, sexism, and homophobia.

But you won't find a hint of this in AA's program. For example, it's a well established fact that the level of alcohol abuse rises (as do the rates of child abuse and wife beating) when unemployment levels rise. Alcoholics Anonymous, however, totally ignores this and all other social factors which contribute to alcoholism. Instead, AA lays the entire blame for alcoholism on the shoulders of alcoholics with its references to "our wrongs," "our shortcomings," and making "amends." In so doing, it provides tacit support for the social and political status quo. In regard to this, *The Christian Century's* comments about the Oxford Group Movement in 1936 are equally true of AA today:

> Indeed, perhaps the worst thing about a religion which undertakes to be purely individualistic and to concern itself not at all as to the way in which the corporate life of society is organized is that it cannot succeed in that undertaking—it is forced to take a political position, and its utter lack of understanding of political realities predetermines what that position shall be.
> Such a religion enters the social arena inevitably on the side of reaction.[16]

9. Made direct amends to such people wherever possible, except when to do so would injure them or others.

This is sometimes a useful thing to do, as it can deepen the appreciation of what effects one's actions had on others, and it can give a sense of closure to an unhappy period in one's life. But in place of this step's emphasis on individual culpability and atonement, it would be healthier to substitute a step that emphasized working to change the social conditions that contribute to alcohol abuse. This could, conceivably, lead to direct social improvements; and at the very least it would enhance personal empowerment. Active engagement, rather than passive acceptance, increases self-esteem.

10. Continued to take personal inventory and when we were wrong promptly admitted it.

This is essentially a restatement of step 4. It's also an expression of the Oxford Group principle of "Continuance." Unfortunately, step 10 doesn't state what *kind* of personal inventory we should continue to take. Since the only type mentioned earlier in the steps was a *moral* inventory, one can only conclude that a *moral* inventory is what's intended. This can only lead to more guilt, low self-esteem, and groveling "humbly" before the "Power" that "restore[s]" AA members to "sanity." The tenth step also implies that there is no escape from the AA program—if you accept it, you'll participate in it for the rest of your life.

11. Sought through prayer and meditation to improve our conscious contact with God *as we understood Him*, praying only for knowledge of His will for us and the power to carry that out.

This is still another tiresome call to dependency, other-directedness, and disregard for facts, logic, and rationality. Not incidentally, seeking such "guidance" from God was considered the *only* legitimate reason for prayer by the Oxford Groups. This step is an expression of the Oxford Group belief in "two-way" prayer, in which God both listens and makes its wishes known. In view of this step, with its repeated calls for *prayers* to "God," the claim that AA's program is "spiritual" rather than "religious" sounds downright ludicrous and more than a little dishonest.

12. Having had a spiritual awakening as the result of these Steps, we tried to carry this message to alcoholics and to practice these principles in all our affairs.

This is another expression of the Oxford Group principle of "Continuance." It was an article of faith among Groupers that once they had been "Changed" they should carry the "message" to those who were still "defeated" so that they too could "change." The reference to "practic[ing] these principles in all our affairs" is an obvious echo of the Oxford Group belief that theirs was not an organization but a "way of life," as well as a foreshadowing of the subsequent AA claim that it too is a "way of life."

It should also be noted that active evangelization ("carry[ing] the message") puts one in a position of relative knowledge and power, and so provides a certain measure of ego gratification for the evangelizer. This tends to cement acceptance of "this message" (AA's ideology) by the evangelizer, and to also cement his or her identification of self with the collectivity (AA). The ego gratification gained through evangelizing also makes the bitter pill of a lifetime commitment to AA easier to swallow.

Having said this, I should note that experience has shown that aiding others to become sober is very helpful to recovering alcohol abusers. It makes them feel useful, which builds self-esteem, which in turn promotes self-caring behavior; and it provides a reminder of the unpleasant realities of alcohol abuse, which provides a powerful spur to staying sober.

At the same time, step 12 clearly indicates that AA's program is a program for *life*—no one (in theory) *ever* graduates from it. It's also indicative of AA's self-absorption. Members of AA are not urged to help others overcome alcohol problems regardless of their acceptance or nonacceptance of AA's program. Rather—because AA has *the* answer—they are urged to "carry this [AA] message to alcoholics." And if those alcoholics don't want to hear the message, screw 'em.

In sum, the 12 steps are not a road to recovery, let alone *the* road to recovery. They are, instead, a road to a substitute dependency—a dependency upon AA rather than upon alcohol. Lois Wilson put the matter well in *Lois Remembers*, in her comments on the drunks who lived in her and Bill's home during AA's early days: "We often made the mistake of overprotecting our new prospects, thus encouraging dependence on other people rather than on the AA program."[17]

Quite simply, the 12 steps lead to a lifetime of dependency. Virtually anyone with any real knowledge of alcohol abuse should be able to construct a sturdier set of steps to recovery.

---

1. "Divine Intervention and the Treatment of Chemical Dependency," by Albert Ellis and Eugene Schoenfeld. *Journal of Substance Abuse*, Vol. 2, 1990, pp. 450-468 and 489-494.

2. *More Revealed*, by Ken Ragge. Henderson Nevada: Alert Publishing, 1992. The revised edition of this book is titled *The Real AA: Behind the Myth of 12-Step Recovery*. Tucson, Arizona: See Sharp Press, 1998.

3. *Lois Remembers*. Al-Anon Family Group Headquarters, 1979, p. 113: "How could he bring the program alive so that those at a distance, reading the book, could apply it to themselves and perhaps get well? He had to be very explicit. The six Oxford Group principles that the Fellowship had been using were not enough. He must broaden and deepen their implications. He relaxed and asked for guidance. When he finished writing and reread what he had put down, he was quite pleased. Twelve principles had developed—the Twelve Steps." (Note the capitalization.)

4. *Pass It On*. New York: Alcoholics Anonymous World Services, 1984, p. 204. The wording in the passage is not clear as to the actual speaker, and while it was very likely, given the context, that it was Wilson speaking, it might have been another member of AA in Wilson's company.

5. Quoted in "A.A. at the Crossroads," by Andrew Delbanco and Thomas Delbanco. *The New Yorker*, March 20, 1995, p. 51.

6. *Alcoholics Anonymous Come of Age*, by Bill Wilson. New York: Alcoholics Anonymous World Services, 1989, pp. 58-63, 160-167.

7. Some readers (members of AA and other 12-step groups) will undoubtedly do a double-take upon seeing members of Moderation Management described as "sober." This is because I've used the word "sober" here as a standard English-language term meaning "not intoxicated." "Sober," however, is also 12-step jargon—what Jack Trimpey calls "steptalk" —and the term's "steptalk" meaning differs from its meaning in standard English. In "steptalk," "sober" means "abstinent"—absolutely abstinent—and only that. Thus, 12-steppers would not normally describe someone who is merely unintoxicated as "sober."

8. Ellis and Schoenfeld, op. cit., p. 463.

9. *The Case Against Religiosity*, by Albert Ellis. New York: Institute for Rational Emotive Therapy, 1983, p. 3.

10. Ragge, op. cit., p. 20.

11. *Alcoholics Anonymous Comes of Age*, op. cit., p. 160.

12. "Relapse Prevention with Substance Abusers: Clinical Issues and Myths," by Dennis Daley. *Social Work*, March-April 1987, p. 140.

13. *Outpatient Treatment of Alcoholism*, by Jeffrey Brandsma, Maxie Maultsby, and Richard J. Welsh. Baltimore: University Park Press, 1980, p. 105.

14. *Alcoholics Anonymous*, by Bill Wilson. New York: Alcoholics Anonymous World Services, 1976, p. xxvi.

15. *Thought Reform and the Psychology of Totalism*, by Robert Jay Lifton. New York: W.W. Norton, 1969, pp. 425-427.

16. "A God-Guided Dictator," *The Christian Century*, September 9, 1936, p. 1183.

17. Lois Wilson, op. cit., p. 124.

6

The 12 Traditions

Just as the 12 steps are a set of guiding principles for individual AA members, the 12 traditions are a set of guiding principles for AA as an organization. The traditions were written by Bill Wilson and are a codification of principles developed and practiced during AA's early, turbulent years. The traditions were first published in May 1946 in their "long form" in AA's official organ, *The Grapevine*, and were unanimously ratified in Cleveland at the first international AA convention in 1950.

To a great extent the 12 traditions explain why AA has survived and prospered for over half a century: they're a blueprint for organization according to noncoercive, anarchist principles. It's a tribute to the soundness and wide applicability of these principles that they were adopted as a result of the real-life experiences and problems of the AA fellowship—large numbers of people who, in the vast majority of cases, almost certainly knew nothing of organizational theory. As well, it's a tribute to the wide applicability of these tenets that they were codified by Bill Wilson, a life-long conservative Republican. (While a discussion of anarchist organizational principles might seem out of place in an analysis of AA, it's inescapable in that AA is organized strictly in accord with those principles. Since most readers will probably have little interest in this topic, though, discussion will be kept to the minimum necessary.)

While the 12 traditions are, overall, much sounder and more humane than the 12 steps, the traditions are still a mixed bag of sound, useful concepts and worse-than-useless religiosity. (The comments on religiosity will be perfunctory in this chapter, because extensive treatment would essentially duplicate criticisms of religiosity in the previous chapters.)

The following discussion will use the "short form" of the 12 traditions. Those interested in seeing the "long form" should consult *12 Steps and 12 Traditions*.

1. Our common welfare should come first; personal recovery depends upon A.A. unity.

But for some of the other traditions, the first tradition could be very dangerous. The idea that the individual is less important than the "common welfare" is, of course, the justification for invasive, coercive government and all manner of horrifying violations of individual rights. It's also one of the central principles—in practice, if not always in rhetoric—of all religious cults and all authoritarian political groups. Traditions 2, 4, and 9, however, make it crystal clear that AA is organized on a nongovernmental (that is, noncoercive) basis. So, instead of a call to coercion, the first tradition is basically a call to cooperation.

Unfortunately, it's also a restatement of the AA principle that the individual is powerless in him or herself, and that recovery is possible only through the AA program. The undesirable effects of this belief—especially the substitution of one form of dependency for another and the induced hopelessness that this belief fosters in alcohol abusers who want to quit or moderate, but can't stand AA—were dealt with in the previous chapter.

2. For our group purpose there is but one ultimate authority—a loving God as He may express Himself in our group conscience. Our leaders are but trusted servants; they do not govern.

This tradition makes plain the AA belief that AA is guided directly by God—at least at times. While this may seem an arrogant claim, it pales in comparison with the claims of many religious cults that they're guided by God at *all* times. And the intent of this tradition is certainly benign in comparison with the intents of religious cults.

Stripped of its religious terminology, the first sentence in the second tradition simply means that AA will operate in accordance with the desires of its membership. The second sentence is equally important. The idea that officers (or "leaders") should serve rather than govern is a cornerstone of any group organized along anarchist principles, as AA is. In *12 Steps and 12 Traditions*, Bill Wilson wisely notes, "our group conscience, well-advised by its elders, will be in the long run wiser than any single leader."[1]

This tradition finds expression in AA's organizational form and decision-making process. To ensure that no ruling elite emerges, there are regular elections for all AA offices; all major decisions are made by majority vote at both local and national levels; and officers have neither the power to determine who is or isn't an AA member, nor to control the activities of the membership.

Another safeguard against the formation of a ruling elite which other groups organized on anarchist principles normally take, but which is only "recommend[ed]" in AA, is the rotation of offices.[2] This does not refer to the simple holding of elections at regular intervals, but rather to a prohibition against individuals serving more than one term. Though this is only a "recommend[ation]" in AA, it seems to be vigorously adhered to in practice.

3. The only requirement for AA membership is a desire to stop drinking.

This is another healthy principle. It ensures that anyone who comes to AA for help will not be turned away; and it goes a long way toward explaining why AA's membership is so diverse. This tradition also serves AA well in a pragmatic sense: if the requirement for AA membership was abstinence, AA membership would undoubtedly be much lower than it is now. As Ken Ragge notes, "The only thing more common among AA members than abstinence is binge drinking."[3]

This tradition also means that AA has no formal way to rid itself of troublesome and disruptive members. Perhaps surprisingly, this has not proven to be much of a problem. From my observations, disruptive persons rarely show up at meetings more than once, and when they do they're generally "bad vibed" out of them. Group opinion is a very powerful force for assuring adherence to group behavioral norms. Unfortunately, it is such a powerful force that a great many persons who come to AA for help, but who merely disagree with AA dogma, are also "bad vibed" out of AA meetings.

4. Each group should be autonomous except in matters affecting other groups or A.A. as a whole.

This is the principle of decentralism. It's an additional safeguard against the emergence of a ruling elite. The only conditions AA places on group autonomy are "A group ought not to do anything which would greatly injure AA as a whole, nor should it affiliate itself with anything or anybody else." The prohibition against injurious activities is normal in organizations of any type, though the prohibition against affiliation with other entities or individuals is not. In this particular, AA departs markedly from specifically anarchist groups. Most such groups are interested in a wide range of issues and normally will work with other organizations toward common goals. AA, on the other hand, is a single-interest group which believes that it has *the* answer to alcoholism and is solely concerned with the spread of its "program."

AA does, however, maintain close though informal ties through members with dual affiliations with other organizations. In particular, AA maintains close ties with the alcoholism treatment industry, in which AA "professionals" and "para-professionals" dominate. AA also maintains close ties with the National Council on Alcoholism and Drug Dependence, which was founded by AA member Marty Mann, and which counted Bill Wilson and Dr. Bob Smith among its openly listed sponsors. This is certainly better than the situation today, when the NCADD is essentially AA's "professional" front group and its spokesman on matters of "public controversy."

Thus, AA is adhering to the letter of this tradition, not to its spirit.

5. Each group has but one primary purpose—to carry its message to the alcoholic who still suffers.

There's both a good side and a bad side to this tradition. The good side is that having a single focus promotes group cohesiveness—there's no wrangling about organizational direction—and that this particular focus serves a therapeutic end. Proselytizing to others gives a sense of purpose to AA members and tends to increase their self-esteem by helping them feel useful.

The bad side of this tradition is that it promotes the idea that AA has *the* answer to the problem of alcoholism. (Notice that the primary purpose of AA groups as defined in this tradition is to "carry" the AA "message" to alcoholics—not to help alcoholics sober up.) The negative consequences of this—arrogance, self-absorption, hostility to non-12-step alcoholism recovery programs, etc.—were dealt with in the previous chapter, and will be dealt with further in Chapter 8.

6. An AA group ought never endorse, finance, or lend the AA name to any related facility or outside enterprise, lest problems of money, property, and prestige divert us from our primary purpose.

This is a wise principle. Overt involvement with commercial enterprises would certainly alter the nature of any Alcoholics Anonymous group; it would move it away from being a volunteer, self-help organization. Further, given the sleazy nature of many, if not most, American businesses, open association with commercial ventures could easily give AA a bad name.

Unfortunately, while AA has no *overt* involvement with "outside enterprise[s]," it does have massive *covert* involvement with such enterprises. At this writing, involvement in AA groups is prescribed as part of treatment in well over 90% of inpatient alcoholism treatment programs, and AA "professionals" run the vast majority of treatment programs. As a consequence, approximately 50% of all AA literature sold is sold to these institutions.[4] The profits from these sales make up a significant part of the budget for AA's General Service Office. In 1988, contributions from individual AA groups were $1,045,300 less than the cost of group services, and income from sales of publications to institutions covered this shortfall.[5] While AA is not paid directly for its services by institutional programs, they do provide AA with meeting space, a huge market for its literature, and a huge pool of recruits.[6] As of 1996, fully 40% of AA members had been introduced to AA by a treatment facility.[7]

Thus, AA is adhering to the letter of this tradition, but not to its spirit.

7. Every A.A. group ought to be fully self-supporting, declining outside contributions.

To those inundated by junk mail begging for their hard-earned dollars, AA's seventh tradition sounds strange indeed. But it embodies one of the most intelligent principles AA has adopted.

As Bill Wilson notes in *12 Steps and 12 Traditions*, "Whoever pays the piper is apt to call the tune."[8] One of AA's prime goals is to keep control of the organization in the hands of its membership; and this vow of corporate poverty, the seventh tradition, is an important guarantee of this. The seventh tradition is intended to keep the organization's service structure dependent upon the membership as a whole for financial support. It's also designed to keep individual AA groups self-directed.

If AA as a whole, or individual AA groups, accepted large contributions, those making the contributions could easily end up having undue influence even if they didn't intend to. The way that this normally occurs is that an organization will accept one large donation from an individual, then another, and before anyone notices it, the organization has become dependent on the donor. Then, even if the donor makes no demands, the group becomes *very* careful not to do anything that could alienate the donor. Thus, even if they don't intend it, those who give large sums of money often end up with undue influence.

Unfortunately, AA's dependence upon money derived from literature sales to institutions seems to subvert, at least in part, the intention of this tradition. At present, the services provided to groups by the General Service Office cost more than the groups as a whole donate to meet G.S.O. expenses. Thus, those groups—nearly *half*—that don't contribute a dime toward G.S.O. expenses are to some extent non-self-supporting.

8. Alcoholics Anonymous should remain forever nonprofessional, but our service centers may employ special workers.

On the surface, this seems remarkably similar to the policy of anarchist political groups that employ service workers, but have no "professional" staff. The reason for AA's policy is, however, different in one important respect from that of anarchist groups. Anarchists avoid "professionalization" of their organizations because they wish to avoid creating hierarchies; they wish to keep their organizations as democratic as possible, something which the creation of an "expert" or "professional" class would work against. To that end, when necessary, they employ service workers whose duties and responsibilities are carefully limited, and who it is clearly understood do not set policy.

This wariness of a "professional" governing class certainly seems to be a large part of the reason for the eighth tradition; but AA also feels that professionalism "does not work for us."[9] By this, AA means that professional psychiatric or psychological treatment independent of AA "does not work." This position tends to lock AA into its regrettable we've-got-the-answer mind set. The positive aspect of this tradition is that it does go a long way toward preventing the formation of a professional bureaucracy dictating policy to members.

9. A.A., as such, ought never be organized; but we may create service boards or committees directly responsible to those they serve.

This tradition demonstrates that its author, Bill Wilson, was just as confused as most members of the public are about what does and what does not constitute organization. The discussion of organization in *12 Steps and 12 Traditions* makes it extremely clear that Wilson shared the popular misconception that organization is synonymous with coercion and hierarchy. The clearest expression of this belief is his statement: "Power to direct or govern is the essence of organization everywhere."[10]

This assertion, which assumes that hierarchy and coercion are essential to organization, is demonstrably false. Organization, according to a dictionary definition, is merely "the state or manner of being organized . . . into a whole consisting of interdependent or coordinated parts, especially for harmonious or united action." Another way of stating this is that organization is a form of systematization for the purposes of communication and coordinated action. Thus, the questions of coercion and hierarchy are external to the question of organization. Coercive, hierarchical organizations, such as government, the military, and large corporations, exemplify but one type of organization.

A brief glance at present-day society reveals thousands of organizations that do not employ coercion. Some examples of organization based on voluntary cooperation are the Red Cross, the National Organization for Women, the U.S. Chess Federation, Mensa, the American Radio Relay League (the national ham radio organization), and innumerable food co-ops and other mutual aid groups. Some of these are nonhierarchical in addition to being noncoercive. As well, a glance at history reveals nonhierarchical mass labor organizations, such as the IWW in the U.S. and the Confederación Nacional del Trabajo in Spain, based purely on voluntary cooperation.[11]

But perhaps the most telling argument against the idea that coercion and hierarchy are necessary to organization is AA itself. AA is probably the best current example of a mass organization run along anarchist (noncoercive) lines. It's a tribute to the efficacy of the noncoercive principle of organization that it functions so well in an organization composed overwhelmingly of persons totally ignorant of anarchist theory and history, and almost certainly violently opposed to anarchism (or what they mistakenly suppose it to be) as a political philosophy.[12]

It's more than a bit ironic that the creation of "service boards or committees directly responsible to those they serve" is a cornerstone of the type of organization that Bill Wilson didn't recognize—noncoercive organization.

10. Alcoholics Anonymous has no opinion on outside issues; hence the A.A. name ought never be drawn into public controversy.

This is undoubtedly a wise guiding principle for a single-interest group. It allows members with widely divergent views on other topics to work together effectively in pursuit of their one common interest. For an organization such as a chess club, it makes a lot of sense. Whether this principle also makes sense for an organization dealing with a social problem is open to question.

AA adopted this tradition largely because of the experience of the Washingtonian Society in the 1840s and 1850s. Like AA, the Washingtonians were originally a self-help organization of alcoholics rooted in Protestant evangelicalism. They had considerable success; the society had more than 100,000 members at its high point. But the Washingtonians expanded their activities to embrace other reform causes such as abolitionism and the temperance movement. They were soon mired in internal and external controversy and disappeared within a few years. (Had they confined themselves to social issues directly contributing to alcohol abuse, the outcome of their story might have been different.)

Unfortunately, the tenth tradition is also an expression of the AA belief that alcoholism is purely an individual problem unrelated to political, social, and economic conditions. If AA were to adopt the more realistic view, that alcohol abuse has clear socioeconomic contributory factors, it would be very difficult for AA to avoid "public controversy"—especially if it wanted to actively work to mitigate the socioeconomic factors which help to produce alcohol abuse. Even if AA *didn't* want to deal directly with the social, economic and political factors which contribute to alcoholism, it would still be a huge advance if AA would simply *admit that these factors exist.*

Instead, AA continues to lay total responsibility for alcoholism directly on the shoulders of alcoholics—a position inherently supportive of the socioeconomic status quo. If alcoholism is completely the responsibility of individuals, by definition it has no causes or contributory factors in the social realm; and hence there is no need whatsoever for changes in the social structure in order to eliminate, or reduce the level of, alcohol abuse—all that's necessary is that *individual* alcohol abusers adopt the AA program.

11. Our public relations policy is based on attraction rather than promotion; we need always maintain personal anonymity at the level of press, radio, and films.

This two-part policy has served AA well. The deliberate policy of avoiding organizational self-promotion has resulted in a tremendous amount of favorable publicity for AA in the mass media. The attraction-not-promotion policy has worked well for two reasons: 1) AA is well intentioned and is widely believed to be doing great good in alleviating a serious social problem; 2) AA, with its religious orientation, emphasis on individual culpability and solutions, and disregard of the social factors involved in alcohol abuse, fits snugly into the existing social order. So, it should be no surprise that the corporate-owned media treat AA in a friendly manner. It's doubtful that AA's non-self-promoting policy would work as well for a more controversial organization. (It should be noted, though, that AA has employed televised public service announcements advertising its services; this seems difficult to reconcile with the eleventh tradition. It should also be noted that AA has little need for direct self-promotion, because there are a myriad of 12-stepping addictions "professionals" ready and eager to promote AA—without, of course, revealing their affiliation with AA.)

The second part of this policy, maintaining personal anonymity, is very wise. It's yet another safeguard against any individual(s) gaining undue influence over AA—it's a leveling device. It's also a safeguard against individuals using AA as a means of self-promotion. But these were undoubtedly only secondary reasons for this tradition's adoption, if indeed they were even considered.

The real reason for the adoption of the eleventh tradition was almost certainly the fear that prominent members would announce their membership and then get publicly drunk. This was a major concern in early AA—as witnessed by the lock-up of Morgan R. before his appearance on the "We the People" radio show (see page 33)—and it would be most surprising if this fear weren't the primary motivation for this tradition.

12. Anonymity is the spiritual foundation of all our Traditions, ever reminding us to place principles before personalities.

This is basically a restatement of the latter part of the eleventh tradition, perhaps added for emphasis. It is refreshing, though, to see this call to act from principles rather than from a desire for self-aggrandizement. One can only wish that this principle were far more widely practiced in all spheres of social life—both inside and outside of AA.

Given this call to act from principles, it's quite ironic that many AA addictions professionals use this tradition (and the eleventh tradition) as justification to act in an unprincipled manner that evades personal responsibility. There's really no other way to construe attacks on AA critics and "alternative" approaches, as well as blatant promotion of AA and its central tenets, by 12-stepping "professionals" who won't disclose their affiliation with AA. Thus, the twelfth tradition, a call to principled action, has been perverted into a "spiritual" excuse for unprincipled, dishonest action.

---

1. *12 Steps and 12 Traditions*, by Bill Wilson. New York. Alcoholics Anonymous World Services, 1982, p. 135.

2. *The A.A. Service Manual combined with Twelve Concepts for World Service*. New York: Alcoholics Anonymous World Services, 1989, p. S72. This is another example of one of AA's most attractive traits—its aversion to laying down "the law," and instead making "suggestions" and "recommendations."

3. *More Revealed*, by Ken Ragge. Henderson, Nevada: Alert Publishing, 1992, p. 134.

4. *The A.A. Story*, by Ernest Kurtz. San Francisco: Harper & Row, 1988, p. 180.

5. *A.A. Service Manual*, op. cit., p. 74.

6. In preparation for this revised edition, I asked A.A. World Services for updated financial information regarding sale of literature to institutions, and also updated financial information regarding support of the General Service Office by individual AA groups. World Services told me that no updated information was available.

7. "Alcoholics Anonymous 1996 Membership Survey" brochure.

8. *12 Steps and 12 Traditions*, op. cit., p. 164.

9. Ibid., p. 166.

10. Ibid., p. 172.

11. See *Collectives in the Spanish Revolution*, by Gaston Leval. London: Freedom Press, 1975; *The Anarchist Collectives*, Sam Dolgoff, editor. New York: Free Life Editions, 1974; and *Homage to Catalonia*, by George Orwell. London: Penguin Books.

12. For expositions of anarchist organizational theory, see *Anarchy in Action*, by Colin Ward. London: Freedom Press, 1973; *Fields, Factories and Workshops Tomorrow*, by Peter Kropotkin. London: Freedom Press; *About Anarchism*, by Nicolas Walter. London: Freedom Press. *Anarchism and Anarcho-Syndicalism*, by Rudolf Rocker. London: Freedom Press; *Anarcho-Syndicalism*, by Rudolf Rocker. London: Phoenix Press; and *The ABC of Anarchism*, by Alexander Berkman. London: Freedom Press.

7

How Effective Is AA?

"Of alcoholics who came to A.A. and really tried, 50 percent got sober at once and remained that way; 25 percent sobered up after some relapses . . ."
—Bill Wilson in *Alcoholics Anonymous*, p. xx

"Everything you know is wrong."
—Firesign Theater

The Problem of Definitions

Is AA an effective treatment for alcoholism? That seemingly simple question is far more difficult to answer than one would expect. A major problem is the difficulty of defining the terms "alcoholism" and "alcoholic." Since the terms were invented over 100 years ago, a great variety of definitions have been offered, and there is still no uniformity of opinion among the "experts" about what constitutes alcoholism nor about what constitutes an alcoholic. The safest thing that can be said is that definitions are largely arbitrary and can (and do) change over time. For example, in the "Big Book," Bill Wilson mentions "a certain type of hard drinker. He may have the habit badly enough to gradually impair him physically and mentally. It may cause him to die a few years before his time." Wilson goes on to say that this person is not a real alcoholic because he can learn to "stop or moderate."[1] Needless to say, virtually all AA members, as well as a very large majority of alcoholism professionals, would now label such a person "alcoholic."

Another indication of the difficulties involved in defining the word "alcoholic" can be seen in the wildly varying estimates of the number of alcoholics in the United States. In the 1986 best seller, *The Courage to Change*, Dennis Wholely estimated that there were 20 million American alcoholics at that time (in other words, over 11% of the adult population). Wholely's figure is twice as high as the estimate of 10 million which is found in many professional journal articles and alcoholism reference texts published in the 1970s and early 1980s, and which is still occasionally cited. A facts sheet circulated by the NCADD, which I obtained in 1991, estimates that there are 12.1 million heavy drinkers exhibiting one or more of the signs of alcoholism; a 1997 NCADD facts sheet lists 13.9 million alcoholics. And if you accept the commonly cited figure that 10% of American adults are alcoholics, you arrive at a current figure of 19.7 million.

The primary reason why these estimates vary so greatly is that "alcoholism" is an elusive concept with several defining factors, the limits of which are seemingly arbitrary, with the exceptions of physical damage caused by alcohol consumption, physical dependence (habituation to the extent that physical withdrawal symptoms appear if alcohol consumption ceases), and tolerance (the need to drink a larger amount than the average social drinker in order to reach a similar state of intoxication). In addition to these physical symptoms, commonly cited defining factors include amount consumed per day, number of drinking days per month, number of days intoxicated (according to some number-of-drinks benchmark), legal problems (e.g., DUIs), employment problems, and family/relationship problems. Obviously, any definition based upon such factors must be imprecise and at least somewhat arbitrary. For example, what is the precise amount of alcohol consumption which separates the alcoholic from the social drinker? And what relation does alcohol consumption have to the other defining variables? Would someone who drank 7 ounces of alcohol per day but who had relatively minor problems in other areas be defined as an alcoholic? Would someone who drank only half that amount but had severe problems in other areas be defined as an alcoholic? It's difficult to view answers to such questions as anything other than arbitrary.

For this reason, researchers in recent years have begun to use the somewhat more precise terms "alcohol dependence" and "alcohol abuse" instead of "alcoholism." "Alcohol dependence" refers to the presence of physical dependence and/or tolerance (as well as, almost invariably, additional problems), while "alcohol abuse" refers to the presence (and magnitude) of at least a certain number of the other defining factors. This distinction represents a definite step forward, though definitions of "alcohol abuse" are still somewhat arbitrary, and almost certainly will remain so. But these more precise definitions do allow for more precise estimates.

How Many Alcohol Abusers?

The figures commonly cited for the number of alcohol-dependent persons in the U.S. and Canada are fairly uniform, with most estimates that I've seen being in the 5% range. A 1995 National Institute on Alcohol

Abuse and Alcoholism (NIAAA) news release estimates the percentage of alcohol-dependent persons in the U.S. at 4.38%,[2] while the Addiction Research Foundation (ARF), based in Toronto, estimated alcohol dependence among the local population at 5.3%.[3] Estimates of the number of alcohol abusers vary more widely, with the NIAAA estimate being that only 3.03% of the population are alcohol abusers, while the ARF estimates the number of alcohol abusers at 5%.

Characteristics of AA Members

One thing that is certain is that the typical AA member today is different than the typical AA member in 1940. In the early days of AA, members were primarily "low-bottom" alcoholics who had been hospitalized for their drinking problems, and whose drinking had had devastating effects on their lives. At present, at least a large minority, perhaps a majority, of AA members are "high-bottom" problem drinkers who were never physically dependent upon nor tolerant of alcohol and who still functioned reasonably well socially and economically at the time they quit drinking. Thus, a well-designed study of the effectiveness of AA today would very probably yield a different result than a similar study conducted 50 years ago, simply because of the differences in the makeup of both AA's membership and the much-expanded pool of drinkers from which it now draws.

With the trend toward inclusion of those with shorter and shorter and ever-less-serious drinking problems in AA, the composition of AA's membership will very likely continue to change for some time to come. (According to AA's 1996 membership survey, there are now roughly 12,000 *teenage* AA members. In the 1930s, AA's early members would have considered the idea of teenage "alcoholics" ludicrous.) One question which arises from this is what percentage of AA's members are now "real alcoholics"? A complicating factor is that at least some disturbed persons whose primary problems are almost certainly not alcohol related attend AA because it's an easy way to meet their social needs. A further complicating factor is that a very high percentage of AA's current members, almost certainly at least a third, and probably more than 40%, are coerced into membership.[4]

Biasing Factors

The changing makeup of AA's membership is, however, a minor problem compared with several others. The most important problem is that in attempting to gauge the effectiveness of AA it's very difficult to tell if you're gauging results due to the AA program or results due to the characteristics of AA's membership. There are several factors predictive of a positive outcome to alcoholism treatment—motivation, middle class status, marital stability, employment, relatively mild and short-term problems with alcohol, and absence of serious mental disturbance being probably the most important—with most being found in higher-than-average percentages (for problem drinkers) in AA's membership; and it should be noted that these factors are *pre*determining factors which were operative in a great many AA members *before* they joined AA. An indication of the importance of these predictive factors is found in Frederick Baekeland's evaluation of different varieties of alcoholism treatment. Baekeland compared studies of four group therapy programs serving high socioeconomic status (SES—an important prognosticator of treatment outcome) patients with studies of four group therapy programs serving skid row alcoholics and other low SES patients. The improvement rates of the programs serving skid row alcoholics were only 18%, 7.9%, 2% and 0%, while the improvement rates of the programs serving high SES patients were 32.4%, 46.4%, 55.8%, and 68%.[5]

As is almost universally recognized in treatment literature, the most important favorable prognosticator is "motivation." Like most cliches, the truism that "once you admit you have a problem, it's half-licked," seems to have a basis in fact. Simply showing up at an AA meeting implies that an individual recognizes that s/he has a problem, and in itself this self-selection seems predictive of a successful outcome. Further, certain aspects of AA are so unpleasant—especially the religiosity, anti-intellectuality, and the gas chamber-like, tobacco smoke-filled atmosphere at many meetings—that continued attendance in itself implies a high degree of motivation, at least for nonreligious and critically minded (not to mention nonsmoking) members.

Estimates of AA's Effectiveness

Biasing factors, such as "motivation," are a serious problem, but it does seem possible to draw at least tentative conclusions about the effectiveness of Alcoholics Anonymous. A good starting point is AA's most recently announced membership figures. As of January 1, 1996, AA claimed 1.251 million members in the U.S. and Canada,[6] while there were approximately 218 million individuals 18 years of age and over in the two countries at that time. Taking the ARF estimates of the percentages of alcohol abusers and alcohol-dependent persons and multiplying them by total population figures yields a total of roughly 22 million individuals with alcohol problems in 1996; doing the same calculations using the NIAAA percentages yields a total of roughly 16.13 million persons. Taking these as high and low estimates of the number of alcohol abusers, as of the date of the last available AA membership figures, somewhere between 5.7% and 7.7% of U.S.

and Canadian "alcoholics" belonged to AA. And the percentage of those who will reach the AA goal of lifelong abstinence is much lower than that.

A noticeable feature of AA is that a large number of its members have been in the organization for a relatively short time. Based on my attendance at AA meetings in San Francisco in the late 1980s, I would estimate that over 50% of those attending meetings in that city at that time were members for less than one year and, in fact, that a majority were members for only a few months. The situation appears to have change little in recent years. (The discrepancy between my observations and AA's claim that only 27% of its members have less than one-year's abstinence is probably accounted for by AA's astoundingly high dropout rate; because of it, one constantly sees new faces showing up at AA meetings, with many of them sticking around for relatively few meetings.)

My estimate, however, isn't too far out of line with the figures given by Bill C. in a 1965 article in the *Quarterly Journal of Studies on Alcohol*.[7] In it, he reports that of 393 AA members surveyed, 31% had been sober for more than one year; 12% had been sober for more than one year but had had at least one relapse after joining AA; 9% had achieved a year's sobriety; 6% had died; 3% had gone to prison; 1% had gone to mental institutions; and 38% had stopped attending AA. What makes these numbers even more dismal than they appear is the fact that Bill C. defined a member as someone who attended 10 or more AA meetings in a year's time. When you take into account the "revolving door effect," it becomes apparent that far more persons attended AA meetings than the 393 "members" Bill C. lists. It seems quite probable that he picked the figure of 10 meetings in a year as a membership criterion because AA's success rate would have been revealed as microscopic if he had used a smaller number of attendances as his membership-defining device. (It should also be mentioned that attendance at 10 meetings in itself seems to imply a fairly high degree of motivation.)

The success rate calculated through analysis of the 1996 AA membership survey is hardly more impressive. The survey brochure indicates that 45% of members have at least five years' sobriety. Using the figure of five years' sobriety as the criterion of success, one arrives at an AA success rate of approximately 2.6% to 3.5% (in comparison with the total number of "alcoholics" in the U.S. and Canada). And the success rate is lower than that if one defines "success" as AA does—as lifelong abstinence.

It could be argued that this is an unfair way of evaluating the effectiveness of AA, and that only "alcoholics" who have investigated AA should be considered. That's a reasonable argument, but there's evidence that a very high proportion of "alcoholics" *have* at one time or another checked into AA. Anyone who has attended many AA meetings can testify that droves of newcomers show up, attend one, or a few, meeting(s), and then are never seen again—the "revolving door effect." As well, roughly 270,000 individuals accused or convicted of drunk driving and other alcohol-related crimes are coerced into 12-step treatment every year in the United States.[8] Based on the sheer numbers of such persons, it seems probable that well over 50%, perhaps as many as 90%, of American and Canadian problem drinkers investigate AA at some time during their drinking careers.

There's statistical evidence to indicate that this is so. Well known researcher Robin Room, of the Addiction Research Foundation, reports that a 1990 survey of 2058 Americans aged 18 and over revealed that 9% of American adults have attended an AA meeting at some time in their lives, and that an astounding 3.4% claimed to have done so in the previous year.[9] (The latter percentage is almost certainly incorrect.[10]) If Room's 9% figure is even close to being correct, it's good evidence that a very high percentage of U.S. and Canadian alcohol abusers have attended AA at least once. In 1996, 9% of American and Canadian adults corresponded to roughly 19.6 million individuals. This figure, when compared with the previously mentioned estimates of alcohol abusers and alcohol-dependent persons (16.13 to 22 million individuals), provides persuasive evidence that the percentage of "alcoholics" who have tried AA is high indeed—and that AA's success rate is very low.

AA's Triennial Surveys

AA's own statistics provide perhaps the most persuasive evidence that AA's success rate is minuscule. Since 1977, AA has conducted an extensive survey of its members every three years (though the survey scheduled for 1995 was conducted in 1996). These surveys measure such things as length of membership, age distribution, male-female ratio, employment categories, and length of sobriety. Following the 1989 survey, AA produced a large monograph, "Comments on A.A.'s Triennial Surveys,"[11] that analyzed the results of all five surveys done to that point. In terms of new-member dropout rate, all five surveys were in close agreement. According to the "Comments" document, the "% of those coming to AA within the first year that have remained the indicated number of months" is 19% after one month; 10% after three months; and 5% after 12 months.[12] In other words, AA has a 95% new-member dropout rate during the first year of attendance.

If success is defined as one-year's sobriety, on the face of it this 95% dropout rate gives AA a *maximum* success rate of only 5%; and a great many new members do not remain continuously sober during their first year in AA, which causes the apparent AA success rate to fall even lower. Of course, many of the 95% who drop out within the first year are probably "repeaters" who have previously investigated AA, and this would increase the apparent AA success rate; but at least for the present there is no way to know what percentage of the dropouts are repeaters. Additionally, at least some of the 95% who drop out of AA during their first year do manage to sober up; but to date there's no way to know what their numbers are. As well, it seems quite probable that most of those who drop out early in the program do so because they dislike and disagree with AA, so it could be argued that most of them who overcome their drinking problems do so in spite of, not because of, AA. Finally, at least some curiosity seekers and relatives of alcohol abusers show up at meetings, and this would further increase the apparent AA success rate. But to date, there are no reliable figures on what percentage of those who "walk through the door" fit those categories—though my personal estimate, and that of researcher/author Vince Fox, is that no more than 10% of new faces at AA meetings belong to relatives or curiosity seekers.[13]

One thing, however, is certain: An extremely high percentage of American drinkers who have been hospitalized for alcoholism or who have participated in other institutional alcoholism programs have participated in Alcoholics Anonymous. The number of patients treated for alcoholism is now approximately 950,000 annually,[14] which (because 12-step treatment is used in well over 90% of institutional programs) is a good indication that the proportion of alcohol abusers who have been exposed to AA is very high. It should also be kept in mind that in most parts of the country con-victed drunk drivers are still routinely forced to attend AA as a condition of probation, which pushes the percentage of alcohol abusers exposed to AA even higher. Further, in most areas AA is the only widely available—and widely media-promoted—alcoholism self-help group, so AA has a very high volume of "walk in" traffic.

But let's give AA the benefit of the doubt and estimate that only 50% of U.S. and Canadian alcohol abusers have tried AA. That would double the success rate calculated earlier (based on the total number of U.S. and Canadian alcohol abusers), and it would increase to 5.2% to 7.0% if the criterion of success is defined as five years' sobriety.

In a worst case scenario, where 90% of U.S. and Canadian alcohol abusers have tried AA, where success is defined as five or more years of sobriety, where 45% of AA members have been sober for five or more years (as AA indicates), and where there are 22 million alcohol abusers in the two countries, the AA success rate would be about 2.9% (and even lower than that if the criterion of success is lifelong sobriety rather than five years' sobriety).[15] The true success rate of AA is very probably somewhere between these two extremes, depending, of course, on how one defines "success"; that is, AA's success rate is probably somewhere between 2.9% and 7% (of those who have attended AA).

Spontaneous Remission

This is far from impressive, especially when compared with the rate of "spontaneous remission." Contrary to popular belief, "alcoholism" is *not* a progressive and incurable "disease." Many studies have been conducted on so-called spontaneous recovery by "alcoholics" (that is, recovery without treatment, which can refer to achievement of either abstinence or controlled drinking), and the consensus of these studies is that "spontaneous" recovery occurs in a significant percentage of alcohol abusers, though the calculated rates of recovery vary considerably.[16] Other consistently supported conclusions are that the rate of alcohol abuse and alcohol dependence (or, to use the older term, "alcoholism") declines far faster than can be explained by mortality among individuals past the age of 40,[17] and that "spontaneous" recovery normally occurs for identifiable reasons. In many cases, remission comes suddenly after a particularly dangerous or humiliating incident shocks the drinker into realization of the seriousness of his or her drinking problem. In other cases, recovery occurs as a result of religious conversion or as the result of an "existential" decision to quit based on a gradually increasing realization of the seriousness of the problem.[18] One review of available literature estimates the rate of spontaneous recovery at 3.7% to 7.4% per *year*.[19] More recently, a large-scale longitudinal study of over 4,000 adults with prior, significant, diagnosable alcohol dependence (the National Longitudinal Alcoholism Epidemiological Survey, conducted by the Census Bureau) reported that 20 years after the onset of alcohol dependence, 90% of those who never received treatment were either abstinent or "drinking without abuse or dependence."[20] Compared with these figures, the above-calculated rate of recovery via AA is not impressive. In fact, it appears to be no higher—and could actually be *lower*—than the rate of spontaneous remission.

Controlled Studies of AA's Effectiveness

But haven't there been scientific investigations of the effectiveness of AA? There have been, but there haven't been many. One reason for this could well be that "A.A. does not like to have researchers around,"[21] that it is highly reluctant to "open its doors to researchers."[22] Whatever the truth of these charges, to date there have been only two well-designed studies of the effectiveness of AA—that is, studies which have included control groups and the random assignment of subjects. (Two recent, often-cited studies, Walsh, et al., 1991,[23] and Project MATCH,[24] did not have control groups, and Project MATCH was not even a direct study of AA.) Both controlled studies indicated that AA is *not* an effective across-the-board treatment for alcohol abuse or dependence ("alcoholism"). The subjects in both studies were, however, court-referred alcoholic offenders and hence different from the general alcoholic population in certain respects. Thus one distinguishing feature of the study populations is that they did not voluntarily seek treatment; they were forced to attend AA.

On the surface, these factors—the employment of coercion and the special-population status of alcoholic offenders—seem to lessen the credibility of the two controlled studies of AA's effectiveness. But it could be argued that one factor is irrelevant and the other actually enhances the studies' credibility. If, as is commonly asserted, AA is a universally applicable treatment for *all* alcoholics, the makeup of the study populations shouldn't have mattered a whit as long as the assignment of subjects to AA and control groups was truly random. And the fact that the studies' subjects were coerced into participating could well *increase* the validity of the studies' findings, because a very important biasing factor, subject motivation, was eliminated, and the remaining biasing factors were spread out fairly evenly among the groups studied because of the random assignment procedure. Further, since at least a third of present-day AA participants are coerced into attendance either by alcoholism treatment programs or the courts, through programs for DUI and other alcohol-related offenders, the populations of these studies were perhaps not as different from the general AA population as one might suspect.

The first of these controlled studies of AA's effectiveness was conducted in San Diego in the mid-1960s.[25] In the study, 301 public drunkenness offenders were randomly divided into three groups. One group was assigned to attend AA, another to attend an alcoholism treatment clinic, and a third group, the control, was not assigned to any treatment program. All of the study's subjects were followed for at least one full year following conviction. Results were calculated by counting the number and frequency of rearrests for drunkenness. Surprisingly, the no-treatment control group was the most successful of the three, with 44% of its members having no rearrests; 32% of those assigned to the clinic group had no rearrests; and 31% of those assigned to AA had no rearrests. As well, 37% of the members of the control group had two or more rearrests, while 40% of the alcoholism clinic attendees were arrested at least two times, and 47% of the AA attendees were arrested at least twice. While far from a definitive debunking of AA's alleged effectiveness, these results are certainly suggestive.

The other controlled study of AA's effectiveness was very carefully designed and conducted, and was carried out in Kentucky in the mid-1970s.[26] A large majority of its subjects were obtained via the court system, and seemed to be "representative of the 'revolving door' alcoholic court cases in our cities." The investigators divided 197 subjects into five randomly selected groups: a control group given no treatment; a group assigned to traditional insight therapy administered by professionals; a group assigned to nonprofessionally led Rational Behavior Therapy (lay RBT); a group assigned to professionally led Rational Behavior Therapy; and a group assigned to AA. Length of treatment varied from 202 to 246 days, and subjects were evaluated at the end of treatment and also at three months and 12 months following its termination.

In general, the groups given professional treatment did better than the nonprofessionally treated groups and the control group. A significant finding, however, was that treatment of any kind was preferable to no treatment.

Since a great many alcohol abusers never seek professional treatment, it's particularly important to compare the results of the AA, lay RBT, and control groups. Lay RBT was clearly superior to AA in terms of dropout rate. During the study, 68.4% of those assigned to AA stopped attending it, while only 40% of those attending lay RBT sessions stopped attending them. Further, at the termination of treatment, all of the lay RBT participants who had persisted in treatment reported that they were drinking less than they were before treatment, while only two-thirds of those who had continued to attend AA reported decreased drinking. As well, during the final three months of treatment, the mean number of arrests was 1.24 for the lay RBT group, 1.67 for the AA group, and 1.79 for the control group.

Perhaps most interestingly, the number of reported binges at three months after termination of treatment was far higher for the AA group than for the lay RBT or control groups. The mean number of reported binges by the AA attendees was 2.37 over the previous three months, while the mean number reported by the controls was 0.56, and the mean for the lay RBT group was only 0.26. This finding strongly suggests that the AA attendees had accepted AA's "one drink, one drunk" dogma, and had then proceeded to "prove" it. It's pertinent to note, however, that at 12 months following the termination of treatment there were no significant differences between the AA, lay RBT, and control groups. One possible interpretation of this finding is that the positive effects of Rational Behavior Therapy fade with time in the absence of continued practice, and that the harmful effects of exposure to AA (at least in regard to bingeing) also fade with time in the absence of further exposure to AA.

A particularly intriguing aspect of this study is that the relatively successful (compared with AA and the no-treatment controls) lay RBT group utilized a treatment based on Rational Emotive Behavior Therapy (REBT). The reason that this is interesting is that S.M.A.R.T. Recovery, the newest of the national secular alternatives to AA, is based on REBT. Thus, there's at least some slight reason to think that SMART might be more effective than AA. Unfortunately, no controlled studies of SMART's effectiveness have yet appeared, though one such study is now under way in Tucson, Arizona. But for now, speculation about SMART's effectiveness will remain just that—speculation.

Clearly, there's a crying need for additional controlled studies of AA's effectiveness, as well as for controlled studies of SMART's effectiveness and that of the other secular groups. In the absence of such studies (at least as regards the alternative groups) all that we're left with is educated guesswork.

What Works?

But is the situation hopeless? No. In fact, there's considerable data available that indicates which approaches are effective and which ones aren't. William Miller and Reid Hester, editors of the most comprehensive and most methodologically sound evaluation of treatment methods ever published, state that, "We were pleased to see that a number of treatment methods were consistently supported by controlled scientific research."[27] But they continue, "On the other hand, we were dismayed to realize that virtually none of these treatment methods was in common use within alcohol treatment programs in the United States."[28] Worse, "A significant negative correlation ($r=-.385$) was found between the strength of efficacy evidence for modalities and their cost; that is, the more expensive the treatment method, the less the scientific evidence documenting its efficacy."[29] They list the treatment methods showing the most positive results, as shown by controlled studies, as brief intervention, social skills training, motivational enhancement, community reinforcement approach, and behavior contracting.[30] Importantly, 12-step treatment was nowhere in evidence in the list of effective treatments; but it was quite likely a component of four modalities for which a number of studies show significant negative results: unspecified "standard" treatment; confrontational counseling; milieu therapy; and general alcoholism counseling.[31] As for AA, Miller and Hester list only the two controlled studies discussed above, both of which showed negative results.

What Doesn't—12-Step Treatment

There have been many studies of 12-step treatment, but the vast majority are of little use in determining treatment effectiveness for two reasons: 1) they lacked control groups; and 2) they were short- or medium-short-term studies. It's impossible to draw meaningful conclusions about treatment's effectiveness without control groups. And any apparent benefits from treatment tend to disappear with time. Thus, long-term studies utilizing control groups are necessary to determining the effectiveness of treatment. But there have been relatively few.

One important study was published in 1983. For eight years, its author, George Vaillant, followed 100 patients who had undergone 12-step treatment; he compared this sample to several hundred other untreated alcohol abusers. The treated patients fared no better than the untreated group. Fully 95% of the treated patients relapsed at some time during the eight years Vaillant followed them, and he concluded that "there is compelling evidence that the results of our treatment were no better than the natural history of the disease."[32] He added, "Not only had we failed to alter the natural history of alcoholism, but our death rate of three percent a year was appalling."[33]

Another very important, very scientifically sound study appeared in 1996. The National Longitudinal Alcoholism Epidemiological Survey was designed and sponsored by the NIAAA and was conducted by the U.S. Bureau of the Census. It was notable both for its size (4,585 subjects) and its study period (20 years). Its subjects were divided into a treated group and an untreated group. All of the study's subjects "had to have satisfied the criteria for prior-to-past year DSM-IV alcohol dependence by meeting at least 3 of the 7 DSM-IV criteria for dependence: tolerance; withdrawal (including relief or avoidance of withdrawal); persistent desire or unsuccessful attempts to cut down on or stop drinking; much time spent drinking, obtaining alcohol or recovering from its effects; reduction or cessation of important activities in favor of drinking; impaired control over drinking; and continued use despite physical or psychological problems caused by drinking."[34]

The study's findings were surprising: At 20 years after onset of symptoms, 80% of those who had undergone treatment were either abstinent or "drinking without abuse or dependence." But those who had never undergone treatment were doing even better: 90% of them were either abstinent or drinking nonproblematically. That is, 10% of those who had never been treated were still drinking abusively 20 years after the onset of symptoms, as were 20% of those who had been treated. In other words, *twice* as many of those who had undergone treatment were drinking abusively as those who had never been treated.[35]

Other important findings included the following: of those who had never been treated, fully 60% were drinking nonproblematically 20 years after the onset of symptoms; and even of those who had undergone treatment and had received dire warnings of loss of control, incurability, and progressivity, 28% were drinking nonproblematically 20 years after the onset of symptoms.[36] As well, in both groups, the percentage of those recovered (abstinent or drinking nonproblematically) steadily *increased* with time.[37]

Those who had been treated reported more initial problems than the untreated group, but as anyone who has ever gone to a few AA meetings can attest, there's status in reporting horrendous drinking behavior: the worse the problems overcome, the more impressive the apparent recovery. And in treatment centers, patients are routinely encouraged to exaggerate their problems. Stanton Peele quotes major league pitcher Dwight Gooden on his experiences being browbeaten in 12-step rehab by fellow patients: "My stories weren't as good [as theirs] . . . They said, 'C'mon, man you're lying.' They didn't believe me . . ."[38] There are many similar anecdotal reports. Given such rewards and pressures, it would be surprising indeed if many persons who have undergone treatment didn't "come to believe" their own stories and would thus over-report previous symptoms. Indeed, there's evidence that *only treated individuals display all of the classic symptoms of alcoholism.*[39] As Stanton Peele puts it, "Treatment here seems to be necessary for the *development* of the classical alcoholism syndrome."[40]

Recidivism Rates

Another way of gauging treatment effectiveness is through recidivism rates. By all indications, they're sky high for 12-step treatment. The NCADD reports that in 1992, "nearly 13.8 million Americans had problems with drinking"; and it claims that in that same year 1.9 million Americans underwent treatment.[41] These are astounding figures. If these figures are accurate and are typical of preceding and subsequent years, and assuming that "treatment works" and has a 0% recidivism rate, every single alcohol abuser in the United States should have been treated in an eight-year period (accounting for mortality, population increase, and the development of new problems), and well over 90% of the nation's alcoholism treatment centers should have shut down by now for lack of clients. Obviously, this hasn't happened. Even if treatment were only 50% effective and there were a 50% recidivism rate, the number of alcohol abusers in this country should have dropped by at least a third over the last decade. Again, obviously, this hasn't happened. Instead, the literally billions of dollars spent on treating the nearly two million people per year reported by the NCADD have had seemingly *no effect whatsoever* on the number of alcohol abusers in the United States. This is good evidence that the treatment industry's drumbeat chant, "Treatment Works!," is an outright lie, and it's also good evidence that the recidivism rate in 12-step treatment is astronomical. Reports from those who have undergone treatment indicate that this is so. One report from a pro-AA participant/observer in a 28-day program states that of the 42 patients who made it through treatment, "Twenty were in treatment for the first time, 15 were in treatment for the second time, and seven patients had had at least two previous admissions."[42] As well, the "National Treatment Center Study Summary Report" states that the recidivism rate at the overwhelmingly privately owned inpatient facilities it surveyed is fully 40%.[43] One suspects that the rate at publicly funded facilities is even higher. Anecdotal evidence indicates that this is so: a report written by a client who had undergone treatment in a VA hospital states that 11 of 12 patients in his 28-day program had previously undergone inpatient treatment, and that one of the recidivists had been in treatment *19 times*.[44]

Misinterpretation of Data

One often hears claims that one or another new study has "proven" the efficacy of AA or of 12-step treatment. Invariably, these claims are made about studies that didn't include control groups and that often had other methodological problems as well. The most obvious recent example is Project MATCH.[45] Treatment industry spokesmen claimed variously that it demonstrated the validity of 12-step treatment; that it demonstrated that all of the tested forms of treatment work equally well; and some even claimed that it demonstrated that 12-step treatment was superior to other forms of treatment. In reality, it did none of these things.

Project MATCH was an incredibly expensive study ($27 million—some reports have placed the total at $35 million) funded by the NIAAA that compared three forms of outpatient and aftercare treatment: motivational enhancement; cognitive behavioral coping skills therapy; and 12-step facilitation therapy. All three forms of treatment were delivered in one-on-one counseling sessions, though the number of scheduled sessions was only four for motivational enhancement, compared with 12 for the other two forms of treatment. The significant findings of Project MATCH were that patients in all three groups experienced very similar improvement, as measured by the number of drinking days per month and the incidence of bingeing, and that 12-step-treated clients with less severe psychological problems had more abstinent days than similar clients in the other two groups. The number of days that outpatient clients drank fell from 22 to 6, while the number of days aftercare clients drank fell from 25 to 4; and the number of drinks per drinking day fell from 12 to 3 among outpatient clients, and from 18 to 2 among aftercare clients.[46] Clearly, these are dramatic results, but were they the result of treatment, or of other factors?

Project MATCH was so over-designed that it seems likely that *any* form of treatment used in it would have shown similar results. First, all clients in Project MATCH were volunteers, and their volunteer status in itself shows a fairly high degree of motivation, a very important biasing factor. This is in stark contrast to the coerced status and presumably low motivation of the average alcoholism treatment client. Second, during the screening process approximately 10% of potential clients opted out of the study for reasons such as "the inconvenient location of the study or transportation problems."[47] This helped to narrow the study to only the most motivated clients. Third, more than half of the remaining potential clients were eliminated from the study for reasons such as "failure to complete the assessment battery" and "residential instability."[48] This not only helped to ensure that only the most motivated clients would participate in the study, but also that only the most well-adjusted clients would participate, thus introducing another positive biasing factor: social and emotional stability.

Client expectations were still another positive biasing factor. The clients knew that they were taking part in an expensive study, and the manner in which sessions were conducted undoubtedly led to high expectations: every session consisted of one-on-one therapy with a competent professional; and every session was videotaped. As well, the study's conductors engaged in "compliance enhancement procedures (i.e., calling clients between sessions, sending reminder notes and having collateral contacts),"[49] which certainly must have helped drive home the study's apparent importance, thus reinforcing clients' positive expectations.

Yet another problem with Project MATCH is that the treatments employed were of universally high quality—not only were all sessions videotaped, but supervisors monitored fully a quarter of them; they bore little resemblance to commonly employed treatments. The difference between Project MATCH and real-world treatments was probably most pronounced in the study's 12-step facilitation therapy. It seems highly unlikely that the therapists employing 12-step facilitation in Project MATCH would have engaged in the abusive behavior that is routine in 12-step treatment. It seems very unlikely that they would have bullied clients in order to coerce false confessions from them; it seems equally unlikely that they would have ridiculed clients who questioned the therapy or made comments critical of it or of AA; and one doubts that they would have lied to clients about "inevitable" loss of control after one drink, or about the "inevitable" progressivity of their incurable "disease."

Given all of these biasing factors, it was hardly surprising that all forms of treatment showed remarkably similar positive outcomes; almost *any* form of treatment would probably have shown similar results. The study's conductors even recognized—at least after the fact—this possibility. They note: "Compliance enhancement procedures . . . and the greater attention of individual treatment may have produced a level of overall compliance that made it difficult for differences between treatments to emerge."[50] They continue, "The overall effect of being a part of Project MATCH, with its extensive assessment, attractive treatments and aggressive follow-up, may have minimized naturally occurring variability among treatment modalities and may, in part, account for the favorable treatment outcomes."[51]

We'll never know for sure, though, because, as the researchers put it, "the efficacy of the three treatments cannot be demonstrated directly since the trial did not include a no-treatment control group."[52] But there does seem to be one clear lesson in Project MATCH: if you introduce enough positive biasing factors, almost any form of treatment will "produce" a positive outcome.

What We Know

For now, the best evidence available suggests that AA is ineffective as a means of overcoming alcohol problems, and there's some evidence that exposure to AA worsens at least one significant abusive behavior—binge drinking. But the evidence is not conclusive, and until additional controlled studies are conducted, it will remain impossible to draw firm conclusions about AA's (in)effectiveness. One thing, however, bears repeating: *there's no good evidence to indicate that AA is any more effective than "spontaneous recovery."* Assertions that AA is an effective means of overcoming alcohol problems, let alone assertions that AA is the *most* or the *only* effective means of doing so, are just that—assertions, and groundless ones at that.

As for 12-step treatment programs, we'll deal with them further in the next chapter.

---

1. *Alcoholics Anonymous*, by Bill Wilson. New York: Alcoholics Anonymous World Services, 1976, pp. 20-21.

2. "NIAAA Releases New Estimates of Alcohol Abuse and Dependence," March 17, 1995.

3. "How Many People Are Alcoholic?" page on the Addiction Research Foundation's web site: http://www.arf.org/isd/stats/alcohol.html

4. I base this estimate on AA's 1996 membership brochure. Because of the limitations of the data supplied by AA, my conclusions here must be somewhat tentative. I arrived at my figures as follows: 16% of those attending were openly coerced by the courts or penal system. I started with this as a baseline figure, because it involves undisguised coercion. Adding all of the percentages listed of other "important factors," one arrives at a total of 241%. To arrive at the coercive total percentage, I added the full 40% listed for treatment facilities (clients are almost invariably coerced into AA attendance by treatment facilities), three quarters of 16% listed for counseling agencies (counseling agencies often make counseling contingent on AA attendance), the full 9% listed for "employer or fellow worker" (undoubtedly, almost all of them were coerced into treatment by EAPs or professional diversion programs), 7% out of the 39% listed for family (the "National Treatment Center Study Summary Report" indicates that 17.5% of inpatient clients are adolescents, who would not enter treatment voluntarily), and half of the 8% listed for health care providers (who sometimes make treatment contingent on AA attendance). This yields a total of 65%, which I divided by 2.41, which yields a figure of roughly 27%. Adding that 27% to the 16% who were outright coerced by the legal and penal systems yields a total of 43% of current

AA members who belong to the organization primarily as a result of some type of coercion. Of course, this method is inexact, but it does yield a reasonable ballpark figure.

5. "Evaluation of Treatment Methods in Chronic Alcoholism," by Frederick Baekeland, in *Treatment and Rehabilitation of the Chronic Alcoholic*, Benjamin Kissin and Henri Begleiter, eds. New York: Plenum Press, 1977, p. 392.

6. "Membership" page on AA's web site: http://www.alcoholics-anonymous.org/factfile/doc07.html

7. "The growth and effectiveness of Alcoholics Anonymous in a Southwestern City," by Bill. C. *Quarterly Journal of Studies on Alcohol*, 26:279-284, 1965.

8. *National Admissions to Substance Abuse Treatment Services: The Treatment Episode Data Set (TEDS) 1992-1995*. Rockville, Maryland: U.S. Department of Health and Human Services, 1997. Table 10, p. 46.

9. "Alcoholics Anonymous as a Social Movement," by Robin Room, in *Research on Alcoholics Anonymous*, Barbara McCrady and William Miller, eds. New Brunswick, New Jersey: Rutgers Center of Alcohol Studies, 1993, p. 169.

10. If it were correct, and if it were even roughly comparable to rates for previous years, the full 9% of the population who claim to have attended at least one AA meeting would likely have done so during the previous three years, given minimal attendance overlap. And even if there were a 50% overlap, the full 9% figure would be reached in just over five years. These time periods are simply too short for both the 9% figure and the 3.4% figure to be correct. Further, given that AA grew in the U.S. and Canada by approximately 50,000 members in the year cited (1990), if 3.4% of the adult population had attended an AA meeting in that year, that would have come to 7,000,000 people, giving AA a new-member dropout rate well in excess of 99% for that year. AA has a very busy "revolving door," but it doesn't revolve quite that fast!

Room indicates that only 42% of the 3.4% who claim to have attended an AA meeting in 1990 admitted to doing so because of an alcohol problem. This simply doesn't wash with experience. From my own observations and those of other sharp-eyed former members (including Vince Fox and Ken Ragge), curiosity seekers are not terribly common at AA meetings, and neither are family members of alcohol abusers (though coerced persons, many of whom shouldn't be there, make up a significant percentage of attendees). My best estimate is that well over 90% of newcomers show up at AA either because of their own alcohol problems or because of coercion. It should also be remembered that even in anonymous surveys many individuals lie about things that they consider embarrassing, which would help to explain the low percentage admitting to attendance because of their own problems.

11. "Comments on A.A.'s Triennial Surveys," no author listed. New York: Alcoholics Anonymous World Services, n.d. (probably 1990).

12. Ibid., p. 12, Figure C-1.

13. Telephone conversation with Fox in August 1997.

14. "National Drug and Alcoholism Treatment Unit Survey (NDATUS): Data for 1994 and 1980–1994." Rockville, Maryland: SAMHSA, 1996, Table 10.

15. The minimum success rate I calculated in the original edition of this book was 1.3%. Most of the difference between the two figures is due to AA's reported increase in five or more years' sobriety among its members from 29% in 1989 to 45% in 1996. Most of the rest is a result of AA's having grown faster than the rate of population growth.

16. "Recovery Without Treatment," by Thomas Prugh. *Alcohol Health and Research World*, Fall 1986, pp. 24, 71 and 72.

17. "Alcoholism as a Self-Limiting Disease," by Leslie R.H. Drew. *Quarterly Journal of Studies on Alcohol*, Vol. 29, 1968, pp. 956-967.

18. "Spontaneous Remission in Alcoholics: Empirical Observations and Theoretical Implications," by Barry S. Tuchfeld. *Journal of Studies on Alcohol*, Vol. 42, No. 7, 1981, pp. 626-641.

19. "Spontaneous Recovery in Alcoholics: A Review and Analysis of the Available Research," by R.G. Smart. *Drug and Alcohol Dependence*, Vol. 1, 1975-1976, p. 284.

20. "Correlates of Past-Year Status Among Treated and Untreated Persons with Former Alcohol Dependence: United States, 1992," by Deborah A. Dawson. *Alcoholism: Clinical and Experimental Research*, Vol. 20, No. 4, June 1996, p. 773.

21. "Is Alcoholism Treatment Effective?," by Helen Annis. *Science*, Vol. 236, April 3, 1987, p. 21.

22. Baekeland, op. cit., p. 407.

23. "A Randomized Trial of Treatment Options for Alcohol-Abusing Workers," by Diana C. Walsh, et al. *New England Journal of Medicine*, Vol. 325, No. 11, Sept. 12, 1991, pp. 775-781. This study is sometimes cited as having a control group, when in fact it did not. A true control group would have received no treatment, whereas over 85% of the "choice" group in this study chose either hospitalization or AA attendance, thus rendering the results of the study ungeneralizable. Walsh et al. measured AA attendance only versus coerced hospitalization with AA attendance, and versus a mongrel "choice" group that voluntarily chose in large part either AA alone or hospitalization featuring AA. Thus the data in this study is of very limited use and cannot be cited (at least honestly cited) as evidence that AA or 12-step hospitalization "works" or doesn't "work," except in relation to each other. And even that comparison is of limited value given that this was a short-term study with a relatively small sample.

24. "Matching Alcoholism Treatments to Client Heterogeneity: Project MATCH Posttreatment Drinking Outcomes," by Project MATCH Research Group. *Journal of Studies on Alcohol*, January 1997, pp. 7-29. This amazingly expensive ($27 million) study not only did not have a control group, but did not directly measure AA's effectiveness vis a vis other treatments, and its methods of client selection and client handling probably served to distort the outcome. As the Project MATCH researchers themselves pointed out, "The overall effect of being a part of Project MATCH, with its extensive assessment, attractive treatments and aggressive follow-up [clients were paid, among other things] may have minimized naturally occurring variability among treatment modalities and may, in part, account for the favorable treatment outcomes." (p. 24)

25. "A Controlled Experiment on the Use of Court Probation for Drunk Arrests," by Keith S. Ditman, George G. Crawford, Edward W. Forby, Herbert Moskowitz, and Craig MacAndrew. *American Journal of Psychiatry*, 124:2, August 1967, pp. 160-163.

26. *Outpatient Treatment of Alcoholism*, by Jeffrey Brandsma, Maxie Maultsby, and Richard J. Walsh. Baltimore: University Park Press, 1980.

27. *Handbook of Alcoholism Treatment Approaches: Effective Alternatives*, William Miller and Reid Hester, editors. Boston: Allyn and Bacon, 1995, p. xi.

28. Ibid.

29. Ibid., Chapter 2, "What Works?," by Miller, Hester, et al., p. 13.

30. Ibid., Table 2.4, p. 18.

31. Ibid.

32. *The Natural History of Alcoholism: Causes, Patterns, and Paths to Recovery*, by George Vaillant. Cambridge, MA: Harvard University Press, 1983, p. 284,

33. Ibid., p. 285.

34. "Correlates of Past-Year Status Among Treated and Untreated Persons with Former Alcohol Dependence: United States, 1992," by Deborah A. Dawson. *Alcoholism: Clinical and Experimental Research*, Vol. 20, No. 4, June 1996, p. 772.

35. Ibid., Table 1, p. 773.

36. Ibid.

37. Ibid.

38. "AA Abuse," by Stanton Peele. *Reason*, November 1991, pp. 34-39. Reproduced at http://www.frw.uva.nl/cedro/peele/lib/aaabuse.html (p. 3 of html document).

39. See "Treatment Seeking Populations and Larger Realities," by Robin Room, in *Alcoholism Treatment in Transition*, G. Edwards and M. Grant, eds. London: Croom Helm, 1980, pp. 205-224.

40. "Denial—of Reality and of Freedom—in Addiction Research and Treatment," by Stanton Peele. *Bulletin of the Society of Psychologists in Addictive Behaviors*, Vol. 5 No. 4, 1986, pp. 149-166. The document is reproduced at http://www.frw.uva.nl/cedro/peele/library/denial.html and the quoted text is taken from page 9 of the html document.

41. "Alcoholism and Alcohol-Related Problems: A Sobering Look." Http://www.ncadd.org/problems.html (pp. 1 & 2).

42. "Goal Setting and Recovery from Alcoholism," by Donna Marie Wing. *Archives of Psychiatric Nursing*, Vol. 4, No. 3, June 1991, p. 179.

43. "National Treatment Center Study Summary Report," Paul Roman and Terry Blum, principal investigators. Athens, Georgia: Institute for Behavioral Research, 1997, p. 17.

44. "Twenty-Eight Days in Wilson's Inferno," by Brian Barton. *Journal of Rational Recovery*, Vol. 9, No. 5, May-June 1997, p. 8.

45. "Matching Alcoholism Treatments to Client Heterogeneity; Project MATCH Posttreatment Drinking Outcomes," by Project MATCH Research Group. *Journal of Studies on Alcohol*, January 1997, pp. 7-29.

46. Ibid., Figure 1, p. 15. These figures aren't exact, as there were minor variations in the outcomes for the three forms of treatment, and I derived these figures by interpreting graphs of results.

47. Ibid., p. 10.

48. Ibid.

49. Ibid., p. 23.

50. Ibid.

51. Ibid., p. 24.

52. Ibid., p. 23.

8

AA's Impact on Society

I've relied upon the work of several other investigators in this chapter, and I would particularly like to acknowledge Stanton Peele, Ken Ragge, and Jack Trimpey. Many of the insights contained in this chapter are theirs. In the section, "Suppression of Dissent," I've relied heavily upon Stanton Peele's journal articles, "Denial—of Reality and Freedom—in Addiction Research and Treatment" and "Alcoholism, Politics and Bureaucracy: The Consensus Against Controlled-Drinking Therapy in America."

Most Americans would describe Alcoholics Anonymous simply as meetings of coffee-slurping, cigarette-smoking ex-drunks in storefront meeting halls, libraries, YMCAs, and church basements. But AA's influence and effective structure reach far beyond such community-based meetings.

At first glance this seems odd, because AA's sixth Tradition explicitly states , "An A.A. group ought never endorse, finance, or lend the A.A. name to any related facility or outside enterprise . . ."; the eighth Tradition states, "Alcoholics Anonymous should remain forever nonprofessional . . ."; and the eleventh Tradition states, "Our public relations policy is based on attraction rather than promotion; . . ." But AA's Traditions do not forbid, and implicitly encourage, AA members to promote AA and its ideology while concealing their AA membership. The eleventh Tradition continues, "we need always maintain personal anonymity at the level of press, radio, and films," which certainly seems to encourage both promotion of AA and concealment of membership.

In fact, such promotion/concealment of identity is very far reaching. Through it, AA exerts tremendous influence in American society; and AA ideology pervades several important social institutions. Through its members and supporters, AA/12-step ideology has great influence in the mass media, legal profession, medical profession, judicial system, penal system, and, above all, in the addictions treatment system.

The Mass Media

Since its earliest days, AA has assiduously courted the mass media; and that courting has paid big dividends. It's rare to see or hear a story critical of AA in the media, or to see a movie or TV show that portrays alcohol problems or alcohol-abusing characters in a manner contrary to the stereotypes prescribed by 12-step ideology. This is no accident, and it's certainly not the result of AA's supposed effectiveness. (See Chapter 7.) Rather, it's the result of well over half a century of favorable media coverage of AA produced by AA's friends and concealed AA members. Like the majority of other Americans, most writers and reporters accept AA's rosy public image as reality, and its pronouncements as truthful. This compounds the problem of writer/reporter laziness and overwork. Because of these factors—AA's well-crafted favorable image, and writer/reporter laziness and overwork—writers and reporters are predisposed to accept AA's assertions as fact, and to accept the assertions of "professional" 12-step spokesmen (often posing as medical experts) without conducting any independent investigation.

On its web site, the group that acts as AA's spokesman on matters of "public controversy," the National Council on Alcoholism and Drug Dependence (NCADD), proudly proclaims its influence in the television industry. (This is hardly surprising; the AA members and supporters at the NCADD almost certainly believe that they're providing expert advice.) Among the instances of NCADD influence cited, they mention that during the 1950s and 1960s, "NCADD . . . assisted the producers of the Armstrong Circle Theater and the Alfred Hitchcock show in developing early dramatic programs that sympathetically explored the subject of alcoholism. These programs reached vast new audiences in their living rooms and gave NCADD an incredibly influential audience for its message."[1] Similar "sympathetic" messages have continued to the present day on shows such as *Beverly Hills 90210* and in Ad Council public service announcement campaigns.

AA and 12-step ideology have also had a major impact on American cinema. As in television, it's rare to see alcohol abuse and alcohol abusers portrayed in films in a manner contrary to AA stereotypes. Beginning with *The Lost Weekend* in 1945, and continuing through *The Days of Wine and Roses* (1962), *Clean and Sober* (1988), and *Drunks* (1996), American film dramas have rarely strayed from 12-step stereotypes. Alcohol and drug abuse (at least when a central issue) is uniformly portrayed as a chronic, progressive "disease" whose symptoms include loss of control and "denial," and whose only cure is lifelong abstinence; and those who provide "help"—AA and other 12-step groups—to the victims of this behavioral "disease" are uniformly portrayed in a positive light. It's difficult to know how many of these portrayals are the result of writers simply accepting common stereotypes, and how many are the result of deliberate attempts to promote AA and 12-step ideology by 12-step group members in the film industry. But some films, such as *Clean and Sober* and *Drunks*, are so blatantly propagandistic that it seems quite likely that their writers and/or producers are members of AA or other 12-step groups. We'll probably never know for certain, though, because it's highly unlikely that their writers and producers will ever "break anonymity."

As for the print media, for nearly half a century after AA's founding, very few critical articles appeared in national publications. In fact, according to the *Reader's Guide to Periodical Literature*, during entire decades (the '30s, '40s, '50s, and '70s) no article critical of AA appeared in any indexed periodical. As noted in Chapter 11, though, this situation has changed somewhat over the past decade; but even during that time approximately 75% of the indexed articles have been favorable to AA and the 12-step movement.

Professional Diversion Programs

The primary influence of AA on the legal profession (as distinct from the judicial system) is through professional diversion programs. Such programs exist in all 50 states. It's common for state bar associations, through diversion programs, to coerce "impaired" attorneys into 12-step inpatient treatment.[2] This type of coercion is even more pervasive in the medical system, affecting doctors and nurses, than in the legal system. In all such cases, the primary purpose of treatment is the indoctrination of coerced professionals into the 12-step belief system—not to help them overcome addictions.

Though he wasn't coerced by a diversion program, this intent is clear in the case of Dr. Clifton Kirton, an Ohio physician who had been abstinent for several years when he applied in the mid 1990s to the Veterans Administration for a liver transplant. His abstinent status mattered not a whit to the VA, and it insisted that he undergo 12-step treatment and "aftercare" (that is, attending AA meetings) as a condition of receiving a transplant.[3] Had it wished to do so, the VA could have easily and relatively inexpensively confirmed Kirton's abstinent status through a few breathalyzer tests, blood tests, and/or urine tests; instead, it insisted on expensive 12-step inpatient treatment. This is far from an isolated case.

The Judicial and Penal Systems

For well over three decades, it's been common for the court system to coerce drunk drivers and others accused or convicted of alcohol-related crimes into AA attendance and/or 12-step treatment, through both pre-trial diversion programs and through sentencing. In 1995 alone, roughly 270,000 individuals were coerced into 12-step treatment by the judicial and penal systems,[4] with DUI offenders making up slightly over one-quarter of such coerced persons.[5] The number of offenders coerced into AA attendance rather than formal treatment is likely even higher. One indication that this is so is that AA's 1996 membership survey brochure reports that 16% of AA members were introduced to AA through either court order or correctional facilities. Considering that there are now roughly 1.25 million AA members, this means that approximately 200,000 of AA's current members are there because of judicial/penal system coercion. Because AA has an astronomical dropout rate—95% during the first year, according to AA's own figures[6]— it's virtually certain that literally *millions* of individuals have been coerced into attending AA, and that literally millions more have been coerced into attending 12-step treatment by the judicial and penal systems.

This is unfortunate in that it's very unlikely that coerced participation in AA or in 12-step treatment are effective ways of reducing instances of DUI and other criminal behavior. As discussed in the previous chapter, one of the most significant studies of coerced participation in AA and alcoholism treatment (in that it was well designed and had a no-treatment control group), Ditman et al., reported that the two groups of alcohol offenders who participated in AA and, separately, in a treatment program fared significantly *worse* (as measured by numbers of rearrests) than the no-treatment, no-AA controls.[7]

But perhaps the best-studied group coerced into AA participation is DUI offenders. Study after study has shown that judicial sanctions, specifically suspension and revocation of drivers licenses, are more effective than AA participation in reducing drunk-driving recidivism. To quote the introduction to one such study, "the best research to date has found that drivers convicted of alcohol-related offenses have fewer crashes after their licenses have been suspended or revoked than after being sent through present types of rehabilitation."[8] Another significant study by Philip Salzberg and Carl Klingberg, involving over 2000 individuals who received DUI citations, concluded that, "The DP [diversion program] group accumulated significantly more alcohol-related violations during the 3-yr post-DP time period. The DP group had an adjusted mean of 0.36 alcohol-related violations compared with 0.30 for the control group [who received normal legal sanctions]."[9] Other studies have confirmed this result—those in 12-step diversion programs have more subsequent accidents and DUI convictions than those receiving legal sanctions.[10]

But prosecutors and the judiciary ignore such findings and continue to routinely sentence those convicted of DUI and other alcohol-related offenses to AA attendance and/or 12-step treatment. One can only wonder how much of this seemingly deliberate blindness is a result of 12-stepping judges and prosecutors being eager to "carry the message." An old friend from the Phoenix area recently called to tell me that, after a DUI conviction, he had been sentenced to attend 12-step treatment by a judge wearing an AA (sobriety) chip around her neck as a pendant.

And one can only wonder how many people have died needlessly, and will die needlessly, on our roads and highways because of the continuing diversion of DUI offenders into AA and ineffective 12-step treatment.

Incubation of the Treatment Industry

The rise of the 12-step treatment industry has been a direct result of the rise of "educational" and "medical" organizations founded by AA members with three purposes: to promote AA and other 12-step groups; to promote the disease concept of alcoholism; and to promote the belief that abstinence is the only legitimate goal of alcoholism and drug treatment. AA's "educational" efforts date to 1944, when AA's first female member, Marty Mann, founded the National Council on Alcoholism (now the National Council on Alcoholism and Drug Dependence, NCADD) with the help of E.M. Jellinek and the Yale Center of Alcohol Studies.[11] Since then, the NCADD has acted as AA's spokesman (without, of course, identifying itself as such) on "outside issues" and matters of "public controversy." The NCADD has tirelessly promoted both the disease concept of alcoholism and the belief that abstinence is the only legitimate treatment goal; it has also attempted to suppress studies on controlled drinking, and has virulently attacked those who publicly disagree with its positions on abstinence and the disease concept.[12]

The NCADD also has close ties with the "medical" arm of AA. In 1954, Ruth Fox, MD founded what is now known as the American Society of Addiction Medicine (ASAM). ASAM, like the NCADD, has campaigned relentlessly for the disease concept of alcoholism and for abstinence as the only acceptable treatment goal, publicly stating that, "Abstinence from alcohol is necessary for recovery from the disease of alcoholism."[13] ASAM also recommends that "physicians and the alcoholism treatment agencies with which they work . . . develop relationships of maximum cooperation with the self-help groups, such as Alcoholics Anonymous," because "self-help groups, particularly Alcoholics Anonymous, have been a tremendous help in recovery to many thousands of alcoholics, their friends and families."[14] ASAM further states that "expert" physicians should have "a knowledge of self-help groups such as AA, NA, Al-Anon, etc.," as well as "a knowledge of the spectrum of this disease and the natural progression if untreated."[15]

In 1973, ASAM's membership voted to become part of the NCADD, and it remained part of the NCADD for over a decade. According to the NCADD, "Membership in ASAM, which had begun certifying physicians specializing in addiction medicine, had grown so large by 1984 that it no longer made sense to remain under NCADD's umbrella. However, the two groups continued to meet together annually until 1991 and today are represented on each other's boards [of directors]."[16]

The NCADD maintains close ties with other "medical" advocates of abstinence, 12-step programs, and the disease concept of alcoholism. In the 1970s, NCADD reports that it "offered homes to both the National Nurses Society on Addiction and the Research Society on Alcoholism which, with ASAM, began publishing *Alcoholism: Clinical and Experimental Research.*"[17]

But perhaps the NCADD's greatest coup occurred during the Nixon Administration, with the passage of the Comprehensive Alcohol Abuse and Alcoholism Prevention, Treatment and Rehabilitation Act of 1970, also known as the Hughes Act, sponsored by "recovering alcoholic" (that is, AA member) Senator Harold Hughes. The Act won Hughes "NCADD's highest honor, the Gold Key Award."[18] It also established the National Institute on Alcohol Abuse and Alcoholism (NIAAA) and thus opened the tap which would release rivers of federal cash to the alcoholism movement. Very early on, the NIAAA "logically began contracting with NCADD for assistance. As a result, in 1976 NCADD's budget peaked at $3.4 million, nearly five times what it had been before passage of the Hughes Act. Government funding accounted for more than 75% of the budget."[19] It's little wonder that UPI "called passage of the Hughes Act a 'signal victory' for groups such as NCADD."[20] It's equally little wonder that in the wake of the Act the NCADD opened an office in Washington.

The money that the NCADD received from the government led to huge and rapid growth of both the NCADD and the rest of the treatment industry. Under the subhead, "Federal Government Boosts Marty's Vision," the NCADD boasts that,"This [federal funds] provided seed money for state voluntary alcoholism associations which in turn helped organize local NCADD Affiliates [sic]. Marty [Mann] . . . lived long enough to see how the government had boosted her early vision: the number of Affiliates [sic] had risen to an all-time high of 223 and their advocacy efforts had helped to bring to at least 23 the number of states who [sic] mandated insurance coverage for alcoholism treatment."[21]

The NCADD continues, "The federal government also facilitated rapid growth in the EAP movement." (EAPs, Employee Assistance Programs, funnel "impaired" employees into 12-step treatment, very often through "interventions," threats of job loss, and other coercive means.) "Eleven years of NCADD campaigning culminated in 1974 with AFL-CIO president George Meany[22] and General Motors director James M. Roche agreeing to chair NCADD's all-star labor management [sic] committee. When NIAAA provided NCADD with funding to establish task forces in ten major cities a year later, NCADD published the first labor-approved EAP guidelines. By the end of the 70s [sic], employees had access to 5,000 EAP programs."[23]

Thus, by the late 1970s AA members in government and the mass media, rivers of federal cash, and AA's "educational" and "medical" arms had set the stage for the explosive growth of the 12-step alcoholism treatment industry that would occur in the late 1970s and throughout the 1980s in the United States.

Growth of the Treatment Industry

It's difficult to pinpoint the date of origin of the 12-step treatment industry. One could make a good case that it began with the "hospital work" of "proto-AA" (while it was still part of the Oxford Groups) in Akron in 1935. One could also make a case that it began with the establishment of the first AA group in a mental institution, Rockland State Hospital, in New York in 1939, or with the establishment of the first AA "rest farm" in 1940. But perhaps the best case could be made that it began with the institution of formal AA indoctrination, using the Big Book, by Doctor Bob Smith at St. Thomas Hospital in Akron, Ohio in August 1939. Before his death, Dr. Smith "treated" over 5,000 persons at that hospital.[24]

In all likelihood, this early "formal" hospital treatment was little different from Dr. Bob's earlier "hospital work": isolate the patient in a private room; restrict his visitors to AA (Oxford Group) members; restrict his reading matter to the Bible and/or (after 1939) the Big Book; induce his "surrender"; and thoroughly indoctrinate him into AA's belief system. The 1980 conference-approved AA book, *Dr. Bob and the Good Oldtimers*, contains a description of the experience of Bill D., the first person ever subjected to "hospital work": "There was the identification with them (Bill Wilson and Dr. Bob), followed by surrendering his will to God and making a moral inventory; then, he was told about the first drink, the 24-hour program, and the fact that alcoholism was an incurable disease—all basics of our program that have not changed to this day."[25]

One other thing that hasn't changed to this day is the emphasis on coercive treatment: "the alcoholic himself didn't ask for help. He didn't have anything to say about it."[26] One thing that *has* changed is that the "treatment" Bill D. received was *free*.

Throughout the 1940s, 1950s, and 1960s, the treatment industry grew relatively slowly. One brief history of treatment, by Edgar P. Nace, reports that, "From the 1930s through the 1960s, hospitals either overtly rejected alcoholics or subtly deterred them . . . The exception was state hospitals. In the 1960s, about 40% of admissions to state hospitals were chronic alcoholics . . . Private psychiatric hospitals were reporting only 6% of their admissions to be alcoholics and very few had specialty units."[27] The author then goes on to note, "In place of hospitals, small residential treatment centers, initially located in homes, were formed. . . . Treatment was informal and followed the principles of Alcoholics Anonymous."

But all that changed in the 1970s. Like the NCADD, Nace attributes the change largely to the passage of the Hughes Act. He also attributes it to major insurers, such as Blue Cross, Aetna, and Kemper, offering coverage for alcoholism treatment. Nace states that "recovering alcoholics [that is, AA members] played major roles in starting assistance programs in industry . . ."[28] The result of all this—federal money, insurance money, and "recovering alcoholics" setting up programs—was explosive growth in the treatment field. Between 1973 and 1980 the number of EAP programs leaped from 500 to 4400, and would continue to grow throughout the 1980s. "By 1985 at least one-half of the Fortune 500 companies had an EAP in operation."[29] The number of alcoholism treatment units also skyrocketed. In the 1975–1981 period, there were roughly 1800–2000 alcoholism treatment programs, treating about 200,000 persons annually.[30] By 1982, Substance Abuse and Mental Health Services Administration (SAMHSA) data indicate that there were fully 4233 alcoholism treatment units; by 1987 the number of treatment units had increased to 5627; and by 1990 the number had hit 7766.[31] During these same years, the number of individuals treated rose from 289,933 in 1982 to 563,430 in 1990,[32] and in that year treatment had become an $865 million per year business.[33]

But these numbers understate the size of the industry, because prior to 1992 these figures did not reflect "non-responding providers"; since 1992, SAMHSA has issued figures including such "non-responding providers."[34] Assuming that the percentage of "non-responding providers" was similar in previous years to the percentage in 1992, calculations yield the following corrected figures: 1982, 6947 providers with 563,509 clients; 1987, 8265 providers with 746,774 clients; and 1990, 10,494 providers with 933,680 clients. It's of major interest that the number of clients apparently peaked with an estimated 987,171 in 1991, but that the number of treatment centers continued to increase into the mid 1990s. In 1992, the number of providers had increased to 11,316, but the number of clients had dropped to 944,880. By 1994, the number of providers had increased further to 11,716, but the number of clients had declined further to 943,623. In that same year, utilization rates hit a 15-year low: 74.2% for all providers, and 57.9% for privately funded providers. "Perceived capacity" had increased 27% since 1991 and was at an all-time high, 1.27 million, and the number of providers had increased by 8%, also to an all-time high, but the number of clients had declined 4% during the same period.[35] Thus it isn't surprising that utilization rates were at a 15-year low.

The gravy train had stopped earlier—or had at least slowed considerably —for inpatient treatment. By the late 1980s, the high cost of alcoholism inpatient treatment was coming under increasing scrutiny from insurers and managed care organizations. Because there were no demonstrable benefits of inpatient over outpatient treatment, insurers became increasingly reluctant to pay for inpatient treatment, and the average length of stay in inpatient facilities plummeted. Nace reports that, "at one private psychiatric hospital . . . the average length of inpatient stay in 1988 was 49 days. In 1991, the average length of stay was 16 days, and by mid-1992 the average length of stay had declined to 11 days. At the same time, contractual agreements with managed care companies and insurance carriers have lowered the average daily hospital payment."[36] This trend toward shorter length of stay continued well into the 1990s. In 1994, a flyer I obtained from the marketing director of America's largest treatment provider, Hazelden, stated that average length of stay, nationally, had declined to five to seven days.[37]

The economic pressure from insurers and managed care organizations "was held responsible for a 'barrage' of initial unit closings in the early months of 1990, with some reports that as many as 200 private programs in the United States had been closed."[38] Most treatment providers, however, survived: "Many units made financial recoveries quite soon after implementation of managed care by offering an altered mix of services emphasizing less intensive forms of care such as outpatient treatment."[39] SAMHSA's "National Drug and Alcoholism Treatment Unit Survey" information supports this report of a shift to outpatient services: freestanding outpatient facilities rose from 37.9% of total facilities in 1990 to 43.8% of the total in 1994, while community mental health centers had dropped slightly, from 14.2% of the total in 1990 to 12.3% of the total in 1994.[40] Thus, their combined total had risen from 52.1% of total units in 1990 to 56.1% in 1994; and the percentage of clients that they treated had also increase slightly, from a combined 66.9% of clients in 1990 to a combined 68.2% in 1994.[41]

During this time, in addition to shifting to outpatient services, inpatient treatment providers also survived through other means. Paul Amyx, an intake counselor for several years at a nationally known inpatient treatment facility in the Tucson area, told me that the ratio of alcoholism to other diagnoses changed radically during the period he was employed, from roughly an 80/20 ratio of alcoholism to other diagnoses in 1991, to a 20/80 ratio when he quit in 1994. The reason? Client characteristics hadn't changed, but by the mid-1990s insurers were much more likely to pay for treatment for other disorders, for example, "post-traumatic stress disorder," than they were to pay for treatment for alcoholism.

Despite such adaptations to changing market conditions, there's some indication that there has been a small decline in the number of privately funded inpatient facilities in recent years. Anecdotal accounts of closures abound, and there's some hard evidence as well. The recent "National Treatment Center Study Summary Report" states that of the 450 units it surveyed, 12.1% (55) were one to five years old at the time of the survey.[42] Approximately one year after they were surveyed, 20 of the units (4.5% of the total) had closed.[43] This data indicates, if the one-year closure rate is typical of previous years, that in the mid 1990s inpatient units were closing at roughly twice the rate that new ones were opening; but the apparent decline in the number of units, while significant, isn't precipitate—only about 2% per year.[44] This apparent trend has, however, only existed for the last few years. NDATUS data indicate that the number of specialized hospital and "other residential facilities" was essentially flat in the 1992–1994 period, rising from a combined total of 2027 units in 1992 to a combined total of 2069 in 1994, that is, in the period 1992–1994 the number of such units rose about 1% annually.[45] The most recent data, however, indicates that the trend toward inpatient unit closings is real. The November 1997 update to the "National Treatment Center Study Summary Report" indicates that the percentage of inpatient treatment facility administrators who say that their facitilities have a moderate or high likelihood of closure has doubled in the year since the report was released; it's increased from approximately 9% to 18%, with the percentage of administrators reporting a high likelihood of closure increasing from .2% to 2.3%.[46]

Thus, the treatment industry is still a giant. Despite the apparent slight decline in privately funded for-profit inpatient units in recent years, the total number of units is at or near an all-time high. Data provided by SAMHSA indicates that by 1995 there were at least 12,000 treatment units[47] treating roughly 950,000 individuals for alcoholism annually.[48] Others place the number of treated individuals far higher. The NCADD, citing SAMHSA data, states that 1.9 million Americans were treated for alcoholism in 1992.[49]

The treatment industry is clearly a major force in American society, and it shows no signs of going away. But what exactly does it do?

12-Step Treatment

Abstinence is the near-universal goal in American alcoholism treatment, and the 12-step approach is standard. The recent "National Treatment Center Study" cited above reports that 98.6% of inpatient treatment facilities recommend abstinence, and that 93.1% of them utilize the 12-step approach.[50] In other words, nearly 14 out of 15 inpatient treatment centers utilize the 12-step approach, and nearly 99 out of 100 have abstinence as the goal of treatment.

Because inpatient treatment is the type of treatment most preferred by 12-step treatment providers, and because in many instances 12-step out-patient treatment is just a watered-down version of inpatient treatment, this section will concentrate on inpatient treatment.[51]

When insurers or individuals will pay for it, the standard stay in inpatient facilities is 28 days. The cost of inpatient treatment averages just over $500 per day, with some units charging as much as $1700 per day.[52] Thus, the average cost of a 28-day stay will be in excess of $14,000, and the cost can reach nearly $50,000. Just what do the insurers and individuals who pay for this expensive treatment get for their money?

Many people believe that alcoholism treatment consists largely of detoxification, but this is not the case. According to the NDATUS TEDS data, only about 23% of those treated for alcoholism in 1995 went through detox,[53] and many of them apparently went through it unnecessarily. One physician, Elizabeth Bartlett, MD, reports that after checking herself into a 28-day inpatient treatment facility, "I was placed on 'detox' and medicated, heavily I might add, despite the fate that I had not had a drink in a month and had no physical symptoms of withdrawal."[54] Such unnecessary "detoxification" (that is, unnecessary drugging) seems to be fairly common, but there's no way to know how many patients are subjected to it.

So if detoxification isn't the primary purpose of 12-step inpatient treatment, what is? One 12-step advocate lists the goals of treatment as follows:

(1) Treatment does not "cure" the disease—the expectation is that by instituting an achievable method of abstinence the disease will be put into remission. (2) All therapeutic efforts are directed at helping the patient reach a level of motivation that will enable him or her to commit to this abstinence program. (3) An educational program is developed to assist the patient in becoming familiar with the addictive process, insight into compulsive behaviors, medical complications, emotional insight, and maintenance of physical, mental, and spiritual health. (4) The patient's family and other significant persons are included in the therapeutic process with the understanding that the therapeutic process does not occur in a vacuum, but

rather in interpersonal relationships. (5) *The patient is indoctrinated into the AA program and instructed as to the content and application of the 12 steps of the program.* [emphasis added] (6) Group and individual therapy are directed at self-understanding and acceptance with emphasis on how alcohol and drugs have affected their lives. (7) There is insistence on participation in a longitudinal support and follow-up program based on the belief that, as in the management of all chronic disease processes, maintenance is critically important to the ultimate outcome of any therapy. This follow-up usually consists of ongoing support provided by the treatment facility as well as participation in community self-help groups such as AA, Narcotics Anonymous (NA), Opiates Anonymous (OA), and the like.[55]

Put in plain English, this means that the purpose of "the treatment process" is to "indoctrinate" the patient into "the AA program" and into the disease-concept-of-alcoholism belief system. That is, the purpose of 12-step treatment is to convince the patient that he has an incurable "disease" from which he will never recover; that he is "powerless" over his alcohol consumption; that he will inevitably lose control if he drinks; that should he return to drinking, he will inevitably drink in a progressively more destructive manner; that he is "in denial"; that he must not trust his own thoughts and perceptions; that he must abandon self-direction and turn his life and will over to God (or God's interpreter, AA); and that he must make a commitment to lifelong involvement in Alcoholics Anonymous, because the only alternative to such lifelong involvement is "jails, institutions, or death."

That is the purpose of 12-step "treatment." It really has very little to do with the problem of alcohol abuse. Rather, it's an indoctrination program designed to inculcate both distrust of self and learned helplessness ("powerlessness") in the patient, and to convince him that his only hope of salvation is to abandon self-direction and to plunge himself into lifelong participation in the religious program of Alcoholics Anonymous.

Never mind that every single premise upon which this indoctrination program is built is demonstrably false. As someone once pointed out, smoking is a behavior and lung cancer is a disease, just as drinking is a behavior and cirrhosis is a disease. Alcohol abuse (lifting bottles or glasses to one's lips and swallowing more alcohol than is healthy) is a *behavior*, not a "disease"—terming a behavior a "disease" broadens the term's definition so greatly as to render it almost meaningless. Thomas Szasz puts the matter thusly: "Excessive drinking is a habit. If we choose to call bad habits 'diseases,' there is no limit to what we may define as a disease."[56]

As well, drinkers are *not* "powerless" over their alcohol consumption—it isn't Satan controlling the muscles in the arm lifting the glass to the lips —and they *can* learn to control it."Loss of control" tends to occur only when individuals *believe* that it will occur.[57]

Progression of the "disease" is *not* inevitable, and a very high percentage of alcohol abusers (including those termed "alcohol dependent") eventually "mature out" and either achieve nonproblem drinking or abstinence without participation in AA or any treatment program.[58]

"Denial" is a Catch 22 concept, and as such is essentially useless except as a bludgeon in the indoctrination process—if you admit that you're an alcoholic, you're an alcoholic; and if you deny that you're an alcoholic, you're "in denial," which is evidence that you're an alcoholic. Either way, as with denials of witchcraft in the Middle Ages, you lose.

And, finally, participation in AA is hardly a ticket to salvation; the recovery rate in AA is no higher than the rate of spontaneous remission.[59]

Because they've been thoroughly indoctrinated into the AA/disease-concept belief system, these facts matter not at all to those administering and conducting 12-step treatment programs. For them, having turned their lives and wills over to God, The Program has become a matter of religious faith; and even to question the premises of their belief system is blasphemous. They *know* The Truth—as revealed by Bill Wilson in the "inspired" Big Book. As well, they believe that their sobriety and their very lives depend on "carry[ing] this message" to those not yet saved, so they often carry that message with fearful zeal.

But what is inpatient treatment actually like? Many of the elements of inpatient treatment are little changed from the days of Dr. Bob's early hospital work: the patient is isolated from family and friends; outside contacts are greatly restricted; reading matter is restricted to approved "recovery" materials, such as the Big Book and other 12-step literature; the patient is regarded as sick and as unable to think sanely—thus the need for indoctrination; coercion is regarded as a normal and sometimes desirable part of the recovery process; the patient is given little time alone and is kept very busy; and the patient is placed in a milieu where indoctrination is achieved largely through the pressure of a unanimous majority opinion, and where dissenting views and skeptical attitudes are viewed as sick, as "disease symptoms." In this milieu, all activities—including individual counseling and group "therapy"—are aimed at one goal: indoctrination into the AA/disease-concept belief system, and involvement of the patient in AA.

Dr. Bartlett, quoted above, describes her experiences in treatment:

For anyone who has not been in a 12-step rehab, the daily program is brutal. Mine lasted from 7:30 AM to 10:00 PM. Essentially there was no time to think. If anyone was in his or her room for more than a few minutes, staff went in and announced that "isolating was just going to cause stinking thinking, so get out of your room." Every patient was expected to be at meals exactly on time, and to participate in all scheduled events. Late arrivals resulted in the loss of the minimal telephone contact we were allowed with the outside world. Almost every group, meeting and lecture began with the Serenity Prayer, and ended with the Lord's Prayer . . . I was told that "addicts do not like following rules," so many arbitrary rules were imposed to essentially break us of the bad habit of thinking independently. They wanted to break my will, so that I would "snap," and become one of them, obedient and grateful to the program. . . .

I was told from the moment that I arrived . . . [that if I] didn't complete their "simple program," *there was a 100% chance I would drink again, and would lose my career and my family, and would ultimately die from drinking.*

. . . I was not allowed to question *anything* about AA, especially the religious aspect[60] . . . They kept telling me that my thinking was stinking, that my intelligence was a liability and was causing my problems, and that I had better check my psychiatric knowledge at the door and *stop thinking.*[61]

Other writers, most notably and eloquently Ken Ragge in *The Real AA*, have pointed out that the attitudes and practices common to 12-step treatment are also common to the indoctrination procedures of religious cults, and to the "re-education" procedures of the Chinese Communists.

What makes matters far worse than they would otherwise be is that a majority of patients in alcoholism treatment programs are coerced into attendance, and often face dire consequences if they leave before completing their programs. The TEDS data place the percentage of those coerced into "alcohol-only" treatment by the criminal justice system at 46% of total clients.[62] And Laura Schmidt and Constance Weisner state that by the end of the 1980s, "the predominant groups found in facilities were now coerced clients, mandated to treatment through court and workplace referrals."[63]

The coerced status of a majority of their clients gives 12-step administrators, counselors, and "therapists" great power—and they often abuse it. They often use their power to force clients to violate their own consciences, to publicly confess their sins and evilness, and to verbally proclaim 12-step/disease-concept beliefs, even if they don't really accept them. Those stubborn and/or courageous enough to resist often face serious consequences. At the very least, they'll be "confronted" in group "therapy" and verbally bludgeoned, sometimes for hours, sometimes for days on end, until they cave in. If they persist in stating their true beliefs, they won't be discharged (as long as their insurance will pay for treatment) or they may be threatened with expulsion, which often carries with it the threats of incarceration, job loss, or loss of professional certification. In extreme cases—as in the case of organ transplant patients—the threat is death.

The abusiveness and coerciveness of some 12-step treatment personnel is well illustrated by the treatment recived by Dr. Clifton Kirton, mentioned above, who was threatened with loss of his liver transplant candidacy because of his resistance to AA, 12-step treatment, and the disease concept.

His description of one treatment coordinator's attitudes is instructive:

"If you think that's what Alcoholics Anonymous is all about, you're really missing the point. Religion has nothing to do with it. Your higher power can be anything. You are not being coerced. Your participation in AA is entirely voluntary. I must caution you, however that your failure to internalize recovery concepts will place your transplant candidacy status in great jeopardy."

This was the response, not necessarily verbatim, but most assuredly accurate in content, from the coordinator of the Chemical Dependency Unit of a major organ transplant center when confronted, by the author, with her own coercive tactics and with the idea that AA is a coercive, proselytizing, religious cult whose main purpose is to strip individuals of personal autonomy and to brainwash them into acceptance of irrational group ideology. This same individual also had the arrogance to state, "We can't always like our *'teachers'* but we must accept what they have to teach us."[64]

Perhaps the most interesting thing in the above passage is the administrator's insistence that Kirton was not being coerced, that he was acting voluntarily by participating in AA, even though he would have "place[d] [his] transplant candidacy [and hence his life] in great jeopardy" if he didn't. One finds similar insistence upon the "voluntary" nature of coercion in other writings and statements by 12-step treatment bureaucrats. For example, the Treatment Contract for "impaired" nurses that is standard in California under the Board of Registered Nursing Diversion Program states in part, "I have voluntarily chosen to participate in the program and agree to adhere to the rules and regulations set forth in this contract." Nurses who don't "voluntarily" participate face loss of certification, possible criminal prosecution, and banishment from their profession. This sort of insistence on the "voluntary" nature of coerced-client treatment is quite common. One could just as easily argue that when an armed robber puts a gun to a person's head, the person "voluntarily" hands over his wallet. All in all, it certainly seems that the 12-step treatment industry is in serious "denial" about its coercive practices.

But while the treatment of Clifton Kirton may seem extreme, it's anything but. Stanton Peele cites the case of a married woman in her 50s whom he calls "Marie." She received a DUI citation after being stopped at a police checkpoint, and chose to pay $500 to attend 12-step treatment rather than lose her license for a year:

Marie's treatment consisted of weekly counseling sessions, plus weekly A.A. meetings, for more than four months. . . . At A.A. meetings, Marie listened to ceaseless stories of suffering and degradation, stories replete with phrases like "descent into hell" and "I got down on my knees and prayed to a higher power." For Marie, A.A. was akin to a fundamentalist revival meeting.

In the counseling program . . . Marie received the same A.A. indoctrination and met with counselors whose only qualification was membership in A.A. These true believers told all the DWIs that they had the permanent "disease" of alcoholism, the only cure for which was lifetime abstinence and A.A. membership—all this based on one drunk-driving arrest!

In keeping with the self-righteous, evangelistic spirit of the program, any objection to its requirements was treated as "denial." The program's dictates extended into Marie's private life: She was told to abstain from all alcohol during "treatment," a proscription enforced by the threat of urinalysis. As Marie found her entire life controlled by the program, she concluded that "the power these people attempt to wield is to compensate for the lack of power within themselves. . . . I find it unconscionable that the criminal justice system has the power to coerce American citizens to accept ideas that are anathema to them. It is as if I were a citizen of a totalitarian regime being punished for political dissent."[65]

This, then, is 12-step treatment. Many have proclaimed its marvels and its life-transforming qualities. But, as we saw in the previous chapter, it simply doesn't work. Given the dismal failure of 12-step treatment, one would hope that 12-step "therapists," "medical experts," and "educators" would actively encourage research into and development of alternative treatment approaches. But this is not the case.

Suppression of Dissent

In the medical/scientific world (at least ideally) when a form of treatment repeatedly fails, it's normal for those administering the treatment to pursue alternative approaches, and to encourage development of such approaches. In the face of the massive, obvious failure of their treatment method, 12-step "therapists," "educators," and "medical experts" have done exactly the opposite: they've clung tightly to their beloved form of treatment, asserting, despite convincing evidence to the contrary, that it's effective, while selectively and desperately clinging to any research, no matter how poorly designed, that seems to support 12-step treatment; they've attempted to suppress research publications on non-12-step forms of therapy; they've blocked programs designed to deliver alternative forms of therapy; they've blackballed non-12-step therapists and psychologists from institutions, conferences, publications, and treatment facilities; and they've unleashed vicious personal attacks on those who have publicly disagreed with their positions or who have published research findings not to their liking.

This is a very serious problem, because AA/the 12-step approach dominates the treatment field, and those in AA's hidden structure (NCADD,

ASAM, etc.) wield considerable power in the medical, psychiatric, and psychological fields. Through their deliberate suppression of opposing views and treatment approaches, they've largely blocked progress in American addictions treatment during the latter half of the 20th century.

The hottest button in the American addictions field is controlled-drinking treatment, and those in the treatment industry and AA's "medical" and "educational" arms have done their best to thwart its development, despite there being good evidence that it's a useful approach for many problem drinkers.[66] But the very idea that *any* alcohol abusers, let alone dependent drinkers, could return to nonproblem drinking contradicts the most sacred tenets of AA and the disease concept. And disease-concept advocates have repeatedly reacted hysterically and abusively to controlled drinking research and researchers.

Perhaps the clearest example of this occurred in the 1970s, when Mark and Linda Sobell published two scientifically sound articles demonstrating that bad-prognosis alcohol abusers given moderation training tended to fare better than a similar group given abstinence training.[67] As a result of these two journal articles, the Sobells were subjected to a decades-long campaign of personal vilification by disease-concept advocates, and, even though they were ultimately cleared of all charges, they were eventually forced to find employment in Canada. Their chief accuser was one Mary Pendery.

Pendery had taken the highly unusual step of contacting the moderation subjects (but not the abstinence subjects) from the Sobells' study, and, with Irving Maltzman and L.J. West, she published an article based on her findings in 1982 in the journal *Science*, disputing the Sobell's results. According to Stanton Peele, "An earlier version of the *Science* article (which the journal rejected on the grounds that it was libelous) had been widely disseminated to the media. In several interviews, at least one of the article's authors repeated his claim that the Sobells had committed fraud."[68] (A panel convened by the Addiction Research Foundation subsequently cleared them of any wrongdoing.) It's also of interest that after being contacted by Pendery, several of the moderation subjects in the Sobells' study sued the Sobells.

Pendery's attack was furthered by the news media. In early 1983, *60 Minutes* aired a report on the Sobells' study which strongly echoed Pendery's views. In one segment, Harry Reasoner asked one of the subjects about the outcome of his moderation training, and the subject laughed; in another segment, Reasoner was shown walking along the side of the grave of one of the four moderation subjects who had died in the decade following treatment. What *60 Minutes* and Reasoner didn't show were the graves of the *six* abstinence subjects who had died in the same period. Pendery evidently loved the *60 Minutes* report, as the report was continuously shown at the 1983 NCADD (then-NCA) convention, at which she delivered an emotional tirade against controlled drinking and those who advocate it.[69]

Similar hysterical reactions greeted another study on controlled drinking, the Rand Report.[70] Don Cahalan reports that, "After valiant year-long attempts by prominent NCA members to have the report suppressed altogether or drastically revised in its findings, it was finally released by Rand in June 1976."[71] The report was met with dire tales that "some alcoholics have resumed drinking as a result of . . . the Rand study,"[72] and with admonitions that it shouldn't have been released to the public: "After all, people's right to know does not mean the people's right to be confused —especially when it is a matter of life and death."[73] Upon the release of the document, the NCA virulently criticized it. Cahalan notes, "The NCA's major press conference criticizing the report revealed a level of anxiety and anger much higher than ordinary concern about fairness and balance in scientific reporting. NCA officials charged that many alcoholics would be 'dying in the streets' as a direct result of publication of the report."[74]

Given such strength of feeling, it's little wonder that abstinence advocates have attempted to prevent establishment of controlled-drinking programs. One such incident involved Peter Nathan, former head of the prestigious Rutgers Center of Alcohol Studies. In the late 1970s, the head of a hospital board approached Nathan and asked him to develop a controlled-drinking program. Nathan and a colleague, Terry Wilson carefully devised a treatment plan and aftercare program, which the hospital board accepted with some minor changes. It then issued a press release describing the program and soliciting clients. Stanton Peele notes that, "When this announcement produced only a small group of potential clients, Nathan and Wilson planned a more aggressive advertising effort. Before they could proceed, however, the hospital withdrew its support for the program because of threats by representatives of AA that they would stop referring patients to the hospital's profitable inpatient program."[75]

Given the depth of feeling against controlled drinking and its advocates, and, for that matter, against virtually all critics of AA and the disease concept, it's equally little wonder that AA/abstinence advocates have often engaged in blackballing when they've had the ability to do so. Blackballing is, in fact, routine in the treatment industry; a great many treatment facilities will simply not hire anyone for *any* position (even as a cook) who does not embrace the 12-step approach and the disease concept of alcoholism.

One local example is illustrative. After moving to Tucson in 1997, Emmett Velten, a well known and well respected psychologist, and co-author (with former American Psychological Association president Albert Ellis) of *When AA Doesn't Work for You: Rational Steps to Quitting Alcohol*, applied to an upscale local treatment facility for an advertised part-time position lecturing on the physiological effects of drugs and alcohol, a position for which he is well qualified. A few minutes after his interview began, the director of the facility entered the room, asked Emmett if he believed in the 12-step approach, and when Emmett said, "no," the director escorted him off the property as if he were a plague carrier.[76]

Those who engage in "public controversy" with AA's front groups face even rougher treatment. Stanton Peele reports that after defending the Sobells in an article in *Psychology Today* in 1983, his column in the *U.S. Journal of Drug and Alcohol Dependence* was dropped; Mary Pendery attacked him in a speech at the 1983 NCA convention; an invitation to deliver the keynote speech to the Texas Commission on Alcoholism's summer school was withdrawn (and then reinstated after Peele protested); and "the number of invitations [he had] received from conferences like that in Texas [had] dropped dramatically."[77]

Peele continues, "My experience with this alcoholism dispute has given me a strong idea of the political power of the alcoholism movement to suppress discordant views. What astounded me most was how academic, professional, and government associates recommended that I drop the matter with the Texas Commission, saying simply that these events were typical. Apparently, those in the field had given up expecting freedom of speech or that a range of views should be represented at conferences receiving government funding and conducted at major universities. What I had uncovered was a matter-of-fact acceptance that those who do not hold the dominant point of view will not be given a fair hearing; that even to mention that there is doubt about accepted wisdom in the field endangers one's ability to function as a professional; and that government agencies reinterpret results of which they disapprove from research they themselves have commissioned."[78]

The Web of Influence

AA is far from being the innocent organization that most people believe it to be. The familiar gatherings of coffee-slurping, cigarette-smoking ex-drunks are only the tip of the iceberg. AA and its disease concept of alcoholism dominate the alcoholism treatment field in this country. Through its hidden members and its carefully cultivated benign image, AA has tremendous influence in the media. It has powerful "educational" and "medical" front groups, such as the NCADD and ASAM, that to a great extent determine the direction of alcoholism research, treatment, and education. (The NIAAA, for example, has funded no controlled-drinking research for a decade.) AA's front groups and hidden members vilify and blackball critics and independent researchers. AA and 12-step treatment advocates attempt to smother alternative treatment approaches. And AA's friends and hidden members in EAPs, diversion programs, the judiciary, and penal system coerce probably half-a-million Americans per year into AA attendance and/or 12-step treatment.

This comprises AA's hidden structure and hidden influence. It is, quite simply, a national disaster.

Stay Tuned

Twelve-step addictions "professionals" and other AA members are evidently quite concerned about the insurance industry's increasing reluctance to pay for ineffective 12-step "treatment," and they're determined to do something about it. Senator Paul Wellstone (D.–Minn.) and "recovering alcoholic" (that is, AA member) Representative Jim Ramstad (R.–Minn.) introduced The Substance Abuse Treatment Parity Act in 1997. The "Act would bar any inpatient day or outpatient visit limits, deductibles, copayments or dollar limits on substance abuse coverage that are more restrictive than those for general health care."[79] That is, if passed, the Act would unleash a river of insurance cash to the treatment industry, something which those in the industry want badly. Roxanne Kibben, president of the National Association of Alcoholism and Drug Abuse Counselors[80] states, "This [Act's introduction] makes a statement that we're not going away. We're not going to let this go."[81]

---

1. Http://www.ncadd.org/50yrs.html (p. 3).

2. *Journal of Rational Recovery*, Vol. 9 No. 3, Jan.-Feb. 1997, p. 15.

3. "The Semantics of the Twelve Step Neurosis," by Clifton W. Kirton. *Journal of Rational Recovery*, Vol. 9 No. 4, March-April 1997, pp. 14-20.

4. *National Admissions to Substance Abuse Treatment Services: The Treatment Episode Data Set (TEDS) 1992-1995.* Rockville, Maryland: SAMHSA, 1997. Table 10, p. 46.

5. Ibid. Table 16, p. 54.

6. "Comments on A.A.'s Triennial Surveys." New York: Alcoholics Anonymous World Services, n.d. (probably 1990). Figure C-1, p. 12.

7. "A Controlled Experiment on the Use of Court Probation for Drunk Arrests," by Keith S. Ditman, George G. Crawford, Edward W. Forby, Herbert Moskowitz, and Craig MacAndrew. *American Journal of Psychiatry*, 124:2, August 1967, pp. 160-163.

8. William Hadden in Introduction to *Deterring the Drinking Driver: Legal Policy and Social Control*, by H.L. Ross. Lexington, MA: Lexington Books, 1984, p. xvii. Quoted by Stanton Peele in "Denial—of Reality and Freedom—in Addiction Research and Treatment," *Bulletin of the Society of Psychologists in Addictive Behaviors*, (5)4:149-166, 1986. See also "AA Abuse," by Stanton Peele. *Reason*, November 1991, pp. 34-39.

9. "The Effectiveness of Deferred Prosecution for Driving While Intoxicated," by Philip Salzberg and Carl Klingberg. *Journal of Studies on Alcohol*, Vol. 44, No. 2, 1983, p. 303-304.

10. See, for example,"Suspension and Revocation Effects on the DUI Offender," Department of Motor Vehicles Report No. 75, by R.E. Hagen, et al. Sacramento, California: 1980. See also "Intervening with Drinking Drivers" in the 1990 Department of Health and Human Services "Seventh Special Report for the US Congress on Alcohol and Health," p. 247.

11. "Prohibition, Alcoholics Anonymous, the Alcoholism Movement, and the Alcoholic Beverage Industry," by L. Allen Ragels. *Journal of Rational Recovery*, Vol. 8 No. 4, March-April 1996, p.23.

12. See "Denial—of Reality and of Freedom—in Addiction Research and Treatment," by Stanton Peele. *Bulletin of the Society of Psychologists in Addictive Behaviors*, 5(4):149-166, 1986. See also "Alcoholism, Politics, and Bureaucracy: The Consensus Against Controlled-Drinking Therapy in America," by Stanton Peele. *Addictive Behaviors*, 17:49-62, 1992.

13. See ASAM "Public Policy Statement on Abstinence," adopted by ASAM board of directors in September 1974. The resolution is posted at http://207.181.5/ppol1.htm#Abstinence.

14. "Resolution on Self-Help Groups," adopted by ASAM board of directors on October 19, 1979. The resolution is posted at http://207.181.5/ppol1.htm#Abstinence.

15. "How to Identify a Physician Recognized for Expertness in Diagnosis and Treatment of Alcoholism and Other Drug Dependence," adopted by ASAM board of directors on February 28, 1986. Posted at http://207.181.5/ppol2.htm#Abstinence.

16. "For 50 Years, The Voice of Americans Fighting Alcoholism." http://www.ncadd.org/50yrs.html (p. 4).

17. Ibid., p. 6.

18. Ibid., p. 4.

19. Ibid., p. 5.

20. Ibid.

21. Ibid.

22. Meany was, with the possible exception of Samuel Gompers, the worst labor leader ever to head the AFL. He was an enthusiastic supporter of the American Institute for Free Labor Development, which was a CIA-controlled organization used to subvert labor movements in Third World countries during the Cold War. He also enthusiastically supported the war in Vietnam, and once publicly wondered why on earth American labor unions should want to organize the unorganized. It's little wonder that he backed the NCADD/EAP plan to coerce American working people into 12-step treatment.

23. "For 50 Years, The Voice of Americans Fighting Alcoholism." http://www.ncadd.org/50yrs.html (p. 5).

24. *Alcoholics Anonymous Comes of Age*, by Bill Wilson. New York: Alcoholics Anonymous World Services, 1989, p. viii.

25. *Dr. Bob and the Good Oldtimers*. New York: Alcoholics Anonymous World Services, 1980, p. 83.

26. Ibid., pp. 82-83.

27. "Inpatient Treatment," by Edgar P. Nace, in *Recent Developments in Alcoholism*, Volume 11, Marc Galanter, ed., 1993, p. 430.

28. Ibid.

29. Ibid.

30. TEDS, op. cit., p. 4. There are significant differences in estimates of the number of treatment facilities, so all such estimates should be taken with a grain of salt.

31. "Developments in Alcoholism Treatment," by Laura Schmidt and Constance Weisner, in *Recent Developments in Alcoholism*, Volume 11, Marc Galanter, ed.. Table 1, p. 371.

32. Ibid.

33. Table 2, p. 374.

34. "National Drug and Alcoholism Treatment Unit Survey (NDATUS) Data for 1994 and 1980–1994." Rockville, MD: SAMHSA, 1996, footnote 2, Table 5.

35. Ibid., Table 10.

36. Nace, op.cit., p. 445.

37. This information came from a one-page handout given out at the "Addictions Round-table" by Hazelden's marketing director at the American Booksellers Association's annual trade show in Los Angeles on May 30, 1994.

38. Schmidt and Weisner, op. Cit., p. 377.

39. Ibid., p. 378.

40. NDATUS, op. cit., Table 5.

41. Ibid.

42. "National Treatment Center Study Summary Report," Paul Roman and Terry Blum, principal investigators. Athens, Georgia: Institute for Behavioral Research, 1997, p. 10.

43. Ibid., p. 11.

44. I arrived at these conclusions as follows: Dividing the 55 units opened in the previous five years by five yields a yearly opening rate of 11 units per year (2.4% of the total number of units). If 20 units per year are closing, that indicates that roughly twice as many units are closing as are opening, and subtracting the percentage opening from the percentage closing (4.5% - 2.4%) yields a yearly closing rate of roughly 2%.

45. NDATUS, op. cit., Table 5.

46. "National Treatment Center Study Six and Twelve Month Follow-Up Summary Report," Paul Roman and Terry Blum, principal investigators. Athens, Georgia: Institute for Behavioral Research, 1997, p. 13.

47. TEDS, op. cit., Table C.1, p. 69. The data give a total of 11,983 units in 1993, but TEDS also reports that the number of admissions during the years 1992–1995 was nearly constant (Table 17, p. 55), and that "privately administered systems are under represented" in its data (p. 4). The apparent leap in the number of units reported in the year 1991–1992, from 8,928 to 11,316 is largely illusory, because SAMHSA changed its tabulation methods in that year to include 2009 nonresponding (to its survey) units. A sampling and analysis of SAMHSA's 1995 "National Directory of Drug Abuse Treatment and Prevention Programs" confirms the figure of roughly 12,000 units.

48. Ibid., Table 16, p. 54. This information is based on a noncomprehensive survey, so the number of treated individuals is likely far higher than the roughly 700,000 reported. NDATUS (Table 5) reports roughly 944,000 treated in each of the years 1992–1994.

49. "Alcoholism and Alcohol-Related Problems: A Sobering Look." http://www.ncadd.org/problems.html (p. 1)

50. "National Treatment Center Study Summary Report," op. cit., p. 24.

51. Paul Amyx told me that after the treatment center he worked for began providing outpatient treatment, it simply had nonlocal outpatients stay at a local motel, and provided them with the same treatment as inpatients during the day.

52. "National Treatment Center Study Summary Report." op. cit., p. 20.

53. TEDS, op. cit., Table 11, p. 47.

54. "Brainwashing 101, or How I Survived 12-Step Rehab," by Elizabeth Bartlett, MD. *Journal of Rational Recovery*, Vol. 10, No. 1, Sept.-Oct. 1997, p. 4.

55. "Contemporary Issues in the Treatment of Alcohol Dependence," by Gregory B. Collins, MD. *Psychiatric Clinics of North America*, Vol. 16, No. 1, March 1993, p. 35. In the quota-tion, Collins is paraphrasing G.A. Mann.

56. "Bad Habits Are Not Diseases: A Refutation of the Claim that Alcoholism is a Disease," by Thomas Szasz. *Lancet*, 2:84, 1972.

57. Numerous studies have demonstrated that the so-called trigger effect leading to supposed loss of control is dependent upon whether drinkers *believe* that they're drinking alcohol, not whether they are or aren't. (See, for example, "Loss of Control Drinking in Alcoholics: An Experimental Analogue," by Alan Marlatt, et al. *Journal of Abnormal Psychology*, 81(1973):233-241.) As well, if inevitable loss of control were an actual phenomenon, no so-called alcoholic could ever return to moderate drinking, when in fact a great many do. (See Chapter 7 for evidence on this point.)

58. See Chapter 7 for research citations and further discussion of this point.

59. See Chapter 7 for a very detailed discussion of this point.

60. Chris Cornutt, a former "para-professional" counselor at a 12-step inpatient treatment facility, told me in an E-mail message on March 13, 1997 that patients " are virtually trapped in a Kafka nightmare once they admit themselves. If they voice any disagreement to you, they risk the wrath of the treatment team. Other patients 'turn them in' for non-AA or conflicting ideas. 'Narcing' on your fellow patients is a sign that you are working a good program and is heavily promoted."

61. Bartlett, op. cit., pp. 4-5.

62. TEDS, op. cit., p. 3.

63. Schmidt and Weisner, op. cit., p. 384.

64. Kirton, op. cit., p. 17.

65. "AA Abuse," by Stanton Peele. *Reason*, November 1991, pp. 34-39. Reproduced at http://www.frw.uva.nl/cedro/peele/lib/aaabuse.html The quotation was taken from page 4 of the html version of the document.

66. See, for example, "Motivation and Treatment Goals," by William Miller. *Drugs & Society* No. 1, 1987, pp. 133-151. See also "Harm Reduction: Reducing the Risks of Addictive Behaviors, by Alan Marlatt and S.F. Tapert, in *Addictive Behaviors Across the Life Span: Prevention, Treatment, and Policy Issues*, Alan Marlatt, et al., eds. Newbury Park: Sage Publica-tions, 1993. See also "Abstinence or Controlled Drinking in Clinical Practice: A Test of the Dependence and Persuasion Hypotheses," by J. Orford and A. Keddie. *British Journal of Addiction*, No. 81, 1986, pp. 495-504. For further this discussion of this issue see "Alcoholism, Politics, and Bureaucracy: The Consensus Against Controlled-Drinking Therapy in America," by Stanton Peele. *Addictive Behaviors*, 17:49-62, 1992, and "Denial—of Reality and Freedom—in Addiction Research and Treatment," by Stanton Peele, op. cit. Also useful is *Treating Addictive Behaviors: Processes of Change*, by William Miller and Nick Heather. New York: Plenum, 1986, pp. 145-148. For a nontechnical discussion of the issue, see *Moderate Drinking: The New Option for Problem Drinkers*, by Audrey Kishline. New York: Crown Books, 1995. See also *Problem Drinkers: Guided Self-Change Treatment*, by Mark Sobell and Linda Sobell. New York: The Guilford Press, 1993.

67. "Alcoholics Treated by Individualized Behavior Therapy: One Year Treatment Outcomes," by Mark Sobell and Linda Sobell. *Behavior Research and Therapy* 11:599-618, 1973, and "Second Year Treatment Outcomes of Alcoholics Treated by Individualized Behavior Therapy: Results." *Behavior Research and Therapy* 14:195-215.

68. Peele, "Denial," op. cit., p.4 of the html version: http://www.frw.uva.nl/cedro/peele/lib/denial.html

69. Mary Pendery remained a bitter opponent of controlled drinking, and those who advocate it, until her dying day. That came on April 10, 1994 in Wyoming, when an ex-abstinence patient-turned-lover, George Sie Rega, in the midst of an alcoholic binge, murdered her and then turned the gun on himself. According to one report, their house was filled with whiskey bottles.

70. Its authors were D.J. Armor, J.M. Polich, and H.B. Stambul.

71. *Understanding America's Drinking Problem*, by Don Cahalan. San Francisco: Jossey-Bass, 1987, p. 135.

72. Dr. Luther Cloud, quoted by Peele, "Denial," op. cit., p. 4 of html document, citing *Alcoholism and Treatment*, by D.J. Armor, J.M. Polich, and H.B. Stambul. New York: Wiley, 1978, p. 232.

73. An unnamed "director of the community services department of a large labor union," quoted by Cahalan, op. cit., p. 135.

74. Cahalan, op. cit., p. 135.

75. Peele, "Alcoholism," op. cit., p. 8 of html document.

76. Personal conversation with the author, October 1997.

77. Peele, "Denial," op. cit., p. 4 of html document.

78. Ibid.

79. "Ramstad, Wellstone unveil substance abuse parity bill," *Mental Health Weekly*, Vol. 7, No. 34, Sept. 8, 1997, p. 5

80. The NAADAC is another AA front group. CADACs (Certified Alcoholism and Drug Abuse Counselors) are low-paid "para-professionals" with few qualifications other than 12-step group membership, who are responsible for much of the 12-step indoctrination grunt work in treatment facilities.

81. *Mental Health Weekly*, op. cit.

9

Is AA a Cult?
(preliminary considerations)

What Is a Cult?

Alcoholics Anonymous is clearly a religious organization, but is AA a cult? Before answering that question, it's first necessary to define the key term. That's a very difficult task; there are almost as many definitions of the word "cult" as there are experts on the subject. One thing virtually all definitions of the word have in common is that they're quite broad.

Two of the definitions given by the *Random House Unabridged Dictionary* are fairly typical: "a group or sect bound together by devotion to or veneration of the same thing, person, ideal, etc."; and "a group having a sacred ideology and a set of rites centering around their sacred symbols."

Such definitions—as opposed to lists of attributes—could well apply to a great number of groups, many of which most people would never consider cults. Thus, the crucial question becomes what are the *specific characteristics* that distinguish cults, especially cults that are dangerous both to their own members and to society?

In the first edition of this book, I listed 17 such characteristics. At the time I made my list, I was unaware of Robert Jay Lifton's groundbreaking study of totalitarian indoctrination methods, *Thought Reform and the Psychology of Totalism*. In his book, Lifton lists eight characteristics of "ideological totalism."[1] These characteristics closely match those of most cults. Four of Lifton's listed characteristics correspond with some of those listed in the first edition of *Alcoholics Anonymous: Cult or Cure?* (though they're labeled differently), but four were not included or were touched on only tangentially. I've included them here as characteristics 3, 5, 10, and 12, though I've relabeled most of them, and I've reinterpreted all of them to some extent. I've also added two of the characteristics listed by Margaret Singer in her important recent book, *Cults In Our Midst*; here they're listed as characteristics 8 and 17. As a result of these additions, my list of cult criteria now includes 23 characteristics .

Based on Lifton's and Singer's criteria, as well as my own research into and direct contact with a number of groups commonly labeled as cults (especially Synanon, the Church of Scientology, the Unification Church [Moonies], Kerista Village,[2] the People's Temple, the Church of the Blood of the Lamb of God, and the Lyndon LaRouche organization in its various permutations [National Caucus of Labor Committees, U.S. Labor Party, etc.]),[3] I would list the following traits as being characteristic of most cults. (I should note, though, that not even the most obviously dangerous cults always possess all of the following attributes, though some do.)

1) **Religious Orientation.** Cults are usually centered around belief in a "higher power"; they often have elaborate religious rituals and emphasize prayer. Current and recent religious cults include the People's Temple, Branch Davidians, the Church of Scientology, the International Society for Krishna Consciousness (Hare Krishnas), the Unification Church, Kerista Village, the Church of the Blood of the Lamb of God (Ervil LeBaron's murderous Mormon splinter group), Synanon (which declared itself a religion while developing the most unsavory aspects of a cult), the Children of God, The Way International, Jehovah's Witnesses, and, arguably, an organization that I consider on the border between cults and mainstream religions, the Church of Jesus Christ of Latter Day Saints, the Mormons.

While secular cults also exist, they are not as numerous as religious cults. The most obvious example of a secular cult is the LaRouche organization, which has almost all of the characteristics of a totalitarian cult other than religious orientation. Two others which I believe could properly be classified as secular cults are the Revolutionary Communist Party and the New Alliance Party. But these are the exceptions; easily 90% of present-day cults are religious in nature.

2) **Irrationality.** Cults discourage skepticism and rational thought. As James and Marcia Rudin note in *Prison or Paradise: The New Religious Cults*:

> The groups are anti-intellectual, placing all emphasis on intuition or emotional experience. "Knowledge" is redefined as those ideas or experiences dispensed by the group or its leader. One can only attain knowledge by joining the group and submitting to its doctrine. One cannot question this "knowledge." If a follower shows signs of doubting he is made to feel that the fault lies within himself, not with the ideas . . .[4]

It's also common for cult leaders to tell their followers that doubt is the work of the devil. The Unification Church in particular has institutionalized the practices of equating doubt with sinfulness and satanic influence, and of attempting to stamp out independent thought. Some of its most common slogans (for internal use) are "Your Mind Is Fallen," "Stamp Out Doubt," and "No More Concepts."[5] If members of cults persist in having doubts, they're accused of being under satanic influence and excommunicated or, in extreme instances, even murdered, as in Ervil LeBaron's Lambs of God,[6] or in the Catholic Church during the Middle Ages and Renaissance.

3) **Dogmatism.** Cults invariably have The Truth and are highly antagonistic to those who question it. The Truth is invariably revealed in a cult's sacred text(s) or in the pronunciations of its leaders. It is beyond question, and to voice doubts about it is seen as, at best, a sign of confusion, and, at worst, a sign of being under satanic influence. This is clearly the case in the Unification Church, where doubt invariably comes directly from Satan, and it's also common in secular cults. In *Thought Reform and the Psychology of Totalism*, Lifton notes that Chinese Communist true believers attribute deviation from revealed Truth to "bourgeois" influence.[7]

4) **A "Chosen People" Mentality.** Given that cultists are alone in possessing a very precious commodity, The Truth, they almost always view themselves as *better* than other people, which means that nonbelievers and members of rival sects are frequently seen as less than human, if not outright tools of the devil. This attitude of superiority often manifests itself in an "ends justify the means" mentality and in the use of violence against outsiders or against heretics within the group. The most lurid recent examples of such violence have been provided by Ervil LeBaron's Lambs of God,[8] though historical examples abound.

5) **Ideology Over Experience, Observation, and Logic.** Cults not only demonize doubt and doubters, but they are also nearly immune to experience, observation, and logic that contradict their claims. Cult leaders claim to have The Truth—and their followers believe them—so anything that contradicts that Truth *must* be wrong. The Catholic Church's insistence that the earth is the center of the universe, coupled with its persecution of Galileo and Giordano Bruno, and its attempted suppression of the Copernican view of the solar system (well supported by observational evidence, even in the early 17th century), provides but one famous example of this phenomenon. To cite another, the leaders of the Jehovah's Witnesses—claiming inspiration directly from God—stated that doomsday would come in 1914, and then in 1925.[9] Yet when the appointed days came and went, the Witnesses suffered relatively minor defections. When their claims are proven false, cult leaders normally either ignore the contradictory evidence or invoke the fathomless Will of God to explain the turn of events. Their flocks never seem to notice this.

6) **Separatism.** Cult members almost always view themselves as outsiders, as different from the rest of society. This sets up an "us versus them" mentality, and it's common for cult members to believe that only they and their fellow cult members can understand each other—"outsiders" certainly can't.

One manifestation of separatism is the use of specialized terms; almost all cults develop a jargon peculiar to themselves. Another, though less common, manifestation of separatism is the abandonment of "old" personal names and the taking of "new" ones, as was done in the San Francisco-based cult, Kerista Village. A third is the adoption of distinctive dress and/or other alterations in personal appearance. The practice of head-shaving among the Hare Krishnas and in Synanon, and the required wearing of red and orange hues by the Rajneeshees are examples of this.[10]

7) **Exclusivity.** Cults invariably view themselves as the *only* path to salvation. Normally that "salvation" is spiritual, though, as with the LaRouchites and other political sects, it can be secular. Again, this leads to arrogance, dehumanization of nonbelievers, and an "ends justify the means" mentality. The Moonies have even adopted a "spiritual" term (for internal use only) for lying and cheating in pursuit of Church goals: "Heavenly Deception."

8) **Special Knowledge.** This is closely related to the concept of exclusivity. Many cults claim that they are the route to personal and/or social salvation because they hold special, extremely valuable knowledge that's unavailable to the uninitiated. As well, many cults only gradually reveal that "knowledge" to members in order to avoid early defections. (A great deal of this "knowledge" is so absurd that most people would walk away immediately were it to be revealed to them all at once.) As an example of this cult tendency, Margaret Singer, in *Cults In Our Midst*, cites a researcher who quotes L. Ron Hubbard, the founder of Scientology, as follows: "new followers or potential converts should not be exposed to [the language and cosmology of Scientology] at too early a stage. 'Talking whole track to raw meat' is frowned upon."[11]

9) **Mind Control Techniques.** These involve such measures as keeping members malnourished and in a state of exhaustion. The classic example of this was the conduct of Jim Jones' cult in its Jonestown settlement in Guyana prior to the mass murder/suicide in 1978.[12] More sophisticated methods are also used, examples being "self-criticism" (in political cults), the use of chanting and various forms of "sensory overload" in groups like the Hare Krishnas, and the use of "therapy," as in the New Alliance Party.

Another important mind control technique is the destruction of personal privacy. The Moonies, for example, normally do not even allow potential recruits at their retreats to go to the bathroom unless accompanied by a member of their cult. This is a way of never allowing new or potential recruits to regain their mental balance.

Still another important mind control technique is the humiliation and intimidation of members. In Synanon, this took the form of "the game," a warped encounter session in which individuals were attacked by other members of the group.[13] In the People's Temple the technique was cruder, with members being, among other things, sexually humiliated in public.[14]

10) **Thought-Stopping Language.** This is another mind-control technique, but Lifton considers it so important that he made it one of his eight criteria of "ideological totalism."As Lifton puts it, the way that these "thought-terminating cliche[s]" operate is that "the most far-reaching and complex of human problems are compressed into brief, highly reductive, definitive-sounding phrases, easily memorized and easily expressed. These become the start and finish of any ideological analysis."[15]

Put more broadly, thought-stopping phrases include any use of language, especially repeated phrases, to ward off forbidden thoughts. One common example of this is the admonition given to Catholic schoolchildren to recite the Hail Mary or rosary to ward off "impure thoughts." The use of repetitive chanting by the Hare Krishnas serves the same thought-stopping purpose.

Another aspect of thought-stopping terms is that, as Ken Ragge points out, "Loaded language, the language of non-thought, entails more than cliches. Individual words are given meanings or shades of meanings entirely separate from their normal usage."[16] To cite the most obvious example, the use of the word "Father" by members of some cults does not refer to a biological parent, but to the cult's leader. These alternative meanings to common words serve to accentuate the separateness of cult members from "outsiders" or "normies."

11) **Manipulation Through Guilt.** Many cults expertly manipulate their members through arousal of guilt feelings. Guilt is created, according to Lifton, by the setting of impossible-to-meet "demand[s] for purity":

> By conducting an all-out war on impurity, the ideological totalists create a narrow world of guilt and shame. This is perpetuated by an ethos of continuous reform . . . Since each man's impurities are deemed sinful and potentially harmful to himself and to others, he is, so to speak, expected to expect punishment . . . Similarly, when he fails to meet the prevailing standards in casting out such impurities, he is expected to expect humiliation and ostracism.[17]

As one might expect, in addition to proscribed actions, proscribed *thoughts* also give rise to guilt. Any attempt at individual assertion or resistance to the demands of the cult's leader or hierarchy—including even the smallest reluctance to enthusiastically parrot every assertion in the group's ideology —is attacked as selfishness and lack of devotion to "The Cause." Such guilt-arousing attacks are especially effective when made in public. They serve as powerful spurs to orthodoxy in thought and action, and also as powerful goads to members to "donate" their assets to the cult and to prove their devotion through self-sacrifice.

But with truly successful indoctrination, guilt is internalized. The simple surfacing of proscribed thoughts—let alone the carrying out of proscribed actions—is sufficient in itself to arouse intense guilt feelings in indoctrinated cult members. To make these feelings bearable, to preserve their self-images as "good" persons trying to live their lives in accord with revealed Truth, cult members "must also look upon [their] impurities as originating from outside influences, that is, from the ever-threatening world beyond the closed, totalist ken."[18] Thus cult members escape responsibility for their sinful thoughts and actions, at least in part. They're just weak individuals dealing with powerful, insidious forces, which they can successfully resist only with the help of the cult.

12) **The Cult of Confession.** Lifton explains the mechanism as follows:

> It is first a vehicle for . . . personal purification . . . Second, it is an act of symbolic self-surrender, the expression of the merging of individual and environment. Third, it is a means of maintaining an ethos of total exposure . . . The milieu has attained such a perfect state of enlightenment that any individual retention of ideas or emotions has become anachronistic. . . . More than this, the sharing of confession enthusiasms can create an orgiastic sense of "oneness," of the most intense intimacy with fellow confessors and of the dissolution of self into the great flow of the Movement.[19]

Thus confession serves the purpose of fostering identification as a member of the cult rather than as an individual human being. It also serves the purpose of alleviating guilt, thus making the confessor dependent on the cult for that alleviation.

A great many cults and religions—the lines are often blurry—have used confession, both individual and public, for these dual purposes. The Catholic Church is, of course, the prime example of an organization that uses individual confession to these ends. The Chinese Communists are the prime example of an organization that uses public confession to these ends.

As well, there is always the possibility that cults will use information revealed in confessions to threaten, manipulate and control their members.

The Church of Scientology, for example, supposedly maintains extensive files on individuals' "auditing" sessions—therapeutic/confessional sessions in which a great deal of potentially embarrassing information is often revealed; one former Scientologist told me that the Church of Scientology records and retains every minute of every auditing session. The Church's retention of the information disclosed in auditing sessions, and the possibility of its being publicly revealed, could well contribute to the reluctance of some disaffected ex-Scientologists to speak out against the Church of Scientology.

Far worse, the hold of some cults is so intense that they intimidate their members into making false confessions, which they then dangle over their members' heads as a means of controlling them. Perhaps the worst example of this was provided by the People's Temple, in which parents were routinely forced to sign false confessions stating that they had sexually molested their own children.[20]

If confession is good for the soul, it's even better for helping cults cement their control over their members.

13) **A Charismatic Leader.** Present in most cults, the leader can be living (Revolutionary Communist Party, Unification Church, LaRouchites) or dead (Synanon, Scientology, Mormons). In cases where the leader dies, the cult either fades away, is taken over by another charismatic leader, or, as with the Scientologists and Mormons, is taken over by a pre-existing hierarchy.

14) **A Hierarchical, Authoritarian Structure.** While this is a very common feature of cults, it should be noted that relatively new cults often have little structure. But as time passes, hierarchy and bureaucracy usually arise, as is to be expected in authoritarian setups. If a hierarchy does not arise—this sometimes happens because of the charismatic leader's fear of take-over attempts—the cult will probably disintegrate upon the leader's death, unless a new charismatic leader quickly arises to take his or her place.

15) **Submission of the Individual to the "Will of God"** or to some other abstraction, such as the "dictatorship of the proletariat." This means abandonment of individual decision making in favor of obeying the will of the abstraction as interpreted by the cult. In practice, this usually means obeying the orders of the charismatic leader or the hierarchy which controls the group.

One outward sign of individual submission to the charismatic leader is the infantilization of members. In many instances, the People's Temple and Unification Church being examples, members refer to and address the leader as "Father."

In many cults the submission of the individual is so complete that the charismatic leader and/or hierarchy make all significant life decisions for the individual, up to and including choice of sex and marriage partners. In Synanon, the control of its founder, Charles Dederich, was so complete that he forced all of the male members of his cult, save himself, to undergo vasectomies.[21] He later forced all members to switch sex partners.[22] And in the Unification Church, the hierarchy picks the marriage partners of members. In that church, it's common for brides and grooms to meet for the first time at their marriage ceremonies.

But perhaps the ultimate expressions of the submission of the individual to the "will of God" (that is, the cult) are self-mutilation and mass suicide. A recent horrifying example of both was provided by the Heaven's Gate cult. A majority of the male members of that severely anti-sexual religious group—in order to remove themselves from temptations of the flesh—"voluntarily" submitted to castration prior to the cult's mass suicide in 1997, in preparation for joining the (of course, nonexistent) UFO in Comet Hale-Bopp's tail.

16) **Self-Absorption.** The primary focus of a cult is the cult itself. Whatever its ostensible aims, in reality a cult is overwhelmingly self-absorbed. Cults are prone to extreme over self-estimation, to what could be termed organizational narcissism; and so a cult's primary concerns are its own survival and expansion, with the ends justifying the means.

17) **Dual Purposes.** This extreme self-absorption leads to what Margaret Singer terms dual purposes—in other words, cults have their stated purposes and their real purposes. As regards individual members, cults present themselves as ways for members to meet their own needs, grow personally or spiritually, and/or to realize higher social or spiritual goals. In reality, Singer notes, the purpose of cults is to subject their members to mind control techniques in order to control and exploit them.

The dual-purpose aspect of cults is also noticeable in their dealing with outsiders, and it's particularly noticeable in their fundraising activities. Cults frequently raise huge sums of money which they allege will be used to alleviate social problems such as alcoholism, drug abuse, homelessness, and abandoned or abused children, when in reality they spend all, or nearly all, of the money raised to support the cult. For example, in its fundraising materials, the People's Temple routinely represented itself as a do-good organization caring for abandoned children.[23]

Secular cults are every bit as self-absorbed as religious cults. Political cults have long been notorious for infiltrating social change groups and manipulating them for the benefit of the cults, often destroying the social change groups in the process. In the 1960s, the Socialist Workers Party (itself heavily infiltrated by the FBI) and the Progressive Labor Party wreaked havoc in the anti-war movement through this tactic; in the 1970s, the women's movement was targeted by the International Socialists and other sects; and in the 1980s and 1990s the New Alliance Party and the so-called Humanist Party have infiltrated environmental and other progressive groups. The political lines and the names of the cults have changed, but the virus-like infiltrate/manipulate/destroy tactic remains the same.

18) **Economic Exploitation.** Cults not only exploit their own members, but, when they can manage it, nonmembers as well.[24] Some, such as the LaRouchites, Synanon, and the People's Temple, have extensively targeted nonmembers.

Cults which target nonmembers solicit money by presenting themselves —or their front groups—as doing "good works," such as fighting drugs, when in fact virtually all of the money that they raise is spent on their own operations and, often, on enriching their leaders. Synanon fundraisers, for example, routinely represented Synanon as a drug rehabilitation program for years after it had effectively abandoned working with drug abusers.[25] The LaRouchites have gone further and have engaged in criminal fraud—under the guise of fighting drugs and other "good works"—on a massive scale. As a result, many of the top members of the cult, including founder Lyndon LaRouche, Jr., were sentenced to lengthy prison terms in the late 1980s.[26]

Direct economic exploitation of members by their cults is often even less subtle. Many cults, such as the People's Temple, strip their members of assets. In the People's Temple, the technique was crude: members were pressured to "donate" their possessions to the church. The Scientologists have taken a more sophisticated approach—potential members are lured by widely advertised free computer personality evaluations and pay very little to take introductory courses, but then must pay much higher fees (often in the thousands of dollars) to take "advanced" Scientology courses.[27]

Another way in which cults exploit their members is by having them work long, exhausting hours for little or no pay. Cults which employ(ed) such tactics include Synanon, the People's Temple, the various LaRouche front groups, the Unification Church, the Church of Scientology, and the International Society for Krishna Consciousness (Hare Krishnas).[28]

19) **Deceptive Recruiting Techniques.** Some cults routinely deceive potential members, which is understandable: most potential recruits would not find attractive the prospect of slavishly following the orders of a guru-figure while working 16 to 18 hours a day for little or no pay. The Unification Church in particular is notorious for deceptive recruitment tactics.[29]

The primary recruitment targets for the Moonies are unattached young people. They usually have a member of the opposite sex approach the target and invite her/him to dinner. According to those who have attended such dinners, no mention of Moon or the Unification Church is made. Rather, there is general talk of a "family" and improving the world. Next follows an invitation to spend a weekend at a retreat. Those who accept are "love bombed" (showered with attention) by members and are invited to a longer retreat. If they accept, they're again "love bombed," kept constantly occupied, accompanied by a Moonie at all times, and denied adequate sleep. And before they know it, they're selling flowers 18 hours a day for room and board.

Another tactic of the Unification Church is the setting up of front groups, such as the Collegiate Association for the Research of Principles (CARP), and having members of the front groups lie about their association with the Unification Church, if asked. In the late 1970s, CARP appeared on the campus of Boise State University, and I investigated it for the school newspaper, the *BSU Arbiter*. Even though CARP's address was the same as that of the local Unification Church, and its literature was distributed by members of that Church, the Moonies staunchly maintained that there was "no connection" between the Unification Church and CARP.

Other cults also employ front groups. The LaRouchites in particular are notorious for this practice. This amoeba-like cult splits so often that it's difficult to follow its permutations. Some of the names it has operated under included the U.S. Labor Party, National Caucus of Labor Committees, Fusion Energy Foundation, the Schiller Institute, the National Anti-Drug Coalition, and the National Democratic Policy Committee.

20) **Possessiveness.** For financial and other reasons, cults will often go to great, sometimes illegal, lengths to retain members. The most extreme example of this was provided by the People's Temple Jonestown gulag, where members were physically prevented from leaving by Jim Jones' heavily armed goon squad. A less sinister example of this tendency is provided by the Church of Jesus Christ of Latter Day Saints, the Mormons. When a Mormon leaves the fold, the LDS Church *never* gives up its attempts to recover its lost sheep. It will track the apostate for decades, and it's not unusual for LDS representatives to contact former members 30 or 40 years after they left the church in an effort to talk them into rejoining.

21) **A Closed, All-Encompassing Environment.** Again, the classic example of this is Jonestown. Almost all cults attempt to provide a closed environment for at least some of their key members, and some attempt to provide it for all of their members. The less contact that members have with

external reality, the more natural the hothouse environment of the cult seems, the more natural the very peculiar beliefs of the cult seem, and the more natural it seems that everyone should follow the orders of the charismatic leader or the controlling hierarchy. A closed, all-encompassing environment also makes members totally dependent upon the cult for social support, economic support, and a sense of identity; and this tends to make leaving the cult a terrifying prospect. To put it another way, cults are like anaerobic bacteria—they thrive in the absence of cleansing breezes.

22) **Millenarianism.** Many cults, especially Christian fundamentalist cults, prophesy that the world is coming to an end. One of the most prominent millenarian cults, the Revolutionary Communist Party (RCP), is, however, secular in nature. Rather than prophesying a biblical Armageddon, the RCP prophesies a nuclear Armageddon unless, of course, it achieves power within the next few years. (The RCP, unlike the Jehovah's Witnesses, has at least had the good sense not to announce a doomsday date.) If members believe this, it's a powerful incentive for them to put in long, unpaid hours working for the RCP's hierarchy and its *lider máximo*, Bob Avakian.

Millenarianism also provides a powerful insight into the hold of cults over their followers. As mentioned previously, some cults, such as the Jehovah's Witnesses, have had the bad judgment to prophesy the date of doomsday, yet almost all such cults have managed to retain a majority of their blindly believing followers despite their failed predictions. The Witnesses, however, seem to have learned from their past false prophecies, and have recently backed away from their prediction of doomsday in the year 2000. So, Witness faithful no longer have that date to look forward to. They simply have the assurance that doomsday is coming *soon.*

23) **Violence, Coercion, and Harassment.** Coercion is routine in cults. Many cults, such as the People's Temple, maintain(ed) goon squads to control their own members; and many, including Synanon, the People's Temple, and the Church of the Blood of the Lamb of God, have employed violence and even killings to intimidate and silence critics, and to keep members in line. The most famous recent incident of such violence was the rattlesnake attack upon attorney Paul Morantz by members of a Synanon goon squad in 1978.[30] [31]

Other cults, such as Scientology, utilize legal harassment. The Church of Scientology is notoriously litigious and has, on one occasion, gone beyond the filing of lawsuits against its critics. In that case, Church of Scientology members, including very high-ranking members of the Church's hierarchy, attempted to frame a critic, journalist Paulette Cooper, on felony bomb charges and very nearly succeeded. A Scientology agent who "befriended"

Cooper during her ordeal reported to his superiors: "She can't sleep again . . . she's talking suicide. Wouldn't this be great for Scientology!"[32] Fortunately, Cooper escaped the Scientologists' plot—after years of torment—and several of those responsible for the conspiracy against her were eventually sentenced to prison terms.

But the use of violence against nonbelievers is hardly a new phenomenon. Over 100 years ago, John Doyle Lee, the Mormon elder who was scapegoated and executed in 1877 for the 1857 massacre of 120 settlers (including many women and children) at Mountain Meadows, Utah, stated:

> . . . the people in Utah who professed the Mormon religion were at and for some time before the Mountain Meadows massacre full of wildfire and zeal, anxious to do something to build up the Kingdom of God on earth and waste the enemies of the Mormon religion . . . The killing of Gentiles [non-Mormons] was a means of grace and a virtuous deed . . .
>
> The Mormons believed in blood atonement. It is taught by the leaders, and believed by the people, that the Priesthood are inspired and cannot give a wrong order. It is the belief of all that I ever heard talk of these things . . . that the authority that orders is the only responsible party and the Danite [member of the Mormon equivalent of the KGB, the Sons of Dan] who does the killing only an instrument, and commits no wrong . . .[33] [34]

An even older example of the bloodthirtiness of some cults was provided by theologian and papal agent Arnold Amalric at the Beziers massacre of Albigensian heretics in 1209: "Kill them all. God will easily recognize his own."[35]

---

1. *Thought Reform and the Psychology of Totalism*, by Robert Jay Lifton. New York: W.W. Norton, 1969, pp. 419-435,

2. Kerista Village was a San Francisco-based polyfidelitous (group marriage) cult of the 1970s, 1980s, and early 1990s. I include it here because, although it's little known, I'm quite familiar with it.

3. See the bibliography for books on these groups.

4. *Prison or Paradise: The New Religious Cults*, by James and Marcia Rudin. Philadelphia: Fortress Press, 1980, p. 20.

5. *Crazy for God*, by Christopher Edwards. Englewood Cliffs, New Jersey: Prentice-Hall, 1979, pp. 116, 138, and 171.

6. See *Prophet of Blood*, by Dale Van Atta and Ben Bradlee, Jr. New York: Putnam, 1981.

7. Lifton, op. cit., p. 432.

8. Van Atta and Bradlee, op. cit. LeBaron ordered the murder of dozens of persons, mostly members of his own polygamous sect and members of rival sects. One of those he ordered killed was his own brother. It would be pointless to cite specific page references here, as Van Atta's and Bradlee's book is an almost non-stop chronicle of mayhem from end to end.

9. *30 Years a Watchtower Slave*, by Walter J. Schnell. Grand Rapids, Michigan: Baker House Books, 1971, pp. 29-30.

10. See *Paradise Incorporated*, by David Gerstel. Novato, California: Presidio Press, 1982 for examples of cult jargon and alteration of personal appearance.

11. *Cults In Our Midst*, by Margaret Singer. San Francisco: Jossey-Bass, 1995, p. 71.

12. See *Six Years With God: Life Inside Jim Jones's People's Temple*, by Jeannie Mills. New York: A&W Publishers, 1979. Shortly after her book's publication, Mills and her entire family were murdered by persons unknown. There have been persistent rumors that the Mills family was killed by a People's Temple hit squad—not all People's Temple members died at Jonestown —but there have never been any arrests in the case.

13. Gerstel, op. cit., chapter 2.

14. Mills, op. cit., pp. 252-255.

15. Lifton, op. cit., p. 429.

16. *More Revealed*, by Ken Ragge. Henderson, Nevada: Alert Publishing, 1992, p. 136.

17. Lifton, op. cit., p. 424.

18. Ibid., p. 425.

19. Ibid., pp. 425-426.

20. Mills, op. cit., p. 12.

21. Gerstel, op. cit., pp. 207-224.

22. Ibid., pp. 239-252.

23. For a close, detailed look at cult fundraising activities, see Mills, op. cit.

24. Ibid.

25. Gerstel, op. cit., pp. 130-133. See also *Escape from Utopia: My Ten Years in Synanon*, by William Olin (Santa Cruz, California: Unity Press, 1980) for details on Synanon's fundraising activities.

26. *Lyndon LaRouche and the New American Fascism*, by Dennis King. New York: Doubleday, 1989, pp. 314-322.

27. See *L. Ron Hubbard: Messiah or Madman*, by Bent Corydon and L. Ron Hubbard, Jr. Secaucus, New Jersey: Lyle Stuart, 1987 for instances of economic exploitation of members of the Church of Scientology. See also *Barefaced Messiah: The True Story of L. Ron Hubbard*, by Russell Miller. New York: Henry Holt, 1987. A good, short source is "The Thriving Cult of Greed and Power," *Time*, May 6, 1991.

28. Rudins, op. cit., pp. 31-96. For information on the LaRouchites' economic exploitation of their own members, see King, op. cit., chapter 31.

29. See Edwards, op. cit., chapters 1 through 9.

30. Gerstel, op.cit., pp. 253-278.

31. *The Light on Synanon*, by Dave and Cathy Mitchell. New York: Seaview Books, 1980, pp. 192-195.

32. Corydon and Hubbard, op. cit., p. 170. The entire affair is described in pp. 164-170.

33. Quoted in *I Was a Mormon*, by Einar Anderson. Grand Rapids, Michigan: Zondervan Publishing House, 1964, pp. 57-58.

34. See also *The Mountain Meadows Massacre*, by Juanita Brooks. Palo Alto, California: Stanford University, 1950; and *Massacre at Mountain Meadows*, by William Wise. New York: Thomas Crowell, 1976.

35. *The Great Quotations*, George Seldes, ed. Secaucus, New Jersey: Castle Books, 1978, p. 53.

10

Is A.A. a Cult?
(conclusions)

Is Alcoholics Anonymous a cult? That's almost as difficult to answer as the question, "What is a cult?" The difficulty is compounded by the fact that AA has very close ties—indeed, incestuous relationships—with a large number of "related facilit[ies]" and "outside enterprise[s]." These include the NCADD, ASAM, and the 93% of all inpatient alcoholism treatment facilities that utilize AA indoctrination as part—usually the centerpiece—of their programs, and that are for the most part staffed and controlled by 12-stepping "professionals." I believe that these front groups should be considered part of, or at least extensions of, AA, just as I believe that groups that are staffed and controlled by Communist Party members, and that advance Communist Party ideology, should be considered part of, or at least extensions of, the Communist Party.

Both AA and the Communists learned long ago that the setting up of front groups is a convenient means of attracting or influencing the unwary, advancing their own agendas, and avoiding both criticism and responsibility (for the actions of their front groups). Here, I intend to hold AA responsible for the actions of its front groups. I will, however, at times maintain a distinction between what Vince Fox refers to as "communal AA" (free meetings and fellowship of the type described in Chapter 1) and what he refers to as "institutional AA" (the 12-step treatment industry). Where I make no distinction between the two, my remarks apply equally to both.

Rather than attempt to determine whether AA (communal or institutional) fits the very broad definitions of a "cult" offered at the beginning of the previous chapter—definitions which fit many mainstream religions and political organizations, as well as groups generally conceded to be cults—it seems more appropriate to determine how many of the characteristics of the destructive cults can be found in AA.

Considering in order the 21 criteria listed in the previous chapter:

1) Is AA religiously oriented? Unequivocally yes .

While many AA members would assert that AA is a "spiritual" organization rather than a religious one, there is little doubt that they are simply
parroting a rote assertion common in AA. In fact, AA's religiosity is so
obvious that even the courts have taken note of it and appeals courts have
consistently ruled (in cases challenging mandated attendance) that AA is a
religious organization. One lower-court case is illustrative; as the court
stated in a 1984 Wisconsin ruling (Grandberg V. Ashland County):

> Alcoholics Anonymous materials . . . and the testimony of the witness
> established beyond a doubt that religious activities, as defined in
> constitutional law, were a part of the treatment program. The distinction
> between religion and spirituality is meaningless, and serves merely to confuse
> the issue.

It's also important to remember that AA was founded by Bill Wilson, an
enthusiastic member of the evangelical Christian Oxford Group Movement,
and by Dr. Bob Smith (also a member of the Oxford Groups) who insisted
that new members get down on their knees and pray Christian prayers with
him. In addition, and significantly, AA (before it adopted its name) operated
as part of the Oxford Groups in both New York and Akron; and in Akron,
birthplace of AA, members of what was to become AA identified themselves
as the "alcoholic squadron of the Akron Oxford Group" during AA's
formative years.

As well, AA literature is filled with references to "God" and a "Higher
Power," and the so-called Big Book's chapter, "We Agnostics," concludes
with the words, "God restored us to our right minds . . . When we drew near
to Him He disclosed Himself to us!" Further, the 12 steps, the core of AA's
program, are simply a codification of Oxford Group principles; and fully
half of the steps mention "God," "Him," or a "Power greater than ourselves."

In the early days of AA, the religious nature of the AA "program," as
outlined in the "Big Book," was openly acknowledged. Dr. Harry Emerson
Fosdick's review of the "Big Book," which AA submitted unsuccessfully to
the *New York Herald Tribune*, and later managed to have printed in several
religious periodicals, states, "the core of their whole procedure is religious."
Even today, a large majority of AA meetings end with the Lord's Prayer.

In every respect, AA's orientation passes the "duck" test: If it looks like
a duck, waddles like a duck, and quacks like a duck, it's probably a duck. In
this case, the "duck" is AA's religious nature.

2) Is AA irrational, does it discourage skepticism and rational thinking? Again, yes.

AA's emphasis is primarily on emotional experience ("spiritual awakening") and "overcoming" doubts en route to spiritual "knowledge." In the "We Agnostics" chapter of the "Big Book," Bill Wilson approvingly cites a former agnostic who "humbly offered himself to his Maker—then he knew."

AA aphorisms are even more revealing. Two common ones are "Your best thinking got you here" and "Utilize, don't analyze." It would be hard to think of more virulently anti-intellectual epigrams. They're all too similar to the Moonie slogan, "You Think Too Much." The distance between these slogans and their more famous counterpart, "Ignorance Is Strength," from Orwell's *1984*, is frighteningly short.

Another popular AA saying is "Fake it until you make it." In other words, members should sit on their doubts and mouth accepted AA wisdom until they feel comfortable doing it. This sounds more like a recipe for brainwashing than a recipe for "spiritual awakening."

Any doubts about this matter can be quickly resolved by a visit to almost any AA meeting. Newcomers who express doubts are normally assailed with bits of wisdom such as those just cited, and are almost always assured that doubting leads to drinking.

3) Is AA dogmatic? Unfortunately, yes.

It's difficult to label as dogmatic an organization in which the most important guiding principles (the 12 steps) are only "suggestions." But despite this disclaimer, a great many AA members are extremely dogmatic. They regard the 12 steps with the reverence that a fundamentalist has for the Ten Commandments, and they regard the "Big Book" as a fundamentalist would the Bible.

Anyone doubting this should attend a few AA meetings. At most meetings, even mild criticism of the steps or the "Big Book" will be met with sarcasm, anger, and put-downs. For AA true believers, the steps and the "Big Book" are received wisdom (which, indeed, Bill Wilson believed them to be); and they are to be blindly followed, not questioned.

Further confirmation of AA's dogmatism is provided by its attitude toward the very many alcohol abusers who investigate AA but can't stomach its program. Rather than attempt to see *why* so many alcohol abusers reject AA (remember, these are oftentimes desperate individuals urgently seeking help), and whether anything—changes in the AA program, referral to the many existing alternative programs—can be done to help them, AA does *nothing* to help these vulnerable people, and instead blames them for rejecting AA, maintaining that the reason they can't stand AA is their "character defects," their lack of "honesty," or their lack of a genuine desire to stop drinking. This happens In every single case. And there have been millions. To its dogmatic members, the AA program is perfect; the problem lies solely with those who reject it.

This is the attitude of a callous, dogmatic religious sect, not that of a rational, humanistic organization concerned with helping those afflicted by what it insists is a deadly "illness."

4) Do AA members have a "chosen people" mentality? Yes.

Given that AA members believe that they alone have The Truth as regards overcoming alcoholism, it would be surprising if they *didn't* have such a mentality. The callous put-downs of those who come to AA for help and reject it provide confirmation of this, as do the common put-downs of sober former alcohol abusers who reject AA as "dry drunks." Further, one often hears comments at meetings about being "better than well" or the like —testimony to the miraculous effects of working the steps in producing human beings happier and more spiritually developed than "normies."

Granted, the "chosen people" mentality of AA members is relatively mild in comparison with that of members of cults such as the Moonies and Hare Krishnas, but it's still undeniably there.

5) Does AA elevate its own ideology over experience, observation and logic? Again, unquestionably yes.

AA has The Truth, and it assiduously ignores the mountain of evidence that AA is quite probably entirely ineffective as a means of alcoholism treatment, and that AA may actually do more harm than good. This evidence comes from the controlled studies of AA's effectiveness, as well as from AA's own analysis of its triennial membership surveys. (See Chapter 9 for a detailed discussion of these matters.)

The alarm bells would have gone off inside any rational organization when the first controlled study was published in 1961. But AA ignored it, and has continued to ignore it, just as it ignored the more sophisticated, more convincing controlled study published in 1980. AA has also ignored its own analysis of its triennial membership surveys, which shows that the rate of recovery via AA is almost certainly no better than the rate of spontaneous remission, and may in fact be worse. Instead of taking a serious look at all of this data, AA and its supporters ignore it while hypocritically presenting AA as the only road to recovery.[1] This, quite obviously, is the posture of an ideology-driven cult.

6) Is AA separatist? Yes, but only somewhat more so than other special interest groups.

AA members are self-selected "alcoholics," as opposed to the supposedly 90% of the population who are non-alcoholics. The more extreme outward signs of separatism—the taking of new names and the adoption of distinctive dress or other alterations in personal appearance—are, however, absent.

The one area in which AA members definitely show signs of separatism is in their use of jargon. As Ken Ragge points out, in AA terms often take on meanings different from their standard English meanings—for instance, "sobriety," rather than merely meaning "unintoxicated," means "a special state of Grace gained by working the Steps and maintaining absolute abstinence. It is characterized by feelings of Serenity and Gratitude. It is a state of living according to God's will, not one's own. It is sanity."[2]

7) Does AA see itself as the exclusive holder of the truth? Unfortunately, yes—at least in regard to the treatment of alcohol abuse.

If AA didn't believe this, it wouldn't ignore the evidence pointing to its ineffectiveness (see Chapter 9). As well, while there are a few scattered and unimportant acknowledgements in AA literature that at least the occasional alcohol abuser can recover without AA, at the vast majority of Alcoholics Anonymous meetings newcomers are routinely told that participation in AA and acceptance of the AA "program" (basically the 12 steps) is the *only* way to overcome an alcohol problem. Compounding this, the same message is frequently delivered by alcoholism "professionals" and "para-professionals" (who are often zealous AA members, some with little if any medical or psychological training) and by the mass media, which uncritically relies upon these "experts" for much of its information on alcoholism.

8) Does AA claim to have special knowledge that will only be revealed to the initiated? A qualified no.

AA makes no claims that it has special knowledge that will be revealed only to those who are "ready for it." But AA does claim that "working a good program" or "working the steps" leads to "serenity" and (at least often) "a spiritual awakening." Thus, these promises are used to induce members to stay in AA and to immerse themselves in its indoctrination program. This seems at least somewhat manipulative, but it's a far cry from the practice of one well-known cult which charges its members tens, sometimes hundreds, of thousands of dollars for ever more "advanced" courses, the eventual pay-off of which is that they will be "cleared" of "body thetans"—the evil spirits of beings blown up by hydrogen bombs in volcanos 85 million years ago.

9) Does AA employ mind control techniques? For the most part, in communal AA, no. In institutional AA, yes.

While communal AA does employ threats (of jails, institutions, and death), prayer, and innocuous rituals, such as the chanting of "Keep coming back, it works!" at the end of meetings, these things should not be confused with severe mind control techniques such as exhaustion, mal-nourishment, and hypnotic chanting. Communal AA does nothing to alter its members' consciousness beyond the serving of a mild drug (caffeine) at its meetings, and, beyond admonitions, the use of low-key rituals, sacred texts, and group pressure, it does nothing to control their thoughts—with the significant exception of the use of thought-stopping jargon.

In institutional AA, however, coerced participants are kept very busy, given little time alone, deprived of outside contacts, allowed to read only approved (that is, indoctrination) literature, forced into making false confessions, subjected to attacks, threats, and ridicule for raising questions or making critical comments, and subjected to extreme pressure by a unanimous majority to change their belief systems. Clearly, mind-control is the *essence* of institutional AA's indoctrination program.

10) Does AA employ thought-stopping language? Yes, but its employment is less stringent than in many religious cults.

As Ken Ragge points out, the function of many AA slogans, cliches and aphorisms is to short-circuit critical thinking.[3] The purpose of such slogans as "Keep It Simple, Stupid," "Utilize, don't analyze," "Your best thinking got you here," and "Let go and let God," is to get AA members to stop thinking for themselves and, instead, to *accept* divine guidance (that is, guidance from AA). And the function of the in-reality-meaningless term "dry drunk" is to discredit critics and apostates. By labeling such troublesome persons "dry drunks," AA members devalue them as persons and can thus conveniently ignore what they say as merely the ravings of "insanity."

But as insidious as this is, it's not to be compared with the hypnotic chanting employed by the Moonies and Hare Krishnas, which in combination with other mind control techniques render their members so debilitated that it requires months if not years for them to fully recover their critical faculties after leaving these cults.

11) Does AA manipulate its members through guilt? Yes.

Guilt is inherent in AA dogma. It's enshrined in the 12 steps with their references to "our wrongs," "our shortcomings," "defects of character" and a "moral inventory." As well, AA members almost invariably suffer intense guilt when they drink or go on benders (as a great many do at one time or another), and are quite penitent when they return, and thus very likely to embrace accepted AA wisdom as their one and only hope of "sobriety." (Such "slips" lead to a considerable loss of prestige—whether the "slip" involves a single beer or two fifths of whiskey—which amplifies the unpleasant effects of the guilt incurred by not "working a good program" and drinking.)

But there is no guru-figure or authoritarian hierarchy to manipulate AA's members, no matter how guilty they might feel. So, the AA "program" fosters guilt in abundance, but there is no one to manipulate it for personal advantage. It should be added, though, that AA-induced (or reinforced) guilt does make members feel sinful and fearful, and thus tends to tie them to AA, because temporary relief from their unpleasant feelings is available at meetings.

12) Does AA employ "the cult of confession"? Does it use confession for purification and to tie its members to it? Yes.

Confession in AA comes in four forms: 1) private confession from "pigeon" to sponsor (as "suggest[ed]" in the fifth step); 2) public confession by *speakers* at AA meetings; 3) public confession ("sharing") by *participants* at AA meetings; and 4) in institutional AA, false confession.

The purpose of the first type of confession is almost certainly to tie the new member to AA, as it deepens the pigeon's involvement in "working the steps," that is, it deepens his or her participation in AA's sequential indoctrination program. It leads to the next step, and it also (at least often) deepens the relationship with his or her sponsor, the person responsible for overseeing the indoctrination process.

The second type of confession is an odd one in that speaker's confession is normally boastful and carries not a trace of remorse. The purpose of such a confession is to establish credibility with listeners, thus making them more receptive to the speaker's message. So, this type of confession also serves the purpose of tying both listeners and the speaker (who receives enjoyable positive attention from the audience) to AA.

The third type serves both the "purification" and "tying" functions. It allows the confessing member to bare his soul and relieve his guilt feelings; and the acceptance that those making such confessions find binds them more closely to AA.

The fourth type is common in institutional AA. Many unwilling individuals are coerced into attending 12-step treatment centers (usually by the courts, their employers, or professional organizations to which they belong). When such unwilling persons are in treatment, tremendous pressure is often brought to bear to force them to confess that they are "alcoholics," even though they often do not believe themselves to be. Many of the persons so pressured have little choice but to knuckle under and make false confessions.

They are also often forced to exaggerate the bad incidents in their drinking histories, or to make up incidents out of whole cloth. The purpose of these confessions is exactly the same as the false confessions obtained by Red Chinese "thought reformers": the confessions signify the submission of the clients/prisoners to their coercers, and they confirm the coercers' ideology.

13) Does AA have a charismatic leader? No, although it does have dead saints.

To his credit, Bill Wilson never sought dictatorial control of AA, and in fact—through devising AA's anarchist form of organization—did much to ensure that no individual could ever take control of AA. Wilson was content to be a first among equals while alive, though especially toward the end of his life he was the object of unsought veneration.

At present, Bill Wilson and, to a lesser extent, "Dr. Bob" are revered by most AA members, and Wilson's writings have attained the status of scripture in the minds of many. But, thanks largely to Bill Wilson, there is no charismatic leader of Alcoholics Anonymous, and it is exceedingly unlikely that there ever will be.

14) Does AA have an authoritarian, hierarchical structure? As for communal AA, definitely no. As for institutional AA, yes.

Thanks largely to the 12 traditions, communal AA is a model of anarchist organization. All AA groups are autonomous. There is no hierarchy giving orders to members, and it is very clear that the relatively few paid staffers are there to "serve," not to rule. Significantly, the structure of AA is often pictured as an inverted pyramid, with the members on top and the paid staff on the bottom.

The situation is different in institutional AA. There, almost all entities are corporations or government agencies, which, of course, are hierarchically organized and authoritarian in nature, with some giving orders and others taking them. In institutional AA, the staffers are there to rule (i.e., to force clients to accept AA and its premises), not to serve; they hold a great deal of power over their coerced clients.

15) Does AA insist on submission of the individual to the "will of God"? As for communal AA, yes and no. As for institutional AA, yes.

A quick reading of the 12 steps leaves little doubt about AA's position. Step 3 states, "[We] made a decision to turn our will and our lives over to the care of God," although it does add the qualifying phrase, "as we understood Him." Another important qualification is that making this decision is officially only a "suggestion," as are the other steps. In practice, however, at a very large majority of AA meetings a great deal of pressure is placed on members to embrace this and the other "suggestions." (And in institutional AA, the steps—with their submission of the individual to the will of God—are simply crammed down clients' throats.) Those who do not accept the 12 steps are frequently made to feel unwelcome at meetings. There is even a common put-down term for such members: "one steppers." This is a bad situation, though it would be far worse but for the official AA positions that the steps are only suggestions and that the only requirement for AA membership is a desire to stop drinking.

Another very important limiting factor is the fact that there is no charismatic leader, authoritarian hierarchy, or priest caste in AA to act as interpreter(s) of "God's will." There are many members who attempt to take on the priest's role, but, fortunately, thanks to AA's structure and official positions, their influence is somewhat limited. (Of course, in institutional AA, the paid staff often take on this role—at least to the extent of demanding acceptance of the 12 steps and other AA doctrines, and using coercion to force that acceptance—given that a great many of them are true believers and are in positions of authority over their institutions' clients.)

16) Is AA self-absorbed? Absolutely.

In his discussion of the failure of the Washingtonian Society (a 19th-century self-help organization similar in some ways to AA) in *Twelve Steps and Twelve Traditions*, Bill Wilson states, "Had they been left to themselves, and had they stuck to their one goal, they might have found the rest of the answer."[4] The implication, of course, is that AA has *the* answer.

Because AA believes that it has *the* answer to alcoholism, AA has shown a marked disinterest in experimental and clinical studies of alcoholism and alcoholism treatment, and in the many non-12-step approaches to alcohol abuse, some of which show considerable promise. Significantly, *none* of the dozens of books and pamphlets published by AA deal with these important topics. They all deal with AA itself, or, in a few cases, with day-by-day ways to remain sober.

Because of its organizational principles, AA has never contributed a dime toward medical research on the causes and the treatment of alcoholism. Further, because Alcoholics has *the* answer, AA as a whole has not only shown no interest in alternative alcohol-abuse treatments, but many AA members and front groups have shown marked hostility to both professional, non-12-step treatment and to nonreligious self-help programs such as Moderation Management, Rational Recovery, S.M.A.R.T. Recovery, and Secular Organizations for Sobriety.

While I was living in San Francisco in the late 1980s, S.O.S. members who put up flyers at AA hangouts told me that the flyers were ripped down very quickly. (None of the flyers attacked AA; they all simply advertised S.O.S. meetings.) One S.O.S. member told me that before finding S.O.S., he had phoned the local AA intergroup office to see if they could refer him to S.O.S., and the AA volunteer who answered told him, "I don't know how to contact them, and I wouldn't tell you if I did." The S.O.S. newsletter is filled with reports of similar and even more offensive incidents. This type of petty harassment evidently continues to the present, as a few days before sending this book to press I read on S.M.A.R.T. Recovery's web site of similar recent incidents involving SMART flyers.

As for institutional AA, for many years its "medical" experts have conducted a *jihad* against controlled drinking programs for alcohol abusers (and against researchers who advocate such programs—see Chapter 8 for details), despite a great deal of evidence that such programs work well—almost certainly better than AA.[5] One still frequently hears 12-stepping "experts" piously proclaiming, without a shred of evidence, that mere advocacy of controlled drinking causes alcoholics to drink themselves to death.[6]

What makes all of this especially harmful is that (as was shown in Chapter 7) AA is, at best, an effective treatment program for only a tiny fraction of alcohol abusers. Through its self-absorption (and the oft-trumpeted claim that AA is not only effective, but the *only* effective treatment program for alcoholism), AA is contributing *nothing* toward the understanding of alcohol abuse, and, under its own terms, is engaging in a vicious game of blame-the-victim (of what it insists is a deadly "illness") with the approximately 95% of "alcoholics" who are not members of AA. (According to AA, the reasons that they are not members of AA are their "shortcomings," "defects of character," and lack of "honesty.")

The attitudes and behaviors exhibited by AA toward clinical and experimental research and toward alternative treatment programs are not those of a rational organization dedicated to the effective treatment of alcoholism. Rather, AA's attitudes and behaviors are those of a dogmatic, self-absorbed religious cult.

Another facet of AA's self-absorption is seen in its members' attitudes toward the high aspirations some of their number held before they joined AA. Within AA, members generally view such aspirations as contributing to alcoholism, because they believe that lofty goals lead to frustration and feelings of failure, which in turn lead to drinking. Because of this, AA members normally offer very little encouragement of each others' interests and pursuits outside of AA, and sometimes actively discourage non-AA-related aspirations, as Dr. Margaret Bean comments, "This can set up a regressive spiral in which no one suggests that a member can or should strive for anything more challenging or interesting than sobriety."[7] And the proper way to strive for sobriety is within, and only within, AA itself.

17) Does AA have dual purposes? As for both communal and institutional AA, yes.

Communal AA presents itself as *the* answer to alcoholism, and thus a great many persons come to it for help in overcoming alcohol problems. But AA's purpose is *not* to help individuals overcome alcohol problems; rather, it's to indoctrinate them into AA's 12-step religious program. If the true purpose of AA was to help problem drinkers to overcome alcohol problems, AA would be greatly concerned about the research evidence indicating that AA is ineffective. One would further expect that AA would initiate studies of its own effectiveness versus that of other self-help groups and versus that of various forms of professional treatment. As well, one would expect that AA would recognize that one size does *not* fit all and would gladly refer individuals who come to it, but who don't like it, to other self-help groups. AA does none of these things. AA's sole purpose is to "carry this [religious] message to alcoholics."

Institutional AA goes even further. Many of its members make a great deal of money from utilizing AA's religious indoctrination program in a medical setting. The costliness and very questionable effectiveness of this kind of "treatment" seems not to bother them a whit. The evidence that 12-step inpatient treatment does no good and may in fact be harmful (see Chapters 7 and 8) is of no matter to them. They have The Truth, and they're quite content to go on making money from it.

18) Does Alcoholics Anonymous economically exploit its members? As for communal AA, no. As for institutional AA, yes.

All donations to communal AA are purely voluntary; there are no membership dues; and AA even places a cap of $1000 per year on individual donations to the organization by its members; and it will not accept *any* donations by non-members. Another example of communal AA's non-exploitive economic practices is provided by its literature: its books are very cheaply priced, with most selling for less than half of what comparable commercially published books would sell for, and its pamphlets are freely given away at meetings.

Institutional AA, on the other hand, charges many thousands of dollars to its clients for what was once so freely given (the AA program). That program is the centerpiece of most inpatient alcoholism treatment programs, and though they do provide some additional services, the high prices that they charge hardly seem justified.[8] The insurance industry apparently agrees with this assessment, and it has become increasingly reluctant to pay for 12-step inpatient treatment in recent years, with the result that occupancy rates and length of stay have both declined considerably over the last decade. This is hardly surprising given that the costs for a 28-day stay at a *cheap* facility run to about $10,000, and most institutions charge considerably more than that. For example, two swank Tucson-area 12-step treatment centers both charge approximately $20,000 for a 28-day stay[9]; and others charge far more.

19) Does AA employ deceptive recruiting techniques? Yes, arguably.

AA does no recruiting whatsoever in the normal sense of the word, that of actively seeking new members. But it could be argued that AA (or at least many of its members) does engage in deceptive recruiting by falsely representing AA as the only effective treatment for alcoholism. At newcomers' meetings, AA members almost invariably repeat the lies that alcoholism is a progressive, fatal disease, that alcohol abusers have no control after they take the first drink, and that AA is the only alternative to jails, institutions, or death. It should be emphasized, though, that most if not all of those who present this misinformation believe what they say, and are not engaging in deliberate deception as a recruiting tool.

As for 12-step treatment facilities, their ads commonly downplay or don't even mention that their primary focus is introduction to and participation in AA. This is understandable given that most people would be reluctant to pay $15,000 or $20,000 for something that is readily available for free. Newcomers lured through such advertising now form a large part of AA's membership. According to AA's 1996 membership survey brochure, 40% of AA members now list introduction at a treatment facility as one of the three "factors most responsible for [their] coming to A.A."

20) Is AA possessive? Does it go to lengths to retain members? No, absolutely not.

AA makes no organizational attempts whatsoever to retain members, and individual members normally do nothing beyond making a few friendly phone calls to other members who haven't shown up at meetings for a few days. In fact, AA's tendency in this area is so contrary to that of most cults that it creates serious problems for researchers attempting to gauge the effectiveness of AA, because of the difficulty of determining membership status. In AA, membership is purely a matter of self-definition; those who say they're members are members. Similarly, due to the extreme and unnecessary emphasis on anonymity *within* AA, it is next to impossible for anyone (including researchers and service workers within AA) to accurately track AA members.

21) Does AA provide a closed, all-encompassing environment? As for communal AA, no. As for institutional AA, yes.

Communal AA has no live-in facilities, though it does provide a social milieu into which many members plunge when first introduced to AA. This is entirely understandable. Many new members are quite lonely (having driven off friends, lovers, and family while drinking heavily), so the friendliness and acceptance provided by AA is quite attractive to them; in addition, AA provides a "safe" environment (at least at meetings and AA hangouts) in which they won't be tempted to drink.

The closest that communal AA comes to providing a closed, all-encompassing environment is the traditional "90 meetings in 90 days" recommendation. Newcomers who follow this recommendation spend many of their waking hours at AA meetings. Additionally, in the larger cities, there is usually at least one AA hangout, and there are often several clubs and other meeting places. Finally, there is an endless amount of AA volunteer work available to those who want to do it—answering the office phone, making 12th-step calls (to "carry the message" to other alcohol abusers), serving as meeting officers or as group service representatives, etc. So, those who want to can easily spend their entire social lives in the world of AA. In fact, members receive much encouragement to immerse themselves in this manner in "the A.A. way of life."

One anonymous member, in a Mensa special interest group publication, describes his plunge into the world of Alcoholics Anonymous:

> After sixty days in the hospital, I was permitted to go back to my job . . . There I became an A.A. addict. I went to a meeting almost every night. I volunteered for the intergroup desk so my Saturdays were spent talking to drunks on the phone.
>
> During this time, I progressed from closet atheist, to passive acceptance, to starry-eyed faith and entered that strange world where the creator of the universe was looking after minor problems like my sex life and auto battery.
>
> It occurred to me one day with a jolt that I had begun a life of superstitious ritual. It was a sort of magic formula of prayers, meetings, and shallow talk that was "keeping me sober."

As bad as this is, institutional AA is worse. In its guise as 12-step inpatient treatment facilities, institutional AA provides a textbook example of a closed, all-encompassing environment. As in all such environments, its purpose is ideological indoctrination—in this case, getting clients to embrace the AA "program" and its attendant baggage (the disease model, loss of control, etc.); patients' activities are to a very large extent dictated by the staff; many patients are coerced into being there (as an alternative to job loss, imprisonment, or professional decertification) and must at least feign acceptance of the prescribed ideology; institutions routinely restrict what patients may read to AA materials and related 12-step books and pamphlets; TV-viewing and radio-listening are routinely prohibited or greatly restricted; and clients' contact with those outside the institution is normally prohibited or greatly restricted. The only redeeming feature of the closed, all-encompassing environment of institutional AA is that the individuals subjected to it must endure it for a relatively short time—though for some that "short time" can seem like an eternity.

22) Is AA Millenarian? In short, no.

There is not a trace of millenarianism in AA.

23) Does AA employ violence, coercion, and harassment? As for communal AA, no. As for institutional AA, yes—at least as regards coercion.

The use of violence by communal AA is so contrary to AA traditions as to be unthinkable. Communal AA employs no coercion. And to the best of my knowledge, the relatively few incidents of harassment directed against groups such as SMART, which are often perceived as rivals to AA, have been mild—verbal rudeness and the ripping down of flyers—and all of them have been committed by over-zealous individual AA members. As far as I know, not a single incident of harassment of "rival" groups or outside critics has been committed by a paid AA service worker.

The case of dissidents within AA is somewhat different. Within the organization, dissident members (especially atheists) are very much second-class citizens; they're often scorned and belittled; and they find it virtually impossible to have their views presented in AA's literature. But these things are as nothing compared with the violence, coercion, and harassment employed by many cults.

In institutional AA, matters are very different. Institutional AA does not employ violence, but, within its own precincts, it does employ coercion and harassment. In this regard, it's important to remember that most patients are coerced into attendance. In many cases, their alternative to submitting to institutional AA is job loss, imprisonment, suspension or expulsion (from teams/leagues, in the case of sports figures), or decertification (in the case of medical personnel). In a very real sense, such persons are prisoners of the

12-step treatment industry. This gives their warders (the paid staff) tremendous leverage over them, and the warders usually take full advantage of that leverage; they customarily exert a great deal of pressure on such unwilling patients, the purpose of which is to break their resistance to AA. If this sounds like a scenario from *The Manchurian Candidate*, it's hardly surprising.

Conclusions

So, is AA a cult? As seems obvious from the foregoing, the answer will differ if you consider communal AA separately from institutional AA, or if you consider them as a single entity. As regards communal AA, the number of definite "yes" matches to the 23 characteristics listed above was 11, while the number of definite "nos" was 7; as for institutional AA, the number of definite "yeses" was 16, and the number of definite "nos" was only 3.

To put these results in context, I compared the scores achieved by communal and institutional AA with the scores based on my evaluation of five groups often labeled as cults: the Church of Scientology; the People's Temple; Unification Church (the Moonies); Synanon; and Kerista Village. None of these groups scored a "perfect" 23, but some came close. The Moonies came in at 22 "yeses"; the Church of Scientology and the People's Temple came in at 21 "yeses"; and Synanon came in with 20 "yeses." In contrast, the low scorer was Kerista Village, which had a score of 14.

To put these results further in perspective, I chose the ten cult attributes that I consider most important, and for those ten attributes I compared the scores of communal and institutional AA with those of the Church of Scientology, the Moonies, and Kerista Village. The attributes I consider most important are religious orientation; irrationality; dogmatism; mind control techniques; a charismatic leader; a hierarchical, authoritarian structure; submission of the individual to the will of God; economic exploitation; a closed, all-encompassing environment; and the use of violence, coercion, and/or harassment. I assigned the Moonies a score of a "perfect" 10 for these attributes and the Scientologists a score of 9 (their charismatic leader is dead), while Kerista Village came in with a score of 6, institutional AA with a score of 9, and communal AA with a score of 4.

Thus, if you consider communal AA separately from institutional AA, you're left with little choice but to conclude that AA isn't a cult—though it comes close, and does have many dangerous, cult-like tendencies. But if you regard institutional AA as an extension of communal AA and consider them as one, you're inexorably drawn to the conclusion that AA *is* a cult. Communal/institutional AA definitely isn't in the same league with vicious, destructive cults such as the Moonies and the People's Temple, but it does display an alarmingly high number of similarities to such groups. All in all, communal/institutional AA merits the description given to it by Stanton Peele: "Cult Lite."[10]

Finally, it's worth noting that while brazenly destructive cults such as the People's Temple and Heaven's Gate have considerably worse effects upon their individual members than AA has upon its individual members, the commonly cited religious cults have very limited numbers of followers (despite self-serving gross over estimates) and have very little influence in society at large, while AA is a mass organization with a very extensive hidden structure that has *tremendous* influence in society. Thus, it could well be that AA does more harm to society—and to far greater numbers of people—than all other religious cults combined.

---

1. A good example of this is provided by George Vaillant, in his influential *The Natural History of Alcoholism* (London: Harvard University Press, 1983). In his book, Vaillant strongly recommends that alcohol abusers be referred to AA, despite his own research evidence which indicates that AA participation at best does no good, and that relapse rates are higher for AA participants than for those who quit on their own.

2. *More Revealed*, by Ken Ragge. Henderson, Nevada: Alert Publishing, 1992, p. 137.

3. Ibid., pp. 127-138.

4. *Twelve Steps and Twelve Traditions*, by Bill Wilson. New York: Alcoholics Anonymous World Services, 1982, p. 178.

5. For an enlightening discussion of this holy war against controlled drinking and its advocates, see "Denial—of Reality and Freedom—in Addiction Research and Treatment," by Stanton Peele. *Bulletin of the Society of Psychologists in Addictive Behaviors*, 5(4): 149-166, 1986. Also available at http://www.frw.uva.nl/cedro/peele/lib/denial.html with a 1996 addendum.

6. See, for instance, "The American Psychiatric Association's attacks on Moderation Management—does the APA oppose moderate drinking treatment goals?," by Stanton Peele, at http://www..frw.uva.cedro/peele/debate/woody.html

7. "Alcoholics Anonymous," by Dr. Margaret Bean. *Psychiatric Annals*/5:3 March 1975, p. 10/86.

8. One expensive service commonly assumed necessary, detoxification, is actually necessary only to a small percentage of long-term, heavy drinkers. According to researcher Vince Fox, only 15% of heavy drinkers experience significant physical withdrawal symptoms when they stop drinking; and withdrawal symptoms are life threatening in only about 25% of those cases. In other words, only about 4% of long-term heavy drinkers experience life-threatening physical withdrawal symptoms. See *Addiction, Change & Choice: The New View of Alcoholism*, by Vince Fox. Tucson, Arizona: See Sharp Press, 1993, p. 191.

9. Telephone quotations to the author, July 7, 1997.

10. The term is used in Stanton Peele's "Online Library" web site's "Controversy" page: http://www.frw.uva.nl/cedro/peele/debate/

11

The Future of AA

In the first edition of this book, I came to the conclusion that AA and related 12-step groups would continue to expand indefinitely. I no longer believe that's true. I now believe that AA will, instead, begin to shrink within the next decade, and perhaps within the next five years, for reasons which I didn't cover in the 1991 edition of *Cult or Cure?*, even though the factors I cited in the earlier edition militating toward AA's growth are still operative.

AA is the direct spiritual descendant of Frank Buchman's Oxford Group Movement, and AA's program, the 12 steps, is a codification of the Oxford Group Movement's principles of individual powerlessness, divine guidance, confession, restitution, and continuance; as well, AA inherited many attitudes, tendencies, and stylistic features from the Oxford Groups, including anti-intellectualism, informality, wariness of formal organization (at least in communal AA), and a fondness for slogans and aphorisms. AA also inherited one other important Oxford Group Movement tendency, and one which has proven important in AA's history: *expansionism.*

Frank Buchman and the other members of the Oxford Groups were convinced that their "way of life" was the panacea for all of the world's ills. So, their overriding goal was to persuade *everyone* to adopt their it. Similarly, a great many AA members are equally convinced that the "AA way of life" (that is, following the 12 steps) is the panacea for all alcohol abusers. Many go further than that and, like their Oxford Group forebears, assert that their "way of life" is a panacea which should be adopted universally—by non-alcoholics as well as by alcoholics. One enthusiastic AA member put it like this: "I think we're talking about a revolution—ending war, people getting rid of their anger . . . I honestly think that if everyone worked the 12 steps it would change the world.[1] A most interesting aspect of this statement is that its author refers to 12-step programs as a "revolution," just as Oxford Group members referred to their reactionary religious program as a "revolution."

Additionally, AA members are told to "carry this message [AA's program] to alcoholics" in the 12th step, the culminating step of AA's program of "recovery." It's no surprise then, that expansionism has been one of the hallmarks of AA; and it's virtually certain that it will continue to be so.

This expansionism can easily be seen in the changing composition of AA's membership. As mentioned in the preceding chapter, the criteria defining an "alcoholic" (thus defining who is eligible for AA membership) were very restrictive in AA's early days. AA even refused to classify as alcoholic some drinkers who showed marked alcohol-related physical deterioration. At present, anyone showing *any* level of physical dependence, let alone deterioration, is automatically labeled "alcoholic" by AA members, and many persons who display no physical symptoms and whose drinking problems are relatively mild and of short duration are also so labeled. Thus, the pool of potential AA recruits has vastly expanded.

While the percentage of drinkers with serious drinking problems is probably no higher now than when AA was formed, the percentage of drinkers labeled "alcoholic" is far higher now than it was during AA's formative years in the late 1930s. Given the current mania for labeling nearly *everyone* an addict of some sort, it remains near certain that the criteria for defining someone as an "alcoholic" will remain very broad, though it's doubtful that they will expand much further; about the only way that that could happen would be to label anyone who drinks any amount of alcohol, no matter how tiny, as an "alcoholic."

Another sign of expansionism can be seen in the age of AA's members. In AA's early days, there were very few members under 30 years of age; and many members were doubtful that anyone younger than 30 *could* be an alcoholic, or at least doubtful that their problems were serious enough to cause them to want to stop drinking. Yet by 1989, 22% of AA's members were 30 or younger, and 3% of AA's members were *teenagers*.[2] Again, the pool of potential recruits for AA has greatly expanded.

Further evidence of AA's expansionism can be found in its attitude toward coercion. In its early days, AA was proud of being an all-volunteer organization. Today, AA embraces coercion. AA willingly cooperates with courts which routinely coerce drunk drivers and others guilty of alcohol-related offenses to attend AA meetings. As well, coerced participants make up a majority of the "clients" in 12-step treatment programs administered and overseen by AA addictions "professionals." In 1996, fully 40% of respondents to AA's triennial survey stated that a treatment center was one of the (up to) three most important factors "responsible for [their] coming to A.A.," and another 16% listed counseling as an important factor. As well, 9% listed"employer or fellow worker" (that is, EAP coercion); 8% listed "health care provider"; and those who were openly coerced made up a full 16% of the sample: 13% listed court orders; 3% listed correctional facilities.[3]

As well, at least some of those who listed "family" were certainly introduced to AA as a result of coercive "interventions," though it's impossible to tell what percentage from the data supplied. Thus, because of the multiple-choice option in the survey, as well as the vagueness of its wording, it's impossible to state what percentage of AA members belong to it primarily because of treatment centers, 12-step counseling programs, coerced attendance via court mandates or correctional facilities, or other forms of coercion. But it's a certainty that it's a very high percentage. In all likelihood, the percentage of current AA members who joined AA because of coercion is at least a third, and is probably in excess of 40%.[4]

As well, a huge number, probably a large majority, of the "professionals" and "para-professionals" employed by both inpatient and outpatient alcoholism treatment programs are zealous AA members who consider AA the be-all and end-all of alcoholism treatment. In many ways, AA serves *their* needs very well (though not the needs of most of their clients). It provides them with a program with all the answers, a simple program which they can "utilize" and "not analyze"; and if that program doesn't work for many clients, it's the fault of the clients' "defects of character" or "lack of honesty." So, not only does AA supply a ready-made program, it also supplies a convenient excuse for treatment failures. For these reasons, for the near future AA will undoubtedly continue to be a key part of a very large majority of treatment programs, and all too many inpatient programs will continue to consist of little more than a 14- or 28-day drying out period punctuated by daily AA meetings and group "therapy" sessions in which clients are pressured to admit that they are diseased "alcoholics" who need the intervention of a Higher Power to overcome their "alcoholism." And all this with a $20,000 bill falling due at the end of "treatment."

This is a comfortable arrangement for both AA and the 12-step treatment centers. The treatment centers provide AA with meeting space, a huge market for its literature, and a steady stream of new members, while AA provides the centers with cheap help (zealous, underpaid para-professionals) and the cheapest method of "treatment" imaginable. Given these realities, it would be very surprising if AA didn't continue to cooperate with agencies that coerce drinkers to attend its meetings, and didn't continue to be an integral part of a large majority of alcoholism treatment programs in the United States, at least for the next several years. In sum, AA's embracement of coercion is perhaps the clearest sign of AA's expansionism.

AA has also been expanding "overseas" (which, strange as it seems, includes Mexico), as well as in the United States and Canada. As of 1996, AA's overseas membership totaled 614,466—nearly 33% of AA's total membership of 1,866,281.[5] One area of particularly rapid expansion has been Latin America.

Given the inherent anti-political activism bias of AA's program, with its inward focus, its total neglect of social factors involved in the production of alcohol abuse, its emphasis upon individual powerlessness, and its insistence upon divine guidance as a panacea, one can only look upon AA's Latin American expansion with trepidation. Alcohol abuse is a terrible problem in many parts of Latin America, and it's unlikely that AA will be any more effective there than it has been elsewhere; AA, in fact, will undoubtedly *block* progress in dealing with alcohol abuse problems there. As well, it's difficult to see the political quietism inherent in AA's ideology as being anything other than a buttress for the inequitable social systems within which alcoholism flourishes in Latin America. Given the dimensions of the alcohol abuse problem, the lack of alternative treatment programs, the presence of business-as-usual regimes that welcome a message of political quietism, and the religion-soaked atmosphere in these countries (a not-surprising reality in lands where social misery reigns), it seems likely that, for better or for worse, AA will continue to expand in Latin America.

A development related to the expansion of AA is the proliferation of non-AA 12-step groups. In 1990, there were approximately 200 non-AA 12-step organizations, with a membership estimated in excess of 2 million.[6] That might have been a rosy estimate, as a Hazelden document I obtained in 1994 stated that there were "2,700,000 12-step individuals" and that "12-step membership has been flat for the last 3 years."[7] If correct, that would yield a non-AA 12-step membership of around 1.5 million in 1994. The figure is probably about the same today, given the "flat[ness]" of 12-step membership and the slight, but noticeable, decline in popular interest in 12-step organizations over the last few years.

One indication of this decline can be found in the number of articles about AA and other 12-step groups in *The Reader's Guide to Periodical Literature.* In the period 1985–1987, a total of 6 articles on AA appeared in indexed periodicals. That figure jumped to 8 articles in 1988 alone, and during the period 1988–1991, a total of 22 articles appeared. But during the following five years, 1992–1996, only 8 articles on AA appeared, with none at all in 1996. The numbers are similar for other 12-step groups. The category "Twelve-Step Organizations" first appears 1988, in which year 2 articles on non-AA 12-step groups were indexed. Interest in such groups peaked in the years 1990–1992, when indexed periodicals ran 13 articles on them. But during 1993–1995, only 3 articles appeared, with none at all in 1996.

(One feature of these articles bears comment: from the late 1980s on —for the first time since the mid 1960s—articles critical of AA have been appearing in the national media. Of the 32 articles on AA listed in the period 1987–1996, 6 were critical. The proportion of critical articles on other 12-step groups was almost twice as high. Of the 18 articles listed from that same period, 6 were critical. In 1997, one national news magazine even ran a cover article headlined, "What AA Won't Tell You."[8])

What is most surprising about the AA spinoffs is that groups having nothing to do with addictions have adopted the 12 steps as their "program," with only the most minimal alterations. Perhaps the most extreme example is Incest Survivors Anonymous. If the AA program, the 12 steps, were truly tailored to fit the needs of alcoholics (or addicts of any sort), it would seem grotesque that it be adopted as the program for *victims* of hideous, cruel abuse. (Should rape and molestation victims really adopt guiding principles which emphasize that *they* should make "amends" to those *they've* "harmed," take a *moral* inventory of *themselves*, and admit *their* "wrongs"?)[9]

But the 12 steps are *not* tailored to fit the needs of alcoholics and addicts. In fact, they're not tailored to fit the needs of *any* particular group. But for the mention of alcohol in the first step and the mention of alcoholics in the twelfth step, they are purely a set of religious principles advocated by Oxford Group Movement/Moral Re-Armament founder Frank Buchman and crystallized by AA co-founder Bill Wilson.

This fact explains a great deal. From early childhood, most persons the world over are taught that God and religious faith are the very essence of goodness; so, they're favorably inclined toward anything overtly religious, such as the 12 steps. At least in Christian countries, most are also taught, as part of their religious training, that their problems are purely their own responsibility, the results of their sins, and that only God has the power to remove those sins. So, most people are predisposed to accept 12-step religiosity with its insistence upon individual responsibility for alcoholism (or other "addictions"), individual helplessness, and the necessity of divine guidance.

But their inherent religiosity is only a partial explanation of the popularity of 12-step programs. There are many other reasons for their spread. One is loneliness. Loneliness is a terrible problem in American society, and people will flock to almost *anything* that relieves it—even 12-step meetings. In the case of AA, this factor is undoubtedly very important in the recruitment and retention of members. Alcohol abusers often drive off all or almost all of those close to them, and are quite socially isolated when they finally decide to quit drinking. Thus, AA, with its innumerable meetings, social functions, and opportunities for 12th-step work, becomes an important —sometimes the only—social outlet for many new members. One young AA member's comments lend support to this view of AA as a refuge from loneliness: "This is a place where I come and I don't feel alone anymore the way I used to when I was drinking and doing drugs."[10] While it's uncertain whether loneliness is as potent a motivating force in drawing new members to other 12-step groups, it is undoubtedly an important factor.

Another reason for the popularity of 12-step programs is the prevalence of rampant psychological pain in contemporary America society. The problems which 12-step programs presume to address are, in many cases, all too real. Because of the absence of affordable or free alternatives (or lack of knowledge of their existence), it seems only natural that a great many people turn to 12-step programs for help. Unfortunately, it's a virtual certainty that for the foreseeable future the socioeconomic system will continue to act as a human meat grinder, churning out generation after generation of emotionally damaged people replete with "addictions" and other "dependencies." If the current trends toward regressive distribution of wealth and income, and sadistic, punitive "solutions" continue—jails rather than job training, savage drug laws rather than a socially tolerant legal code, etc., etc.—it seems likely that the social meat grinder will accelerate the pace of its grisly work. So, it's a virtual certainty that these factors in the growth of AA and other 12-step groups will continue to operate and could well become even more potent than they are now.

Another factor explaining the popularity and expansion of 12-step groups is AA's tremendously effective propaganda machine. Until fairly recently, the portrayal of AA in the print media was uniformly favorable, with many articles being near adulatory, and having titles such as "The drunk who helped millions get sober"[11] and "Alcoholics Anonymous: the heart of treatment for alcoholism."[12] The film industry and television have, if anything, been even worse; they've painted an unrelievedly rosy picture of the group, as in movies such as *The Days of Wine and Roses* and *Clean and Sober.* There are three reasons for this favorable portrayal of AA in the mass media: 1) AA members have set up front groups to promote the 12-step approach under the guise of professional organizations, the NCADD being the prime example; 2) most reporters are woefully ill informed about addictions, tend to believe the misinformation they've been fed over the decades by AA and its allies, and tend to regard and rely upon AA's unidentified (anonymous) spokesmen and front groups, such as the NCADD and ASAM, as disinterested experts; and 3) because of AA's anonymity provisions, many AA members in the addictions professions and in the mass media are free to issue pro-AA pronouncements and to produce pro-AA pieces (as well as to attack AA's critics) without revealing their affiliation with AA. This is unlikely to change anytime soon. Even over the last decade, magazine articles critical of AA and the 12-step movement (as listed in *The Reader's Guide to Periodical Literature*) have been outnumbered by pro-AA/pro-12-step pieces by a ratio of more than 3 to 1.

Yet another, and undoubtedly the most important, reason for AA's growth over the last three decades has been the systematic use of coercion by the courts, prisons, employers, and 12-step treatment industry to force people into AA. This has been tremendously important in AA's growth; as indicated in Chapters 7 and 8, at a bare minimum, a third of AA's current members were coerced into first attending, and the figure could be considerably higher.[13] In many ways, over the last three decades AA has been in the position of a snake being force-fed mice—not that the snake was all that unwilling.

A final reason for the popularity and growth of 12-step groups is their anti-intellectualism. As Luther Burbank once remarked, "The greatest torture in the world for most people is to think." Sadly, this appears to be true, and 12-step programs, with their "utilize, don't analyze," "your best thinking got you here" philosophy, seem ideal social vehicles for those wishing to escape the "torture" of critical thought. For many members, 12-step group-think organizations form a comfortable herd in which they can submerge themselves. (This may seem extreme, but consider the cliched remarks of many members, often consisting almost entirely of time-worn AA slogans and folk sayings, at almost every meeting; consider also the many "AA successes" who have virtually no social life outside of AA.) Given the miserable state of the educational system and the smothering influence of fundamentalist Christianity and other anti-intellectual religions, it seems virtually certain that the anti-intellectualism of 12-step programs will continue to be a powerful attractive force.

But there is also reason to think that the growth of AA (and the 12-step movement) will soon end, and that AA will in fact begin to shrink in size in the near future. I believe that the shrinkage will begin within the next ten years, and perhaps within the next five. There are several reasons that this seems probable.

First is the shrinkage of the inpatient treatment industry. Over the last decade, the average length of stay, and occupancy rates have both dropped, and over the last two or three years it seems as if the number of inpatient facilities has begun to decline. As insurers become even more reluctant to pay for expensive, ineffective 12-step inpatient treatment, these trends seem likely to continue.

Second, because of recent state and federal court decisions, coercion into 12-step group attendance/12-step "treatment" by the courts and penal system is on the way out. While it's still common in many parts of the country, as more and more suits against mandated attendance are filed and won, this source of members for AA will simply shrivel up, as it's already doing.

Taken together, these two factors will diminish the number of persons coerced into AA membership. Coerced persons now constitute at least a third—and probably considerably more—of AA's members, so this will be a serious blow to AA. There's some indication that at least one of these factors is already having an effect: since 1989, the percentage of teenagers in AA has fallen by two-thirds, from 3% to 1%. One likely explanation for this drop is a decline in the number of "interventions" with teenagers and their coercion into 12-step treatment. (I simply can't conceive of any significant number of teenagers being attracted to AA meetings with their bad coffee, cigarette smoke, drunkalogues, and predominance of older folks.)

A third reason for AA's probable decline is that it simply doesn't work very well. As discussed in Chapter 7, the controlled studies of AA have found that it is, quite simply, ineffective—no better than no treatment at all. And in the end the truth will out. Despite AA's well-oiled propaganda machine and its unmerited near adulation in the mass media, in the long run an organization that purports to be *the* answer to a serious personal and social problem, but which is utterly ineffective, cannot endure.

A fourth reason to believe that AA will begin to shrink in the near future is that the stranglehold of AA upon the mass media is loosening. Over the last decade, as indicated above, a number of articles critical of AA have appeared in the mass media (while there were *none* over the previous 20 years), and during the same time a spate of books critical of AA and its concepts has also appeared. Titles such as Stanton Peele's *Diseasing of America*, Ken Ragge's *The Real AA*, Jack Trimpey's *The Small Book*, Vince Fox's *Addiction, Change and Choice*, Albert Ellis's and Emmett Velten's *When AA Doesn't Work for You*, and the present volume come to mind. The continuing appearance of a steady stream of critical books, periodicals, and magazine articles seems a near certainly, and it thus seems almost equally certain that AA's stranglehold upon the media will be a thing of the past within the next 10 to 20 years. And with a more realistic portrayal of AA in the mass media, AA's volume of walk-in traffic will undoubtedly greatly diminish.

A related development is the appearance and endurance of the various nationwide "alternatives" to AA. In the early 1980s, there was only one such group: Women for Sobriety (WFS). Today, there are five: in addition to WFS, we have Moderation Management, Rational Recovery, Secular Organizations for Sobriety, and S.M.A.R.T. Recovery. All of these groups have now survived for at least several years, and it seems reasonable to expect that at least two or three of them will prosper in the coming years. As they do so, they'll become better known, and AA's reputation as the only game in town will disappear; and with its disappearance, AA's volume of walk-in traffic will again decline.

A final reason to believe that AA will shrink significantly over the next decade or two is AA's ideological fossilization. AA will not be able, as it has not been able, to adapt its program to changing social realities. AA's membership characteristics and organizational structure ensure this.

To a great extent, AA's direction in the coming years will be determined by its members, especially those members actively involved in AA's administration. For the most part, these people are quite conservative; AA's service structure is staffed by members deeply imbued with AA tradition who love the 12-step program just the way it is, and who would fight to keep it from changing.

This is strongly related to the religious nature of AA's program. For many, probably most, AA members, the 12 steps and related beliefs are articles of faith; and it would be as unrealistic to expect AA believers to alter their central beliefs as it would be to expect Catholics to alter theirs. Additionally, as indicated in AA's *Service Manual*, approval by three-quarters of *all* registered AA groups would be required to make any changes in the heart of AA's program, the 12 steps. Anyone familiar with AA will recognize that this makes changes in the steps, AA's ideological core, utterly impossible. In spite of changes in the composition of its membership, it seems certain that as long as AA survives it will continue to be what it has been since its articles of faith were first published in 1939: a religiously oriented ideological fossil.

These six things—the shrinkage of inpatient treatment; the drying up of court/penal-mandated attendance; AA's ineffectiveness; the loosening of its stranglehold on the media; the appearance and endurance of the "alternative" self-help groups; and AA's inability to adapt its program to changing social conditions—virtually ensure that AA will begin to shrink significantly within the near future, perhaps within the next five to ten years; and they make it entirely possible that AA will cease to exist as a significant social movement by the second quarter of the 21st century.

---

1. "Setting Store by Personal Recovery," by Joan Smith. *San Francisco Examiner*, December 16, 1990, p. F6.

2. "Comments on A.A.'s Triennial Surveys." New York: Alcoholics Anonymous World Services, 1990, p. 2.

3. "Alcoholics Anonymous 1996 Membership Survey" brochure.

4. Figures taken from AA's 1996 membership survey brochure. For the calculations used in determining the percentage of AA's members there because of coercion, see Chapter 7, p. 86, endnote 4.

5. "1996 Survey," op. cit.

6. "Going to Church the 12 Step Way," by Don Lattin. *San Francisco Chronicle*, December 17, 1990, pp. A1 & A6.

7. This information came from a one-page handout given out at the "Addictions Roundtable" by Hazelden's marketing director at the American Booksellers Association's annual trade show in Los Angeles on May 30, 1994.

8. "The Drinking Dilemma," by Nancy Shute. *U.S. News & World Report*, September 8, 1997, pp. 55-65.

9. Apparently some 12-steppers think so. In *More Revealed* (Henderson, Nevada: Alert Publishing, 1992, p. 178), Ken Ragge recounts an instance from his personal experience in which an AA member who as a boy had been sexually molested by a priest, made "amends" to the priest by apologizing for being angry about the molestation. Ragge also recounts another episode in which a woman who had been gang raped was urged to make "amends" to the rapists.

10. "Sobering Times for A.A." *Time*, July 10, 1995, pp. 49-50.

11. *U.S. Catholic*, February 1989, pp. 10-12.

12. *Aging*, No. 361, 1990, pp. 12-17.

13. See Chapter 7, footnote 4, page 86.

A

Secular Self-Help Groups

Important changes for the better have taken place in the American self-help field over the last 15 years. In the early 1980s, there was only *one* secular alternative to Alcoholics Anonymous for problem drinkers, and that alternative—Women for Sobriety—was available to only half the population. At present, five significant secular self-help groups exist here. Four are abstinence programs, and the fifth, Moderation Management, is a moderation program.

It is, perhaps, also significant that whereas all previous alcohol abuse self-help groups were based on their founders' personal experiences and theories, the two most recent entries in the field, Moderation Management and S.M.A.R.T. Recovery, are, respectively, based on modern research findings and modern psychological theory.

To avoid any appearance of favoritism, I invited all five secular self-help groups to submit self-descriptive statements of up to 1500 words that I would run unedited, if they so desired. Four of the groups, Moderation Management (MM), Rational Recovery (RR), S.M.A.R.T. Recovery (SMART), and Women for Sobriety (WFS), submitted such statements. Only Secular Organizations for Sobriety (SOS) did not respond to my request for a self-descriptive piece. (I contacted SOS twice in writing, but received no reply.) Hence, I've retained the section on SOS that appeared in the original edition of this book, but I've updated it, edited it, and shortened it.

The pieces on the various groups were written by the following persons: MM—Audrey Kishline (MM's founder); RR—Jack Trimpey (RR's founder); SMART—Phil Tate (SMART's vice-president) and Emmett Velten; SOS—Chaz Bufe; WFS—Jean Kirkpatrick (WFS's founder). The authors of all of these descriptions, and not the author, editors, or publisher of this book, are responsible for the accuracy of the statements they make here (with the single exception of the section on SOS, written by the author). As well, all of the material in these descriptions remains the copyrighted property of its authors. Finally, I want to make plain that there are a number of assertions in some of these self-descriptions with which I flatly disagree. I also want to make plain that I do not endorse any of these programs over any others. Different approaches work for different people.

Here are the groups in (mostly) their own words:

Moderation Management

Moderation Management is a program for people who are concerned about their drinking. It is a program for people who want to take action to cut down or quit drinking *before* they experience serious personal or health problems. The MM program provides a simple nine-step approach to help members take "small steps" toward leading healthier, balanced lives.

I had a drinking problem nine years ago, and when I sought help was immediately labeled an "alcoholic" and told that I had a "disease" which could not be cured, but that could be arrested by total abstinence and attendance at A.A. meetings for life. The alternative, they said, was death, jail, or insanity. I was told that there was only one way to solve my problem: the 12-step A.A. program. I bent—and was bent—to their will.

In the hospital ward my vital signs were routinely taken. I obediently swallowed my daily vitamin pill and attended individual and group therapy, both of which included a heavy dose of religious/spiritual instruction for my supposed "disease." The expensive "medical treatment," as it turned out, was little more than prolonged indoctrination into the 12-step program of A.A. Fine for some, not for me.

The result? Things got worse. I felt depressed. I had been told that I was powerless, sick, and diseased. I was told that after one drink I would lose all control and would drink myself into oblivion. Initially after treatment my drinking became worse, and I became a binge drinker. Then after a number of years, during which time I grew up, took on more of life's responsibilities, and matured, I began to question the alocholic diagnosis. I began to drink again and was successful at drinking moderately.

I wondered why I had not been offered the option of moderation when I was in treatment, and why I had never been told that such an option even existed. This motivated me to do some research. I read the major authors in the field of alcohol studies and discovered that a large number of them had rejected many of the conventional ideas about heavy drinking, including the notion of "alcoholism as a disease." My research also revealed that ideas about the alleged inevitable progression (of the "disease"), loss of control, and genetic transmission were not defensible.

I learned that drinking is not like pregnancy—an either/or proposition—but a position on a scale from total abstinence to alcohol dependence (as measured by many diagnostic tools.)

My greatest discovery was that the achievement of moderate drinking is not only a reasonable and acceptable recovery goal for many people who have had a problem with alcohol, but that it was the most frequently chosen and attained form of recovery for beginning stage problem drinkers.

In treatment-outcome studies it is now common to report the number of clients who have returned to moderate, responsible drinking. Controlled studies, under laboratory conditions, have conclusively shown that a significant number of problem drinkers are capable of moderating their drinking, given the motivation and opportunity to do so.

In time I recognized that the abuse of alcohol is something a person does, not something—a condition—that a person has. It's a behavior, exacerbated by habit, and although not a disease as such, it can produce diseases such as hypertension and cirrhosis. The 20-cup-a-day coffee drinker does not get "caffeineism," nor does the heavy smoker get "nicotineism"; both, however, can suffer physical and psychological damage as a result of their behaviors.

Armed with the facts, I wondered how many people could benefit from a program oriented toward needs similar to mine. I wondered how many problem drinkers would be motivated to address their drinking problems sooner if a support program were available to them that did not insist on total abstinence, or a religious/spiritual program as essential to change, or a program that would not label them with that nasty word "alcoholic." Would a support program for them be of help?

Sure, why not? Again, I went to work and wrote dozens of letters of inquiry to significant people in the field of alcohol studies. I offered my ideas and asked for help. The replies were many and encouraging.

I read papers in which I learned that the option of moderated drinking had long been offered in Great Britain, Germany, Australia, and the Scandinavian countries. Then I discovered a Canadian moderation training program started by Martha Sanchez-Craig, on which I based MM's guidelines and limits for moderate drinking.

Heavy drinkers have long had their choice of total abstinence programs —S.M.A.R.T. Recovery, Rational Recovery, Alcoholics Anonymous, Women for Sobriety, Secular Organizations for Sobriety, and others. But the millions of problem drinkers in the United States did not have the benefit of a program tailored to their needs. They were often misdiagnosed as alcoholics or simply wouldn't enter the system at all.

That is why I started MM.

The first MM group met in Ann Arbor, Michigan in December of 1993. For one whole year we only had this one group. Then in 1994 there were five groups, and today there are 50 in 38 states. Two groups in Canada are forming, and now that the program has received media attention in Great Britain, a group is forming there.

MM is neither a panacea nor a viable option for everyone; some people need a total abstinence program. In MM, we provide information concerning all self-help-support programs (I invite all support programs to do the same.) MM stresses personal responsibility. It is up to the individual with the drinking problem to decide on the best course of action. Most people will try to moderate before they go on to abstinence. In MM we support their right to make their own choice. Though MM is primarily a program for moderated drinking, we also have some members who remain in the MM program, even though they have chosen abstinence as their recovery goal. This is consistent with the goal of our program: to reduce one's alcohol consumption to a *level* which no longer causes life problems. For some this level must be zero.

The premises of the MM program are, in part, a development of ideas by Dr. Martha Sanchez-Craig, Dr. Stanton Peele, Dr. Herbert Fingarette, Vince Fox, John Craig, Dr. William Miller, and Dr. Alan Marlatt, in addition to many problem drinkers who have shared their experiences with me.

In summary, MM is an educational and early prevention program designed not for the chronic and heavy drinkers whose lives have been shattered by their consumption of alcohol; MM is designed for people who have perceived a potentially serious problem with alcohol and who want to do something about it so as to achieve a healthy and non-destructive approach to responsible and moderated drinking and living. We insist that people are responsible for their own lives and behaviors. But sometimes they need a little help, and that help is now available to them.

We offer information about alochol, a suggested reading list, a web site (http://comnet.org/mm/), an on-line support group, and a support group for chairpersons in MM. We also provide our entire MM Group Folder on our web site, for those interested in starting and chairing a group. To find out where your local group is located, be sure to check out our web site. Moderation Management Network, Inc. is a nonprofit, tax-exempt organization. Our groups are anonymous, and there is a suggested $4.00-per-meeting membership fee.

Our entire program is detailed in the book *Moderate Drinking: The Moderation Management Guide* (published by Crown).

Contact information: Moderation Management Network, Inc.
P.O. Box 27558
Golden Valley, Minnesota 55427
http://comnet.org/mm/

Rational Recovery

Rational Recovery (RR) is largely the work of Jack and Lois Trimpey, a handful of RR Center directors, and several thousand self-recovered people who have volunteered to disseminate information on self-recovery in their own communities. RR began in 1986 as a tiny consumer revolt in California that grew into an international self-recovery movement. After over a decade of trial and error, RR has finally developed a highly sophisticated method for immediate self-recovery from any substance addiction, Addictive Voice Recognition Technique® (AVRT). AVRT, which is a set of instructions on how to summarily quit an addiction, is more important than all of the research that has ever been done on the subject of addiction.

Rational Recovery takes the mystery out of addiction and recovery, and introduces some order into a field characterized by linguistic and theoretical chaos. We do not label participants or their families "alcoholics" or "co-dependents," and we point out blatant logical errors such at the idea that people can be "enabled" to do what they fully intend to do. We understand clearly that the yearning to continue using a substance that has already caused serious problems is the Addictive Voice, and that people who are capable of moderation do not experience such yearnings. AVRT is the foremost abstinence program, since it is based on the experience of self-recovered people, and actually teaches the ability to unconditionally and permanently abstain.

One of the early errors was the use of cognitive-behavioral therapy as a substitute for the spiritual prescriptions of Alcoholics Anonymous. We discovered that it is fruitless to undertake personal improvement as a condition of abstinence, no matter what means is chosen to improve oneself. Abstinence alone, we found, is the sine qua non of addiction recovery, and produces improvements that exceed the most optimistic hopes of facilitated self-improvement. This discovery has extreme importance at a time when alternatives to AA are finally being sought in some quarters.

Another error was the emphasis on the group experience as an ingredient of addiction recovery. AVRT is not a group-oriented approach, although local RR Coordinators meet in person or by phone with addicted people to assure them that self-recovery is commonplace and relatively easy. AVRT is the collected wisdom of self-recovered people, condensed into a simple, easy-to-learn, educational format. With AVRT, anyone who wants to quit drinking may completely recover in less than one week. One study of RR participants by New York University Medical School found 74% abstinent, without regard to the substance used. Accordingly, the abstinent outcomes at our RR Centers nationwide are in the 75% to 80% range. The outcomes we describe, however, are commonplace and well-supported by scientific studies showing that the large majority of addicted people, in the 70% to 80% range, self-recover. You probably know someone yourself who one day simply quit drinking or using. That person probably didn't make a big deal of it, and I doubt that a network TV anchor pulled up with a satellite hookup to announce to the world that someone had actually quit drinking without attending recovery groups or entering an expensive treatment center. People just get fed up and quit. They do it all the time. AVRT is approximately how each one of them did it.

Health professionals call this quitting behavior "spontaneous remission," or "maturing out." These science-spouting professionals don't know what they are talking about. They were, for the most part, never addicted to anything more potent than iced tea. There is nothing spontaneous about addiction recovery, and people don't mature out of addictions. They struggle against addictions, from fear for their lives, and many of them fail and die. But those who do make it have a common story, one which RR has identified and named AVRT. It sounds like this:

> Something bad happened, for the umpteenth time. I got up the next day and thought about the big picture, about my whole life, and I decided that there was no place for alcohol/drugs in my life any longer. I knew that moderation was not realistic, because my desire for the substance exceeded moderation, and the substance impaired my ability to stop as planned. So I decided that I would never drink or use again, and when I made that decision I felt good inside. I knew that I was taking responsibility for myself and my behavior, and that my life would eventually become more enjoyable. But the next day, it wasn't easy. I woke up wanting a drink/fix, and my body screamed out for it. I knew it was just the physical addiction talking to me, so I ignored it, and it went away. The next day was easier, but now the voice in my head sounded different, more friendly, more seductive. But I knew what I was dealing with, an inner enemy that didn't care about me or anything I loved; it would sacrifice it all for a little drink right now. I started learning how this thing worked, and soon it was easy to spot it anywhere I went. It followed me around, trying to get me to drink for many months, but it grew weaker, as if it somehow knew I was in control. It's been many years now since my last drink, I forget how many. I don't even remember so much why I quit doing alcohol and drugs, but I know for sure that I will never drink or use again. The thing inside still haunts me every once and a

while, just to check me out, but I always chuckle at it, my old enemy which is now a faint, pathetic whisper. Today, I am reasonably happy and free to go where I choose and associate with whomever I choose. I have no purpose in attending recovery group meetings, or associating with people simply because they have also had troubles with alcohol or drugs. In fact, those people give me a bad name, "alcoholic," and their self-imposed burden of lifelong recovery is sometimes shifted onto me, such as when I mention that I don't drink, I may be asked, " what's your home group?" or when I apply for insurance I may be considered at risk. I can live down my own stupidity back then, but it seems I will never live down the disease idea, which haunts me from time to time.

There are many variations on this theme, but it all boils down to the same thing, which is so simple that even a child can understand it, or even explain it to an alcoholic or drug addict. Any addicted person, which includes all those who consider themselves "in recovery," might possibly recover completely just by reading the above passage. Addiction is a big problem; recovery is not.

In our culture, however, addiction recovery is practically forbidden. When people act as in the passage above, it is said that they didn't really have "the problem" in the first place. Ironically, they know something more important than all the research ever done on addictions: how to quit once and for all. Were it not for a nonprofit organization, Alcoholics Anonymous, self-recovered people would stand as examples for others who still drink or use against their own better judgment. Instead, the failure of AA founder, Bill Wilson, to remain sober on his own has been held up by the United States government as the moral standard for every single addicted American. Consequently, America has the greatest problem of mass addiction of any society in human history.

Wilson's followers, all of whom stubbornly refuse to quit drinking and using drugs for good, have succeeded in convincing mainstream America that those who have independently quit drinking or using drugs are fundamentally different from those who still drink in spite of problems. To anyone who still drinks, they say, "You have continued to drink/use in spite of your problems, and that proves beyond doubt that you are incapable of doing so. Your way obviously doesn't work, so the only means for you to quit is our way. We are the ones with real problems like yours, and we are the only ones who have lived to tell the story. If you do not accept what we say, you will continue to drink, just as you have all along. To continue doing the same thing and expect different results is insane, but you are not truly insane, just diseased with alcoholism like the rest of us. We are restored to sanity, but we are still diseased, so we keep coming back because, like you, we cannot succeed on our own."

Now, this is pretty powerful stuff to be foisted upon a desperate, addicted person, especially when backed by professional sanction and courts of law. Add to this, that addicted people, by definition, are impassioned to continue drinking or using, and you have a lethal concoction. "Take what you like and leave the rest," the groupers say, when they notice wide-eyed incredulity typical of the newcomer. And that they do. Ninety five percent of all newcomers leave the group within one year, fifty percent within one month, taking with them the disease concept which "marks" them to continue drinking/using, and of course, they leave the rest, the insipid steps, behind. When trouble returns, as is often the case when people continue drinking or using, the newcomers are no longer newcomers. They are becoming seasoned veterans, crawling back to mother group, increasingly vulnerable to the persistent message of powerlessness, surrender of critical judgment and control, and above all, mistrust of their own thought processes. Many people struggle for decades, in and out of AA and treatment centers, never suspecting that they are victims of a cult which uses highly sophisticated techniques to entangle addicted people in their snares.

A most important discovery by Rational Recovery is that newly abstinent people immediately feel better and do better—across the board. Making a Big Plan—a commitment to permanent abstinence—results in a sense of relief and hope for a better life. This contradicts the predictions of doom by recovery groupers for people who "just" quit drinking without accepting AA as their personal savior.

Nearly 100% of Rational Recovery participants have had substantial exposure to Alcoholics Anonymous. AVRT is rapid deprogramming, a jolt back to one's own senses and original family values. Where we have groups, they are limited to brief exposure. Participants are warned, "Don't keep coming back here. This isn't a support group, and is not a healthy practice to mingle with other people who are insecure about their own abstinence. Please do not form new relationships here; make friends with normal people based on common interests—not common problems. Be sure to read *Rational Recovery: The New Cure for Substance Addiction* (Pocket Books, 1996) so we don't have to repeat what's in print. Subscribe to *The Journal of Rational Recovery* to keep abreast of issues that directly affect you. No, we do not sign attendance slips for courts; we will not participate in any court's misguided policy of forcing people to attend recovery groups. If you have questions about self-recovery or AVRT, ask them now. Most people catch on to AVRT very quickly and recover right away, never to drink or use again; if you want to take strong action beyond a few visits here, contact a Rational Recovery Center, where you can receive skilled instruction on AVRT."

Rational Recovery has two related agendas, (1) to disseminate information on planned abstinence, and (2) to bring about social change. RR has achieved many important "firsts" thus far, including being the first to announce that addiction treatment is dead, the first to declare addiction treatment a fraudulent practice, the first to identify the professionals in the addictions field as merchants of misguidance, and the first to identify the recovery group movement as a prime cause of mass addiction. These insights come solely by looking through the lens of AVRT, which exposes our entire addiction care system as a creation of the Addictive Voice itself. AVRT, now a finished product, contains all of the information America needs to solve the problem of mass addiction and build a better future on its original platform of values.

Rational Recovery Political and Legal Action Network (RR-PLAN) is an association of activists who challenge federal, state, and local governments which perpetuate the AA cartel. We use freedom of information laws and public records acts to document the universal fact that no public addiction treatment agency collects or reports abstinence outcome statistics for addiction treatment programs. We also request records indicating the extent to which AA members are employed in public addiction programs. The agencies invariably conceal this information, even though everyone knows that grossly disproportionate numbers of AA members work at addiction programs and their funding and licensing agencies, demonstrating that AA members in public agencies have a higher loyalty to AA than to the society they purport to serve.

RR has ushered in the post-treatment era, when addiction recovery is the responsibility of addicted people and not of society. We present a new image of formerly addicted people who, by holding themselves to a higher standard than tentative sobriety, have become first-class citizens. Our centers nationwide are vital resources providing information on AVRT, one of the most important bodies of information in the modern world. Put the word out, and we can cause a very pleasant revolution.

Contact information: Rational Recovery
P.O. Box 800
Lotus, CA 95651
Phone: 530-621-4374 or 530-621-2667.
http://www.rational.org/recovery/

Secular Organizations for Sobriety

Secular Organizations for Sobriety's (SOS's) origin dates to a magazine article, "Sobriety Without Superstition," written by Jim Christopher, which appeared in the Summer 1985 issue *of Free Inquiry* magazine. It recounted

Christopher's struggle to overcome his drinking problem, and the non-religious approach he had devised to achieve sobriety. The article generated an enthusiastic response, and two years later *Free Inquiry*'s publisher, the Council for Democratic and Secular Humanism (CODESH), decided to sponsor the new nonreligious recovery program, SOS (Save Our Selves/ Secular Organizations for Sobriety).

Christopher convened the first SOS meeting in November 1986 in North Hollywood, California. At the time, SOS didn't have an office; all it had was one weekly meeting, a telephone and an answering machine. In October 1987, CODESH began its support of the new organization, and within a few months SOS began to publish its quarterly newsletter. Despite having no office, an unpaid coordinator, no literature beyond the newsletter and a few amateurishly produced flyers and brochures, in 1988 SOS expanded into a national organization with, reportedly, over 100 chapters scattered across the country, many of them in Northern California. In that year, SOS received a boost with publication of Jim Christopher's book, *How to Stay Sober: Recovery Without Religion.* In 1989, SOS published *Unhooked: Staying Sober and Drug Free,* Christopher's second book; and in that same year, SOS began the process of formal incorporation.

SOS has no structured recovery program comparable to those of AA, MM, RR, SMART or WFS. SOS does have, however, Suggested Guidelines for Sobriety, which boil down to "acknowledg[ing] that we are alcoholics or addicts" and that "we can not and do not drink or use, no matter what. Since drinking or using is not an option for us, we take whatever steps are necessary to continue our Sobriety Priority lifelong." In other words, SOS places great emphasis on overcoming "denial," making sobriety one's most important priority in life, and doing whatever it takes to stay sober (in the AA sense of the word—totally abstinent).

In form, SOS meetings resemble nothing so much as the most informal of AA discussion meetings, albeit without a hint of religiosity. They're generally held in schools, hospitals, library meeting rooms, and even, occasionally, in churches. As of the late '80s and early '90s, however, the ratio of men to women was different in SOS than in AA; whereas only 35% of AA members are female, roughly 50% of SOS members were female at the time. (I have no information about the ratio today.)

One major difference between AA meetings and SOS meetings is that nonreligious refugees from AA often show up at SOS meetings and, at least at first, spend quite a bit of time venting about the condescension, hostility, and put-downs they were subjected to at AA meetings. SOS meeting facilitators normally recognize the value of such venting, but generally try as quickly as possible to steer discussions back to methods of staying sober.

In early 1990, Jim Christopher moved to Buffalo, New York, the home of *Free Inquiry* and CODESH, where he accepted a CODESH-funded position as coordinator of the SOS National Clearinghouse and began to work full time for SOS. One result of this was an improvement in the quantity and quality of SOS printed materials. In 1996, however, Christopher moved back to Southern California, which is where SOS headquarters is now located. Despite the move, I believe that CODESH is still providing financial support to SOS.

It's difficult to say how large SOS is at present, as SOS did not respond to my two written requests for a self-descriptive piece. SOS's web site, however, lists 23 meetings scattered across the nation as of mid-July 1997. It seems probable that there are at least some additional SOS meetings in various parts of the country.

Contact information: Secular Organizations for Sobriety
6632 Grosvenor Blvd.
Marina del Rey, CA 90066
Phone: (310) 821-8430

Self Management and Recovery Training

Introduction

Self Management And Recovery Training, usually called SMART or SMART Recovery, was incorporated in 1992 and has been operating under the name, S.M.A.R.T. Recovery, since 1994. It is a not-for-profit program of free, rational self-help and support for people who cause themselves problems through alcohol, drugs, or other addictions and who want to stop doing so. SMART focuses on teaching practical ideas and methods many people find helpful as they work to build less painful, happier, healthier lives.

SMART uses cognitive-behavioral self-help methods, especially those of Rational Emotive Behavior Therapy (REBT), originated by Dr. Albert Ellis, including its famous ABC format. While the primary focus in SMART is helping people overcome addictive behaviors, SMART offers people ways to address problems in living, such as anxieties, depression, and anger, in addition to addictive behaviors. SMART also teaches relapse prevention methods and ways that people can resolve ambivalence about quitting substance use and other addictive behaviors.

SMART's self-help meetings are discussion groups, not counseling or therapy, and they focus on SMART's four-point program: (1) build and maintain motivation to abstain; (2) learn how to cope with urges; (3) learn to manag e thoughts, feelings, and actions, using REBT's ABCs and other methods; (4) build an enjoyable life that constructively balances momentary and enduring satisfactions.

History and Background

The SMART program was founded in 1994 when a split over program content and direction developed between Rational Recovery's founder, Jack Trimpey, and the majority of the members of the Board of Directors of Rational Recovery's nonprofit arm, who then established SMART. Though SMART and Rational Recovery are now two, they retain some similarities. One difference is that SMART remained a non-profit organization, whereas Rational Recovery did not.

In its program, SMART retained the use of cognitive-behavioral self-help methods to help people learn to address problems in living in addition to addictive behaviors. RR originally did so—the "rational" in Rational Recovery came from Rational Emotive Behavior Therapy. Trimpey, however, made RR's focus AVRT, addictive voice recognition technique, itself a cognitive intervention directly targeting desires for alcohol or other drugs. In 1994 he publicly eschewed REBT and most other cognitive-behavioral interventions, holding that they could often be harmful in self-help for addictions. The then-RR board of directors did not agree with this change in direction, and made a clean break with RR's for-profit arm by changng the nonprofit organization's name to S.M.A.R.T. Recovery. Since that time SMART has continued to provide free self-help meetings using the approach upon which RR was originally based—Rational Emotive Behavior Therapy, and other forms of cognitive-behavioral therapy.

The Structure of SMART

Besides its volunteer Board of Directors, SMART has two part-time employees, and a professional office manager, who staff the central office. All other participants are volunteers. They include "coordinators" and "advisors." Coordinators lead the self-help meetings. Most are lay persons, usually with a history of addiction, who like and use the SMART principles. Besides establishing and leading self-help meetings, coordinators do local public relations. SMART also includes "advisors." Advisors work with some of the SMART meetings and usually are trained mental health professionals. Advisors assist the coordinators in technical aspects of running a meeting, and they sometimes help with publicity. New meetings are formed as people develop an interest, either through their experience in a SMART meeting or from their hearing of SMART through the media or from readings.

A noteworthy accomplishment by SMART was its acquisition of a training grant, which funded training seminars throughout the country. The attendees included SMART coordinators and addictions counselors from various prison systems. Currently, a project is being considered in coordination with a private organization seeking a grant to establish work in prisons.

What Does SMART Believe and How Does It Differ From AA?

SMART is a non-12-Step approach. It can be especially attractive to people who have tried the 12-Step approach without success or who don't feel comfortable with it. While SMART is similar to AA in goals and cost (most SM ART meetings pass the hat, like AA), it is different from AA in key ways:

● SMART appeals to individuals who want to learn to rely upon themselves and take responsibility for their feelings and actions rather than "turn it over" to a Higher Power. It does not emphasize spiritual or religious values, and it is based on common sense, ability to learn and reason, and scientific knowledge.

● SMART sees itself as just one of many possibilities, including the self-help alternative of doing it by oneself. SMART is not the only way to do things. People have figured out how to change their bad habits throughout history. Recovery is part of a natural human capacity that, at most, attendance at SMART can augment.

● SMART does not teach that people's emotional disturbances and problem behaviors are created mainly by past events or by a disease, but instead by their present beliefs.

● SMART encourages the use of medication when prescribed by a licensed professional having prescription privileges.

● People are welcome to attend and coordinate SMART meetings if they're interested in helping people, including themselves, learn self-management skills. Participation in SMART does not depend on having had a history of substance abuse or anything else other than being human.

● SMART supports abstinence as a sensible choice for some people who have given themselves a problem with addictive behaviors. In its meetings, SMART constructively views lapses and relapses as unfortunate, but as experiences from which much can be learned on the journey to recovery.

● SMART views addictive behaviors as bad habits, not diseases.

● SMART discourages self-labeling: people have bad habits, such as chronic indulgence in alcohol, but they are not the same thing as their bad habits.

● SMART meetings are discussion groups, and crosstalk is encouraged.

● SMART encourages people to come to meetings for as long as it seems helpful, rather than forever.

● Substance abuse and other addictive behaviors have some biological roots. So does everything else people do—including their abilities to recover and change how they act, to take responsibility for their lives, to learn better habits, and to feel happier.

● SMART Recovery encourages self-acceptance, not self-worth. One's worth as a human being does not depend on one's actions, addictive or otherwise.

● SMART does not say that people are "in denial" or unmotivated if they don't like or profit from SMART. Different strokes for different folks.

Meeting/ Discussion Group Format

SMART is new and is experimenting with different formats for its meetings. Its meetings use some simple self-management methods, which have been widely disseminated in self-help books for the general reader, and many of these methods are derived from cognitive-behavioral therapies. SMART is not counseling or therapy, however; rather, its format is that of a lay-led self-help discussion group. Participants in the discussions often offer each other ideas that they themselves have created or heard about and found helpful in their own lives.

Most discussions are an hour long, though some are 1.5 hours. In some of the hour and a half meetings, a half hour is set aside for newcomers. The most common meeting format begins with a brief introduction to SMART by the coordinator and the request—usual in most kinds of self-help meetings—that "what's said here stays here." Next is the personal update, in which participants, using first names only, briefly tell (1) something significant that happened to them in the last week that bears on why they are at the meeting and (2) what benefits they want to get out of the discussion. If nothing happened of significance in their weeks, then they are asked to tell briefly why they chose to attend SMART meetings. Newcomers go last and are asked why they've chosen to attend meetings.

Next the meeting agenda may be set. The coordinator asks who would like some time in the meeting to work on an addiction-related problem, or other problem, whether dealt with successfully or unsuccessfully. Usually these situations were mentioned in the personal update. Most of the rest of the meeting involves those present working with participants with agenda items, using the ABC method and elements of the SMART 4-point plan mentioned above. The coordinator may ask participants what they could do during the next week that would help them with the problems they brought up. Finally, the coordinator will review the meeting (or ask another participant to do so) and passes the hat for voluntary donations. The meeting then closes, with enough time for socializing, signing papers, etc.

Contact information: S.M.A.R.T. Recovery
24000 Mercantile Road, Suite 11
Beachwood, OH 44122
Phone: 216-292-0220
http://home.sprynet.com/sprynet/mike888/

Women for Sobriety

Women for Sobriety is both an organization and a self-help Program for women alcoholics. It is, in fact, the first national self-help program for women alcoholics.

There are an estimated 7,500,000 women alcoholics in the United States alone. That number of women alcoholics is equal to the *total* population of Maine, Idaho, Nevada, Montana, New Mexico and Utah! Surely this large number of women deserves a program that speaks to their specific needs in recovery.

WFS has been providing services to women alcoholics since July, 1976. The WFS "New Life" Program grew out of one woman's search for sobriety—mine. Now hundreds of WFS self-help groups are found all across the country, and a few abroad.

Based upon a Thirteen Statement Program (affirmations) of positivity that encourages emotional and spiritual growth, the "New Life" Program has been extremely effective in helping women overcome their alcoholism and learn a totally new lifestyle.

The WFS Program is being used not only by women alcoholics in small self-help groups, but also in hospitals, clinics, treatment facilities, women's centers and wherever alcoholics are being treated.

The activities of WFS are the establishment of self-help groups and the distribution of literature to women who ask for our help.

Unfunded by any agency, WFS derives its operational money from group donations, sale of literature, speaking engagements, workshops, and outside donations.

Until the founding of WFS in 1976, it was assumed that any program for recovery would be just as effective for women as for men. When it became obvious that recovery rates for male alcoholics were higher than for females, it was then declared that women were harder to deal with and they were seen as less cooperative than male alcoholics.

WFS came forth with the belief that women alcoholics require a different kind of program in recovery than the kinds of programs used for male alcoholics.

The success of the WFS "New Life" Program has shown this to be true. Although the physiological recovery from alcoholism is the same for both sexes, the psychological (emotional) needs of women are very different from those of male alcoholics.

When I first put the Program together, it was 13 affirmations that I had jotted down and found to be useful in each morning's period of meditation.

It wasn't until a number of years later that I found I was grouping them whenever I gave speeches. So the 13 Statements (affirmations) are now presented for recovery in levels:

The WFS Program as first written:

1. I have a drinking (life-threatening) problem that once had me.
   We now take charge of our life and our disease. We accept the responsiblity.
2. Negative thoughts destroy only myself.
   Our first conscious sober act must be to remove negativity from our life.
3. Happiness is a habit I will develop.
   Happiness is created, not waited for.
4. Problems bother me only to the degree I permit them to.
   We now better understand our problems and do not permit problems to overwhelm us.
5. I am what I think.
   I am a capable, competent, caring, compassionate woman.
6. Life can be ordinary or it can be great.
   Greatness is mine by a conscious effort.

7. Love can change the course of my world.
   Caring becomes all important.
8. The fundamental object of life is emotional and spiritual growth.
   Daily I put my life into a proper order, knowing which are the priorities.
9. The past is gone forever.
   No longer will I be victimized by the past. I am a new person.
10. All love given returns.
    I will learn to know that others love me.
11. Enthusiasm is my daily exercise.
    I treasure all moments of my new life.
12. I am a competent woman and have much to give life.
    This is what I am and I shall know it always.
13. I am responsible for myself and for my actions.
    I am in charge of my mind, my thoughts, and my life.

When presented in the form of levels for recovery, the Program is thus:

Level I: *Accepting Alcoholism as a physical disease.*
   "I have a drinking (life-threatening) problem that once had me." (#1)

Level II: *Discarding negative thoughts, putting guilt behind, and practicing new ways of viewing and solving problems.*
   "Negative thoughts destroy only myself." (#2)
   "Problems bother me only to the degree I permit them to." (#4)
   "The past is gone forever." (#9)

Level III: *Creating and practicing a new self-image.*
   "I am what I think." (#5)
   "I am a competent woman and have much to give to life." (#12)

Level IV: *Using new attitudes to enforce new behavior patterns.*
   "Happiness is a habit I will develop." (#3)
   "Life can be ordinary or it can be great." (#6)
   "Enthusiasm is my daily exercise." (#11)

Level V: *Improving relationships as a result of our new feelings about self.*
   "The fundamental object of life is emotional and spiritual growth." (#8)
   "I am responsible for myself and my actions." (#13)

To make the Program effective, we ask that women arise each morning 15 minutes earlier than usual and go over the 13 Statements. We ask too that women use this time to tune into themselves—to ask where they are going and how they are caring for their spiritual life.

This time is very important to a recovering alcoholic person for it is a time of coming to grips with stark reality. Who am I? What is my life about? Must I make more changes?

The sum of the WFS Program is for women to move toward a state of empowerment, a place in which they are in charge of themselves.

We do not believe that women need to attend meetings forever. This sometimes continues dependency and this is what women need to change. Our Program helps women to free themselves from the myriad dependencies women experience in our society. Our Program aims at women freeing themselves from dependence upon alcohol and other drugs and freeing them from dependence upon others. To this end, women in WFS groups do not have a one-on-one sponsor. In WFS, the whole group serves as a sponsor in the early months.

Our Program urges meditation every morning. We emphasize nutrition, and we also urge women to see their lives in a more dynamic way by asking them to set goals and have plans—a goal a month and plans for a year to five years. More immediately, we ask every woman to have at least one thing planned for each week other than a WFS meeting.

Because we do not have groups everywhere, we urge women who can not attend a WFS group to join our pen pal program and subscribe to our newsletter. Over the years we have developed a large amount of literature—cassette tapes of meetings, videos of meetings, a number of workbooks, and several diaries. Our most important piece of literature is our small program booklet—all these can be used when no meeting is available.

Perhaps it should be noted that WFS was the first program to start since the beginning of AA in 1935. WFS began in 1976 and has been publishing a monthly newsletter ever since that time.

We strongly believe that women have issues that are different from males and should have a program taking that into account. The most important is for women to be empowered—to know about self and to believe in that person. At the close of each meeting, we join together in saying, *"We are capable and competent, caring and compassionate, always willing to help another, bonded together in overcoming our addictions."*

Contact information: Women for Sobriety
P.O. Box 618
Quakertown, PA 18951
Phone: (215) 535-8026

B

AA and the Law

AA has grown remarkably over the last quarter century, and a good part of that growth is directly traceable to coercion. In the 1992 AA membership survey, 3% of respondents reported a correctional agency as responsible for their AA attendance, and another 8% listed a court order as being responsible. In 1996, the percentage forced to attend by the penal system remained at 3%, but the percentage forced to attend by court order had risen to 13%—a 60% increase in the space of a mere four years. So, in 1996 one out of every six AA members was attending AA as a direct result of government coercion.[1]

When you add those who were coerced to attend through interventions and/or threats of job loss, suspension, or decertification (in the case of professionals, such as lawyers, doctors, and nurses), the figure rises substantially, to over 30%, probably. And if you add those who unwarily entered treatment and were then coerced to embrace AA, the figure likely rises to over 40% of AA's total membership. (See the discussion of these points in Chapter 7, endnote 4.) Thus, coercion has become very important to AA's growth and survival.

To date, the only significant challenges to coerced membership in AA have come from those forced to attend 12-step meetings by the courts or penal system. Since 1984, there have been approximately 15 cases brought against the authorities for forcing inmates or probationers to participate in AA or NA (Narcotics Anonymous—NA's program is a carbon copy of AA's). All of these cases have focused on violation of the establishment clause of the First Amendment to the U.S. Constitution (which prohibits any "establishment of religion" by government). The plaintiffs lost most of the cases in the lower courts, but the plaintiffs have won all three cases which have reached the higher courts, that is, courts with precedent-setting authority. Two of these cases involved federal Courts of Appeal, and the third involved New York State's highest Court of Appeals.

All three cases are quite significant, but the New York case, Griffin v. Coughlin, 1996, is the only one that has been appealed to the Supreme

Court, which in January 1997 refused to hear the case. Thus the New York Court of Appeals' decision now stands as highly influential precedent in New York State, and as persuasive but nonbinding precedent in other states.

In its decision, the 5 to 2 majority of the New York Court of Appeals noted that "doctrinally and as actually practiced in the 12-step method-ology, adherence to the A.A. fellowship entails engagement in religious activity and religious proselytization."

The reasoning in both federal court cases has been similar.

In August 1996, the Seventh Circuit Court of Appeals found for the plaintiff, who had been forced to attend NA by prison authorities, in the case Kerr v. Farrey. In its 2 to 1 decision, the court first commented, "We find . . . that the state has impermissibly coerced inmates to participate in a religious program [NA]." It went on:

> The district court [which ruled against the plaintiff] thought that the NA program escaped the "religious" label because the twelve steps used phrases like "God, as we understood Him," and because the warden indicated that the concept of God could include the non-religious idea of willpower within the individual. We are unable to agree with this interpretation. A straight-forward reading of the twelve steps shows clearly that the steps are based on the monotheistic idea of a single God or Supreme Being. True, that God might be known as Allah to some, YHWH to others, or the Holy Trinity to still others, but the twelve steps consistently refer to "God, as we understood Him." Even if we expanded the steps to include polytheistic ideals or animistic philosophies, they are still fundamentally based on a religious concept of a Higher Power.

This decision now stands as non-binding but highly influential precedent in the court's jurisdiction, an area encompassing most of Indiana, Illinois, and Wisconsin.

The decision by the Second Circuit Court of Appeals in Warner v. Orange County [New York] Department of Probation was made on similar grounds the following month. In its unanimous decision, the court stated:

> The A.A. program to which Warner was exposed had a substantial religious component. Participants were told to pray to God for help in overcoming their affliction. Meetings opened and closed with group prayer. The trial judge [who ruled in favor of the plaintiff] reasonably found that it "placed a heavy emphasis on spirituality and prayer, in both conception and in practice." We have no doubt that the meetings Warner attended were intensely religious events.
>
> There can be no doubt, furthermore, that Warner was coerced into participating in these religious exercises by virtue of his probation sentence. . . . The County argues further that the non-sectarian nature of A.A.

experience immunizes its use of religious symbolism and practices from Establishment Clause scrutiny. The argument is at the very least factually misleading, for the evidence showed that every meeting included at least one explicitly Christian prayer.[2] Furthermore, the claim that non-sectarian religious exercise falls outside the First Amendment's scrutiny has been repeatedly rejected by the Supreme Court. . . .

We have little difficulty concluding that the constitutional line was crossed here.

So, with these influential precedents now in place, it looks as if the days of court- and penal system-ordered coercion into AA attendance are numbered. It's highly unlikely that the Supreme Court will ever hear a case regarding coerced 12-step attendance—especially considering its refusal to hear the Griffin case. Rather, it seems likely that change will proceed piecemeal across the country. Given the three precedent-setting cases cited here, it seems equally likely that courts across the land will gradually rule coerced 12-step attendance unconstitutional in their jurisdictions.

In fact, as Vince Fox points out in his monograph, "The Constitution of the United States, Tax Dollars, the Law, Alcoholics and Narcotics Anonymous," a snowball effect seems entirely likely. Fox credits this to "the American Civil Liberties Union, Rational Recovery (especially), S.M.A.R.T. Recovery, the Prison Law Office, [and] enhanced communications through the Internet." One of the next steps will in all likelihood be a major class action suit filed by Rational Recovery. In preparation for that suit, RR is currently seeking the names of persons who have been coerced into attending 12-step programs or 12-step treatment and who want to take part in the suit. Those wishing to participate in this class action suit should contact Rational Recovery directly. RR's contact information is listed in Appendix A on page 176.

Although it looks as if coercion into *some* kind of treatment will continue, it seems quite likely that the government will stop coercing individuals into attending *12-step* groups and treatment programs within the next five to ten years, perhaps sooner. That leaves what Fox terms "a gray area" in which employers or professional associations (lawyers, physicians, nurses), coerce employees or members into attending 12-step programs or 12-step treatment. Rational Recovery is already assisting such persons, and it seems likely that there will soon be a spate of lawsuits—including the RR class action lawsuit— challenging professional and employer mandates. Given the precedents already established, it seems likely that such challenges will succeed.

All of this does not mean that the flow of coerced members to AA will entirely stop. It seems likely that the courts will rule that coerced treatment or self-help group attendance is constitutional as long as those being coerced have the choice between AA (or NA) and at least one secular alternative. But given AA's reputation as something akin to a religious cult, and the distaste with which a great many alcohol abusers regard it, it's a safe bet that when given a choice between attending AA or a secular group, a good majority of those being coerced will choose the secular group.

The effect of this upon AA will be profound.

Addendum: In November 1997, the Tennessee Supreme Court ruled in Evans v. Tennessee Department of Paroles—on establishment clause grounds, citing Griffin v. Coughlin—that mandated AA attendance as a condition of parole is unconstitutional. The snowball effect predicted by Vince Fox seems to be gaining momentum.

---

1. The membership surveys asked the respondents to list up to three reasons for their attendance. But, given the fact that the individuals represented in these two categories were directly coerced—and faced dire consequences if they didn't cooperate—it's fair to regard any other reasons that they might have cited as inconsequential.

2. Undoubtedly the "Our Father" at the end of meetings.

Afterword
Why it is Good to Speak Out Against AA

Alcoholics Anonymous (AA) is an American icon, the great hope of mainstream society that mass addiction will subside. AA is seemingly immune to criticism and public scrutiny. Very few people, including public officials who actively support the AA cartel, have actually read AA doctrinal literature, or even the Twelve Steps, which are obviously religious. Even fewer have sat down in a typical meeting of the recovery group movement, to observe the indoctrination of newcomers into the ideology of power-lessness, helplessness, and dependence. AA sows the seeds of addiction before itself, then poses as a solution as it advances. AA shows the friendly side of tyranny, proclaiming honorable values to the public and media, while imposing its will upon addicted people behind closed doors. AA's methods of indoctrination are an offense to common decency; they result in many addicted persons paying tribute to AA, even while their own addic-tions progress toward despair and death. AA has found a niche in the dark side of the human psyche, and made it into a lair from which it preys on human vulnerabilities. Why is it good to speak out against AA?

1) By speaking out against AA, you will warn others to stay away from recovery groups of all kinds, and thus prevent harm to addicted people. Recovery groups create an illusion of hope during desperate times. You will also be encouraging addicted people that they can do the obvious—quit their addictions once and for all, rather than adopt the foolishness of abstaining one-day-at-a-time. Most addicted people recover on their own, and we must expect and encourage them to do so. AA doesn't believe in people at all. It believes in AA: when people improve, they must praise AA, not take credit themselves. America must start believing in people, not programs, so that addicted *people* may finally shoulder a burden that no *society* can—the burden of self-recovery from substance addictions.

By speaking out against AA, you will put the helping professions, particularly medicine, on notice that they have already committed a grave offense against the society they were sanctioned to protect. They have accepted money to perform services that they are not qualified to perform. There is no treatment, medical or otherwise, for addiction, for there is no disease. This was well known in the medical and psychiatric professions until rivers of tax dollars gushed forth. Then, those who were licensed to bill—stole. The professionals may eventually be forgiven for this ethical catastrophe, but not until they have admitted that they were wrong.

2) If you love your country, speak out against AA. America is a unique society in human history, built on values of individualism, self-reliance, moral virtues, personal liberty, justice, and religious freedom. What appears to be a fellowship of recovered people offering encouragement to addicted people is actually the drug culture of America between drinking and using episodes. These are not the kind of people from whom to seek help of any kind. They have not recovered from their own addictions, and admit this freely. They have abandoned their own family values for the ersatz religion of AA. They have renamed the ultimate self-indulgence, addiction, a "disease," and accordingly do not know right from wrong. Their group norms are sharply at odds with religious values, moral intuitions, and traditional mental health concepts.

People are arrested for alcohol or drug use, convicted of crimes, and are then required to profess that they are not responsible for their own actions. The disease concept gives them a doctor's excuse for their illegal behavior. This corruption of justice is eating at the fabric of our society. Most people recognize that something is wrong with America, that we are becoming a nation of victims dependent on an ever-expanding array of government services. The engine of this disturbance is the 12-step recovery group movement, which proselytizes its mentality of victimhood and entitlement via government decree and popular media. By speaking out against AA, you can help stop our progress toward becoming a therapeutic state, in which prisons and hospitals are one and the same.

3) If you are a religious person, it is good to speak out against AA. The keystone of American society is the separation of organized religion from government affairs. AA has gutted the First Amendment of the U.S. Constitution and has become our de facto state religion. We can't stop this from happening; it has already happened. No one spoke out against Alcoholics Anonymous.

AA is bad religion. It is a Gnostic heresy, easily recognizable as such by any trained theologian. AA teaches addicted people to expect miracles on demand, a juvenile attitude discouraged by legitimate religions. AA's homogenized deity can be a toad or a bedpan, but this idolatry is ignored by clergy who have been taught that addiction is a disease and idolatry is treatment. AA stole the sin of addiction from the churches of America and made it into a disease which no physician can treat or cure. In sharp contrast to any of the world's great religions, which view abstinence or temperance as a way to find or to honor God, AA poses God as an obstacle to the moral act of recovery through planned abstinence. The AA deity must be worshipped as a condition for abstinence from alcohol and drugs. Legitimate religious charities never hold back bread on condition of religious conversion. They give freely, expecting no tribute or submission, and welcome those who, once fed, enter freely into the faith. AA threatens addicted people with death unless they come to believe the AA creed. They use our courts, prisons, and social institutions to enforce their rule over desperate, addicted people. This is exactly what our Founding Fathers most feared—that America would succumb to the tendency of nations to impose religion upon their citizens.

Why didn't organized religion speak out as AA grew in membership and might? Some didn't criticize AA because they were afraid of AA, afraid that they would be criticized for criticizing. (This is common in all lands; it's how "good" citizens, the "silent majority," help tyrannies to gain power.) But others didn't criticize AA because they thought that they saw another religion. Interdenominational disputes are rare in the land of the free, and AA has been granted a shield against criticism which is common to religions. But AA is cunning, baffling, and powerful. It denies that it is religious—it's only "spiritual." In this way, AA has it's cake and eats it too: other religions perceive it as being religious, and hence don't criticize it; and because of its dishonest assertion that it's "spiritual, not religious," it has infiltrated our public institutions, where it grows in power and influence.

Twelve-step enthusiasts have written books depicting AA founder, Bill W., as the reincarnated Christ. This is simple idolatry. AA is not "spiritual." AA is a dangerous religious cult which seeks world domination. Churches must unite to resist AA, using their legitimate moral authority.

4) The United States, with the worst record in managing substance abuse of all nations, exports a product far more dangerous than narcotics or other drugs. We export AA to other nations which have always had adequate means to manage substance abuse. Those nations will copy our errors, and will succumb to mass addiction. AA ambassadors preach disease hysteria, announcing grave consequences unless foreign governments employ its members at new 12-step treatment centers. AA seeks a new world order based on God-control of all nations. By speaking out against AA, you will help other lands avoid repeating America's addictions tragedy.

5) If you are an addicted person, it is good to speak out against AA because you have been misled about the nature of addiction and the nature of recovery. There is not a word or suggestion in the 12-step program concerning planned abstinence. To the contrary, newcomers are immediately informed that they are powerless to immediately and independently quit their addictions. Instead of directing seriously addicted people toward this direct, powerful, life-saving action, groupers routinely distract newcomers from this direct, powerful decision by drawing them into disorienting discussions of metaphysics, pop psychology, and AA lore.

Anyone can quit an addiction if they want to and know what they are doing. AA is not about addictions or abstinence; AA is about AA. The recovery group movement diverts millions of people away from the most obvious and significant focus of recovery—abstinence from alcohol and drugs. If you criticize AA, you will discover that you have no friends in AA but only partners in the fellowship. AA is a cult which values its unity above any individual, and its members believe that their survival depends on the truth of its doctrine. If you criticize AA, you also threaten them, and they will cut you loose with a grim prediction—a jinx—that you will self-destruct by drinking. It's good to know who your friends are—and aren't.

If you were required to attend AA by force, professional intimidation, court mandate, or by lack of information about other means to recover, your rights were certainly abused, including your Constitutional rights. As you criticize AA, you will feel stronger and you will see more clearly that the 12-step program is in truth the philosophy of addiction itself, wrapped up in God-talk to fool the larger society. When you see this, you will understand that you were on the right track while struggling alone, and that it is not you, but the groupers, who are crazy.

The AA cartel exists solely because people do not criticize AA. If we don't raise our voices now, mass addiction will grow worse, billions more of our tax dollars will be wasted, liberty and freedom be further limited, and it will become ever more difficult to throw the rascals out of our public institutions. Don't be fooled by people who say that AA shouldn't be criticized because it has helped so many people. AA has helped no one, failed millions, fooled almost everyone, and taken credit for the success of its relatively few members who have stopped drinking. Speak up for your rights! Help people recover from addictions! Help your country! Be true to your religious faith! It is good to speak out against Alcoholics Anonymous and the recovery group movement!

—Jack Trimpey, founder/president, Rational Recovery

Bibliography

AA HISTORY AND IDEOLOGY

Alexander, Jack. "Alcoholics Anonymous: Freed Slaves of Drink, Now They Free Others. *Saturday Evening Post*, March 1, 1941.

Bean, Margaret. "A.A. and Religion." *Psychiatric Annals*, March 1975, pp. 36–42.
—"Alcoholics Anonymous Principles and Methods." *Psychiatric Annals*, February 1975, pp. 7–21.
—"A Critique of A.A." *Psychiatric Annals*, March 1975, pp. 7–19.

Blumberg, Leonard. "The Ideology of a Therapeutic Social Movement." *Journal of Studies on Alcohol*, Nov. 1977, pp. 2122–2143.

Cain, Arthur. "Alcoholics Anonymous: Cult or Cure?" *Harper's*, February 1963, pp. 48–52.
—"Alcoholics Can Be Cured—Despite A.A." *Saturday Evening Post*, September 19, 1965, pp. 6–8.

Dick B. *Turning Point: A History of Early AA's Spiritual Roots and* Successes. San Rafael, CA: Paradise Research, 1997.
—*Design for Living: The Oxford Group's Contribution to Early A.A.* San Rafael, CA: Paradise Research, 1996.
—*The Good Book and the Big Book: A.A.'s Roots in the Bible.* San Rafael, CA: Paradise Research, 1997.

Ellis, Albert and Schoenfeld, Eugene. "Divine Intervention and the Treatment of Chemical Dependency." *Journal of Substance Abuse*, No. 2, 1990, pp. 459–468 and 489–494.

Ellison, Jerome. "Alcoholics Anonymous: Dangers of Success." *The Nation*, March 2, 1964, pp. 212–214.

Gelman, Irving. *The Sober Alcoholic: An Organizational Analysis of Alcoholics Anonymous.* New Haven, CT: College and University Press, 1964.

Hunter, T. Willard. *It Started Right There: AA & MRA.* Salem, OR: Grosvenor Books, n.d. (probably 1995)

Katz, Stan and Liu, Aimee. *The Codependency Conspiracy.* New York: Warner Books, 1991

Kurtz, William. *Not God: A History of Alcoholics* Anonymous. Center City, MN: Hazelden, 1979.

Markey, Morris. "Alcoholics and God." *Liberty,* September 30, 1939, pp. 6–7.

Peele, Stanton. *Diseasing of America.* Lexington, MA: Lexington Books, 1989.

Pittman, Bill. *AA The Way It Began.* Seattle, Glen Abbey Books: 1988.

Ragge, Ken. *The Real AA: Behind the Myth of 12-Step Recovery.* Tucson: See Sharp Press, 1998.

Robertson, Nan. *Getting Better: Inside Alcoholics Anonymous.* New York: Wm. Morrow, 1988.

Rudy, David. *Becoming Alcoholic.* Carbondale, IL: Southern Illinois University Press, 1986.

Salomone, Guy. *Religious and Spiritual Origins of the Twelve Step Recovery Movement.* Lotus, CA: Lotus Press, 1997.

Thomsen, Robert. *Bill W.* New York: Harper & Row, 1975.

Trimpey, Jack. *Rational Recovery from Alcoholism: The Small Book.* Lotus, CA: Lotus Press, 1989.

Wilson, Bill. *Alcoholics Anonymous (3rd ed.).* New York: Alcoholics Anonymous World Services, 1985.
—*Alcoholics Anonymous Comes of Age.* New York: Alcoholics Anonymous World Services, 1957.
—*Twelve Steps and Twelve Traditions.* New York: Alcoholics Anonymous World Services, 1953.

Wilson, Lois. *Lois Remembers.* New York: Al-Anon, 1979.

Anonymous.
—*Dr. Bob and the Good Oldtimers.* New York: Alcoholics Anonymous World Services, 1980
—*Pass It On: Bill Wilson and the A.A. Message.* New York: Alcoholics Anonymous World Services, 1984.
—*The A.A. Service Manual Combined with Twelve Concepts for World Service.* (No author listed for "Service Manual"; Bill Wilson listed as author of "Twelve Concepts.") New York: Alcoholics Anonymous World Services, 1989.

THE OXFORD GROUP MOVEMENT/MORAL RE-ARMAMENT

Bennett, John C. *Social Salvation.* New York: Charles Scribner's Sons, 1946, pp. 53–59.

Clark, Walter. *The Oxford Group: Its History and Significance.* New York: Bookman Assoc., 1951.

Devine, Frank. "Salvation for the Select." *American Mercury*, March 1933, pp. 313–319.

Driberg, Tom. *The Mystery of Moral Re-Armament.* New York: Alfred A. Knopf, 1965.

Eister, Allan. *Drawing-Room Conversion: A Sociological Account of the Oxford Group Movement.* Durham, NC: Duke University Press, 1950.

Ferguson, Charles. *The Confusion of Tongues: A Review of Modern Isms.* Grand Rapids, MI: Zondervan, 1940, pp. 89–109.

Harrison, Marjorie. *Saints Run Mad.* London: John Lane the Bodley Head, 1934.

Henson, Herbert, D.D. (Bishop of Durham). *The Oxford Group Movement.* New York: Oxford University Press, 1933.

Howard, Peter. *Britain and the Beast.* London: Heinemann, 1963.
—*Frank Buchman's Secret.* New York: Doubleday, 1961.

MacIntosh, Douglas Clyde. *Personal Religion.* New York: Charles Scribner's Sons, 1942, pp. 372–395.

Niebuhr, Reinhold. "Hitler and Buchman." *The Christian Century*, October 7, 1936, pp. 1315–1316.

Richardson, John A. *The Groups Movement.* Milwaukee: Morehouse Publishing, 1935.

Trillin, Calvin. "U.S. Letter: Chicago." *New Yorker,* December 16, 1967, pp. 128–136.

Van Dusen, Henry. "Apostle to the Twentieth Century." *Atlantic Monthly*, July 1934, pp. 1–16.
—"The Oxford Group Movement." *Atlantic Monthly,* August 1934, pp. 240–252.

Anonymous.
—"Buchman's Kampf." *Time*, January 18, 1943, pp. 65–66.
—"A God Guided Dictator." *The Christian Century*, September 9, 1936, pp. 1182–1183.
—*Ideology & Co-Existence.* Moral Re-Armament, 1959.
—"Less Buchmanism." *Time*, November 24, 1941, p. 59.
—"Moral Re-Armament RIP." *National* Review, October 20, 1970, p. 1099.
—"The Moral Re-Armer." *Time*, August 18, 1961, p. 59.
—"New Man at M.R.A." *Time*, October 30, 1964, p. 74.
—"The Oxford Group—Genuine or a Mockery?" *Literary Digest*, January 28, 1933, pp. 18–19.
—"Oxford Group: God-Guidance and Four 'Absolute Principles.'" Newsweek, June 6, 1936, pp. 26–27.
—"Report on Buchmanism." *Time*, January 4, 1943, p. 68.
—"When the White Begins to Fade." *The Christian Century*, June 28, 1972, pp. 704–705.

EFFECTIVENESS OF AA/12-STEP TREATMENT

Annis, Helen. "Is Alcoholism Treatment Effective?" *Science*, April 3, 1987, pp. 20–22.

Baekeland, Frederick. "Evaluation of Treatment Methods in Chronic Alcoholism." *Treatment and Rehabilitation of the Chronic Alcoholic*, B. Kissen and H. Begleiter, eds., pp. 385–440. New York: Plenum Press, 1977.

Bebbington, Paul. "The Efficacy of Alcoholics Anonymous: The Elusiveness of Hard Data." *British Journal of Psychiatry*, Vol. 128 (1976), pp. 572–580.

Bill C. "The Growth and Effectiveness of Alcoholics Anonymous in a Southwestern City, 1945–1962. *Quarterly Journal of Studies on Alcohol*, Vol. 26 (1965), pp. 279–284.

Brandsma, Jeffrey, et al. *Outpatient Treatment of Alcoholism*. Baltimore: University Park Press, 1980.

Cahalan, Don. *Understanding America's Drinking Problem*. San Francisco: Jossey-Bass, 1987.

Daley, Dennis. "Relapse Prevention with Substance Abusers: Clinical Issues and Myths." *Social Work*, March-April 1987, pp. 138–142.

Dawson, Deborah. "Correlates of Past-Year Status Among Treated and Untreated Persons with Former Alcohol Dependence: United States, 1992." *Alcoholism: Clinical and Experimental Research*, Vol. 20, No. 4, June 1996, pp. 771–779.

Ditman, Keith, et al. "A Controlled Experiment on the Use of Court Probation for Drunk Arrests." *American Journal of Psychiatry*, August 1967, pp. 64–67.

Drew, Leslie. "Alcoholism as a Self-Limiting Disease." *Quarterly Journal of Studies on Alcohol*, Vol. 29 (1968), pp. 956–967.

Fingarette, Herbert. *Heavy Drinking: The Myth of Alcoholism as a Disease*. Berkeley, CA: University of California Press, 1988.

Finney, John and Moos, Rudolf. "The Long-Term Course of Treated Alcoholism." *Journal of Studies on Alcohol*, Vol. 52, No. 1 (1991), pp. 44–54.

Finney, John and Monahan, Susan. "The Cost Effectiveness of Treatment for Alcoholism: A Second Approximation." *Journal of Studies on Alcohol*. Vol. 57 (1996), pp. 229–242.

Fox, Vince. *Addiction, Change & Choice: The New View of Alcoholism*. Tucson, AZ: See Sharp Press, 1993.

Glaser, Frederic and Ogborne, Alan. "Does A.A. Really Work?" *British Journal of Addiction*, No. 77 (1982), pp. Pp. 123–129.

Hester, Reid and Miller, William. *Handbook of Alcoholism Treatment Approaches: Effective Approaches (second edition)*. Needham Heights, MA: Allyn and Bacon, 1995.

Nace, Edgar. "Inpatient Treatment." *Recent Developments in Alcoholism, Vol. 11* (1993), Marc Galanter, ed., pp. 429–451.

Ogborne, Alan and Glaser, Frederick. "Evaluating Alcoholics Anonymous." *Alcoholism and Substance Abuse: Strategies for Clinical Intervention*, Thomas Bratter and Gary Forrest, eds. New York: The Free Press, 1985, pp. 176–192.

Peele, Stanton. "AA Abuse." *Reason*, November 1991, pp. 34–39.
—"Denial—of Reality and Freedom—in Addiction Research and Treatment." *Bulletin of the Society of Psychologists in Addictive Behaviors*, Vol. 5, No. 4, 1986, pp. 149–166.
—"Alcoholism, Politics, and Bureaucracy: The Consensus Against Controlled-Drinking Therapy in America." *Addictive Behaviors*, Vol. 17 (1992), pp. 49–62.
—*The Truth About Addiction and Recovery* (with Archie Brodsky). Lexington, MA: Lexington Books, 1995.

Project MATCH Research Group. "Matching Alcoholism Treatments to Client Heterogeneity: Project MATCH Posttreatment Drinking Outcomes." *Journal of Studies on Alcohol*, January 1997, pp. 7–29.

Roizen, Ron. "The Great Controlled-Drinking Controversy." *Recent Developments in Alcoholism, Vol. 5*, pp. 245–279.

Schmidt, Laura and Weisner, Constance. "Developments in Alcoholism Treatment." *Recent Developments in Alcoholism, Vol. 11* (1993), pp. 369–396.

Tuchfeld, Barry. "Spontaneous Remission in Alcoholics: Empirical Observations and Theoretical Implications." *Journal of Studies on Alcohol*, Vol. 42, No. 7 (1981), pp. 626–641.

Zinberg, Norman. "Alcoholics Anonymous and the Treatment and Prevention of Alcoholism." *Alcoholism: Clinical and Experimental Research*, January 1977, pp. 91–102.

Anonymous/Multiple Author
—"National Treatment Center Study Summary Report." Athens, GA: Institute for Behavioral Research, 1997.
—"National Treatment Center Study Summary Report: Six and Twelve Month Follow-up" Athens, GA: Institute for Behavioral Research, 1997.
—"National Admissions to Substance Abuse Treatment Services: The Treatment Episode Data Set (TEDS) 1992–1995." Rockville, MD: SAMHSA, 1997.

CULTS

Anderson, Einar. *I Was a Mormon*. Grand Rapids, MI: Zondervan, 1964.

Anderson, Jon Lee and Anderson, Scott. *Inside The League*. New York: Dodd Mead, 1986.

Appel, Willa. *Cults in America*. New York: Henry Holt, 1983.

Atack, Jon. *A Piece of Blue Sky: Scientology, Dianetics and L. Ron Hubbard Exposed*. Secaucus, NJ: Lyle Stuart, 1990.

Bradlee, Ben, Jr. and Van Atta, Dale. *Prophet of Blood: The Story of the "Mormon Manson."* New York: Putnam Pub. Group, 1981.

Brinton, Maurice. *The Irrational in Politics: Sexual Repression and Authoritarian Conditioning*. Tucson, AZ: See Sharp Press, 1993.

Brodie, Fawn. *No Man Knows My History*. New York: Knopf, 1946.

Corydon, Bent and Hubbard, L. Ron, Jr. *L. Ron Hubbard: Messiah or Madman?* Secaucus, NJ: Lyle Stuart, 1987.

Edwards, Christopher. *Crazy for God: The Nightmare of Cult Life.* Englewood Cliffs, NJ: Prentice-Hall, 1979.

Gerstel, David. *Paradise Incorporated: Synanon.* Novato, CA: Presidio Press, 1982.

Hassan, Steven. *Combatting Cult Mind Control.* Rochester, VT: Park Street Press, 1988.

King, Dennis. *Lyndon LaRouche and the New American Fascism.* New York: Doubleday, 1989.

Lifton, Robert Jay. *Thought Control and the Psychology of Totalism.* New York: W.W. Norton, 1969.

Martinez, Thomas and Guinther, John. *Brotherhood of Murder.* New York: McGraw Hill, 1988.

Miles, Austin. *Don't Call Me Brother: A Ringmaster's Escape from the Pentecostal Church.* Buffalo, NY: Prometheus Books, 1989.

Miller, Russell. *Bare-Faced Messiah: The True Story of L. Ron Hubbard.* New York: Henry Holt, 1987.

Mills, Jeannie. *Six Years with God: Life Inside Rev. Jim Jones's Peoples Temple.* New York: A & W Publishers, 1979.

Milne, Hugh. *Bhagwan: The God That Failed.* New York: St. Martin's Press, 1986.

Mitchell, Dave and Cathy, and Ofshe, Richard. *The Light on Synanon.* New York: Seaview Books, 1980.

Penton, James. *Apocalypse Delayed: The Story of the Jehovah's Witnesses.* Toronto: Toronto University Press, 1986.

Reich, Wilhelm. *The Mass Psychology of Fascism.* New York: Farrar, Straus & Giroux, 1970.

Rudin, James and Martha. *Prison or Paradise: The New Religious Cults.* Philadelphia: Fortress Press, 1980.

Sanders, Ed. *The Family.* New York: E.P. Dutton, 1971.

Schnell, William. *30 Years a Watchtower Slave.* Grand Rapids, MI: Baker Book House, 1971.

Singer, Margaret. *Cults In Our Midst.* San Francisco: Jossey-Bass, 1995.

Stoner, Carroll and Parke, Jo Ann. *All Gods* [sic] *Children: The Cult Experience—Salvation or Slavery.* New York: Penguin, 1977.

Underwood, Barbara and Betty. *Hostage to Heaven.* New York: Clarkson S. Potter, Inc. 1979.

Williams, J.L. *Victor Paul Wierwille and The Way International.* Chicago: Moody Bible Institute, 1979.

A Final Note: For readers interested in the latest developments regarding Alcoholics Anonymous, the best single source is *The Journal of Rational Recovery*, P.O. Box 800, Lotus, CA 95961.

Index

Dear Reader,

With the drastic decrease in the number of reviews published by newspapers and magazines, and the drastic increase in the number of books published annually, reader reviews have become very important.

If you enjoyed this book, please consider writing a reader review for your favorite e-retailer, online bookstore, or book review site.

You'd not only help the author and a small publisher, you'd help other readers discover this book.